365 DAYS OF RICHER LIVING

OTHER BOOKS BY ERNEST HOLMES

Creative Mind

Creative Ideas

How to Use the Science of Mind

The Science of Mind

What Religious Science Teaches

Creative Mind and Success

The Voice Celestial

This Thing Called You

365 DAYS OF RICHER LIVING

DAILY INSPIRATIONS

ERNEST HOLMES
Author of *The Science of Mind*
and
Raymond Charles Barker

573 Park Point Drive | Golden, CO 80401

Copyright © 2021 by Science of Mind Publishing

First Edition: 1953

Science of Mind Publishing
573 Park Point Drive
Golden, CO 80401-7402

All rights reserved.
No part of this book may be reproduced in any form
without permission in writing from the publisher,
except in the case of brief quotations.

Printed in the United States of America

COVER: MARIA ROBINSON, DESIGNS ON YOU LLC

Library of Congress Catalog Card Number: 53-9599
ISBN: 978-1-956198-04-1

About the Authors

ERNEST HOLMES, one of the foremost spiritual teachers of the last century, blended the best of Eastern and Western spiritual philosophies, psychology, and science into the transformational ideas known as the Science of Mind. He formulated a specific type of prayer, known as spiritual mind treatment, that has positively changed the lives of millions. Basing his techniques for living a free and full life on sacred wisdom—from the ancient to the modern—Ernest Holmes outlines these ideas in a collection of inspiring books. Written with simplicity and clarity, these books provide the means for every reader to live a more satisfying life.

RAYMOND CHARLES BARKER served as minister of the First Church of Religious Science of New York City, and his Sunday morning lectures in New York's Town Hall and Lincoln Center reached thousands of people seeking to improve their lives. He lectured throughout the United States, Canada, and Europe.

Introduction

IN APRIL OF 2017 it will be 50 years since I received my first copy of this book you hold in your hands. It was given to me after I attended a lecture by Raymond Charles Barker in New York City. He was teaching the Science of Mind lessons by Ernest Holmes. This treasure-chest-in-a-book, in its many editions since that time has been my most trusted guide and compass.

It is important as we read the Daily Lessons that we remember the saying of the American transcendentalist, Ralph Waldo Emerson, "The genius of man is a continuation of the Power that made him and has not done making him." This simply implies stay connected to that Power and Truth that sets us free for there is always more to learn and apply.

By <u>daily</u> reading these truths and affirmations, we are, in essence, "Priming the Cosmic Pump". This describes the action of God's Presence in us as Subjective Mind. The words in these lessons, and the thoughts and feelings they evoke in us are the primer for the pump. Thus, the Subjective Mind in us responds to these Truths and gushes forth the ideas of the Infinite of like quality.

Stir up the gift of God within you. The method in order to accomplish this all resides in the lessons contained herein.

Lovingly shared,
Lloyd George Tupper, Jr., D.D.
July 2016

Foreword

THIS BOOK IS A JEWEL and an important support for staying spiritually centered in our world at this time. As a citizen on our planet I consider it my responsibility as well as my opportunity to bring awareness and consciousness daily to the things taking place across our globe. And what a swirl of events, media coverage and points of view there are! Technology makes all that is taking place instantaneously available to us in dizzying amounts as every climate challenge, violent act, loss of life, moment of societal change and opinion is reported. The up side of this for people on the spiritual path is that everything is available to our consciousness and our Truth-knowing and condition-shifting thoughts and prayers. Each event is a planetary call for people of spiritual awareness to stand resolutely in the Truth we know, and to continue to embrace the oneness of Life, the sacredness of creation, the divinity of individual being, the creative power of thought, the Presence of Love and the Power of Good. It is not ours to be caught in the trance of conditions or to fall into fear, despair or negative reaction.

365 Days of Richer Living is a valuable companion for our personal spiritual walk as well as our collective one. The daily readings pour blessings of spiritual principle into our consciousness—opening our minds and hearts to greater possibility and peace and lighting the way to the demonstration of change. They remind us each day that we dwell in a Divine Reality that seeks its expression through and as our being and our lives. They orient us to the Truth that is above and beyond the appearances and conditions of the world and welcome this Truth into our experience. They center us in the knowing that we live in God and in Good.

Enjoy!

Kathy Hearn, D.D.
July 2016

January 1

I Am Resolved to See the Good in Everyone and in Every Event

...for what fellowship hath righteousness with unrighteousness? and what communion hath light with darkness?
II Corinthians 6:14

Q. Is ignorance produced by anything? A. No, by nothing. Ignorance is without beginning. ...The origin of pain can be traced to ignorance and it will not cease until ignorance is entirely dispelled, which will be only when the identity of the Self, with Brahma (the Universal Spirit) is fully realized.
The Raja Yoga Philosophy

Rabbi Ismael answers, "Not God but ye yourselves, are the creators and supporters of moral evils."
The Talmud

LIGHT can have no union with darkness; evil has no affinity with good. If good is the great reality, while evil is the great negation or denial of reality, then it follows that we should see the good in everything, and recognize the apparent evil merely as a theoretical opposite of good. There is not God and something else. The divine Spirit inhabits eternity; overshadows everything, including human events; indwells our own soul, and is released through our own act. To see good as evil is to becloud our vision, to obstruct the pathway of our progress and to cast a shadow across the sun of righteousness, which, Swedenborg tells us, is forever at an angle of forty-five degrees in the heavens. This spiritual sun was the guiding star which lead the Magi of old to the place where the little child lay. That is, to the place of good in our soul; to the presence of God at the center of every man's being. The humility of the manger is the common place in every man's life. It is here, in the common place, that we must find the good, and finding it here, we shall also discover that the larger issues of our experience are overshadowed by this same good which we have discovered in the common place.

I AM resolved today to see the good in everyone and in every event. I shall call upon the good and shall refuse to accept that anything other than good can come into my experience. In this way I will be praying to the good through meditating upon it.

January 2

Today I Shall Guard My Thoughts, Seeing to It That Nothing Emanates from My Consciousness Other Than That Which Will Bless, Build Up and Heal

> *But if ye bite and devour one another..*
> *take heed that ye be not consumed one of another.*
> Galatians 5:15

> *He who injures others is sure to be injured by them in return.*
> Kwang-Tze

> *I destroy the ignorance-born darkness by the shining lamp of wisdom.*
> The Bhagavad-Gita

THIS lesson teaches us the law of cause and effect, the plaything of the soul. In the long run, as Emerson tells us, if we seek to harm another, we but find that we are beating our own bleeding breast. Men of spiritual wisdom have always taught that our thoughts and acts ride on a return circuit and that they never fail to react upon us until we have transcended the negative causation set in motion by such acts.

This is why we are taught that we should do to others what we would like them to do to us. It is the old law of the returning circle. In this law alone can we find exact justice, and through understanding this law come to realize with Robert Browning: "All's love yet all's law." The universe imposes neither evil nor limitation upon us, nor can we impose evil or limitation upon it. However, being free agents, we may and must experience, at least temporarily, the result of our own acts. As the Gita tells us, the lamp of wisdom shining in the darkness of ignorance alone can free us.

REALIZING that the universe has bestowed upon me the divine right to be affected by my own act, today I shall guard all of my thoughts, seeing to it that nothing emanates from my consciousness other than that which blesses, builds and heals. I shall not worry about the consequences, for they already exist in the mathematical law of cause and effect. This law of cause and effect is not something that governs me. Quite the reverse, it is something which I govern. If nothing goes forth from me that can hurt, then nothing can return to me which can harm. The knowledge of this makes me wise. The consciousness of good at the center of my being is my sanctuary.

January 3

Today I Live

And God shall wipe away all tears from their eyes; and there shall be no more death, neither sorrow, nor crying, neither shall there be any more pain...
Revelation 21:4

Pray not that sinners may perish, but that the sin itself may disappear.
The Talmud

By knowledge of God [deva] all the bonds [of ignorance, unhappiness, etc.] are destroyed.
Upanishad

THE wisest man who ever lived told us that the knowledge of truth shall make us free. All books of spiritual wisdom have taught us that it is not the one who makes the mistake whom we should seek to destroy; it is the mistake itself which must be erased. Now, this means that evil has no existence in itself, it has no history. No matter what the negations of yesterday may have been, the affirmations of today may rise triumphant and transcendent over them. Thus all the evils of our yesterdays disappear into their native nothingness. If we behold beauty instead of ugliness, then beauty will appear. If we persist in seeing the true rather than the false, then that which is true will appear. Where is the false, the untrue and the evil when the knowledge of truth has made us free? Its days are as though they had never been; its cause is neutralized; hence it leaves no effect. Let us, then, cease weeping over the shortcomings and mistakes and evils of our yesterdays, and steadfastly beholding the face of the great and the divine reality, let us resolve to walk in that light wherein there is no darkness.

DEFINITELY I know that every negative condition of the past is cleared away from my consciousness. I no longer think about it, see it, or believe in it. Nor do I believe that it has any effect whatsoever in my experience. Yesterday is not, tomorrow is not, but today, bright with hope and filled with promise, is mine. Today I live.

January 4

I Know Now That My Spirit Is Free from All Limitation—I Know That I Understand the Truth About Myself

I am the almighty God; walk before me, and be thou perfect.
Genesis 17:1

Whoever knows the God who is without commencement, without end, who within this impervious [world] is the creator of the universe, who is of an infinite form, the one penetrator of the universe, becomes liberated from all bonds.
Upanishad

Thus it is that the Tao produces [all things], nourishes them, brings them to their full growth, nurses them, completes them, matures them, maintains them, and overspreads them.
The Tao Te Ching

OUR Chinese text tells us that *Tao*, which means Spirit, produces everything, nourishes everything and maintains everything. It spreads Itself over everything. It flows through everything and is in all things. Indeed, being all that is, there can be nothing outside It. Our Hindu text tells us that in such degree as we understand God, who is the one penetrator of the universe, in such degree we become liberated. And the Hebrew text says, "Walk before me and be thou perfect." We are to recognize the Divine in everything; to speak to the Divine in everything; to see It everywhere—"Lift the stone and you will find me, cleave the wood for there am I." The fragrance of the rose; the beauty of the dewdrop glistening in the sun, are manifestations of Its presence and activity. This Itself as the source and root of all. This source, Hermes tells us, forevermore proclaims itself as "the Oneness, being source and root of all, is in all things as the root and source." And the Christian scriptures tell us, "I am over all, in all and through all." The enlightened of the ages have told us that it is this God within us that recognizes Itself, or Himself, in everything we are.

I KNOW that my spirit is free from all limitation; that my physical body and my objective affairs reflect and manifest the perfection which I feel; the wholeness which I am certain of, and the prosperity which rightfully belongs to me.

January 5

The Unerring Judgment of Divine Intelligence Directs My Faith and Makes Plain and Perfect the Way Before Me

But we speak the wisdom of God in a mystery, even the hidden wisdom, which God ordained before the world unto our glory...
I Corinthians 2:7

The skillful masters [of the Tao] in old times, with a subtle and exquisite penetration, comprehended its mysteries, and were deep [also] so as to elude men's knowledge.
The Texts of Taoism

He who is happy within, who rejoiceth within, who is illuminated within, that Yogi, becoming the eternal, goeth to the Peace of the eternal.
The Bhagavad-Gita

THE hidden wisdom of God is the knowledge that we are one with the divine being. This wisdom, which is hidden from us until we perceive our fundamental unity with reality, is clearly revealed when we seek the eternal in everything. "The skillful masters" who have penetrated the mystery of life which so often eludes the intellect, are those who with utmost simplicity have found direct approach to the supreme reality at the center of their own soul. The Gita tells us that we must become the eternal if we wish to enter into the peace of the eternal. This has an identical meaning with the saying of Jesus that we must be perfect even as God in us is perfect. This calls for the recognition of the Spirit as an indwelling presence, as well as an overshadowing power. The road to self-discovery often calls for the clearing away of the underbrush of ignorance, fear, superstition, and a sense of isolation which has made us feel that we were unworthy, unheld and lost. In the divine providence of good, salvation is unnecessary but self-discovery is essential. We do not save that which was lost, we merely discover that which needs to be found.

I KNOW that God is within me and I know that this divine Spirit is perfect. I enter into Its peace and am secure in a sense of Its protection. Love will guide, and intelligence will direct me. The power of the infinite will sustain and uphold, as well as direct. The unerring judgment of divine intelligence directs my faith and makes perfect and plain the way before me.

January 6

Today I Consciously Live in the Eternal Presence

*But seek ye first the kingdom of God, and his righteousness;
and all these things shall be added unto you.*
Matthew 6:33

*Then, in this way know God; as having all things
in Himself as thoughts, the whole Cosmos itself.*
Thrice-Greatest Hermes

*Jesus saith: "... and the Kingdom of Heaven is within you;
and whosoever shall know himself shall find it. Strive therefore to
know yourselves, and ye shall be aware that ye are the sons of the...
Father; and ye shall know that ye are in the City of God, and ye are that City.*
Fragments of a Faith Forgotten

SINCE the kingdom of God is a kingdom of righteousness, and since it is a kingdom which contains everything, then it becomes of prime importance to seek this kingdom, which Jesus so plainly stated is to be found within the self. Of course he was not referring to the lesser, but to the greater self; that self upon which is set the stamp of the eternal—the God self. The real self is inseparable from God, thus in discovering the self, we also discover God, the cause of the self. Naturally, everything is included within the Divine, and since we are in It and It is in us, true self-discovery is the key to the mysteries of life. Hermes tells us that God has everything within Himself as thought; that the whole cosmos itself is a thing of consciousness. This is the true city of God—the city of right thoughts and right actions; the city which is four square, the length and breadth and thickness of which are equal. This is the city which Saint Augustine so beautifully depicts in his great essay on the relationship of the individual soul to the universal Spirit. All the sages and seers have plainly told us that we already walk the streets of this city, but like the slaves of Plato, blindfolded, our vision is blurred by shadows cast on the wall of human experience. Evil deals with shadows, truth deals with light, which dispels the shadows. We are of the truth. Evil is neither person, place nor thing.

TODAY I consciously live in the eternal presence. The kingdom of heaven is within me and I live in the city of God. I am one with all other citizens who inhabit this celestial metropolis. Here, in a true communion of Spirit, I find unity, peace and joy.

January 7

Today I Stand on the Mountaintop of My Soul and Cause My Spiritual Vision to Encompass More

For as he thinketh in his heart so is he.
Proverbs 23:7

As far as mind extends, so far extends Heaven.
Upanishad

My soul hath built for me a habitation.
Book of the Dead

NOTE that Proverbs does not say that a man is as he thinks he is—quite the contrary. It says he is *as* he thinks. Here is a vast difference. A person might imagine himself to be very clever while remaining quite dull, but if his thoughts are brilliant the man also will be brilliant. "As a man thinketh in his heart so is he." The heart stands for the center of consciousness, the point from which circulates everything that we are. It is said that Moses was led by the divine Spirit into a high mountain and told that all the land that his vision could encompass his feet could tread upon. This high mountain stands for an exalted place in consciousness. As consciousness extends its vision it extends the possibility of its objective experience. This means that objectively we possess that which subjectively we encompass. Our soul is always building a habitation for us, because consciousness is forever dealing with first cause, with the causeless cause, with that which plays with cause and effect as children play ball. Emerson tells us to stay at home with the cause, to build a habitation and therein to dwell. It is wonderful to realize that our true home is not made with hands but is eternal in the heavens.

TODAY I stand on the mountaintop of my soul and cause my spiritual vision to encompass more. I shall push out the horizons of my previous experiences in order that I may have more room. My soul shall look out and see that all is well. I am filled with peace, with joy and with contentment.

January 8

The Changeless Abides With Me.
I Am Calm and Peaceful in the Midst of Confusion

I am the Lord, I change not.
Malachi 3:6

The Tao, considered as unchanging, has no name.
Texts of Taoism

Immovable [is] God alone, and rightly [He] alone; for He Himself is in Himself, and by Himself, and round Himself, completely full and perfect.
Thrice-Greatest Hermes

WE should realize that all the great scriptures have taught one identical message—the unity of good. All the sacred books have been inspired by the one Mind. Each in its own tongue has told the story of reality. "I am the Lord, I change not," was revealed to the Hebrew mystic. To the great Chinese sage came the same message, "The Tao cannot change, it has no name," and to Hermes, God is in Himself, by Himself, full and perfect. If we can add to this glorified conception the realization that this divine being is the breath of our breath, omnipresent, forever within us, then we shall realize that we live in one eternal and perfect Mind. An excerpt from the sacred books on the attributes of God says, "There is no variableness in God since He is eternal, immortal and infinite. Nevertheless He is that from which every transformation arises." This means that, while we live in the eternal which does not change, we are forever drawing from It, or from Him, the possibility of the manifold expressions which give variety to existence and which make living interesting.

I KNOW that the changeless abides with me. I am calm and peaceful in the midst of confusion. I know that nothing moves the soul. Peace, infinite peace, is at the center of my being. I live, move and have my being in that which is perfect, complete within itself. That self is my self.

January 9

Today I Feel That I Merge With the Infinite

Canst thou by searching find out God? Canst thou find out the Almighty unto perfection? It is high as heaven... The measure thereof is larger than the earth, and broader than the sea.
Job 11:7-9

The Tao cannot be heard; what can be heard is not It. The Tao cannot be seen; what can be seen is not It. The Tao cannot be expressed in words; what can be expressed in words is not It. Do we know the Formless which gives form to form? In the same way the Tao does not admit of being.
Kwang-Tze

Realize that thou art "that"—Brahm, which is the cessation of all differentiation, which never changes its nature and is as unmoved as a waveless ocean, eternally unconditioned and undivided.
Raja Yoga

JOB asks us if we can find God by searching. He means that since God is everywhere, and since the subtle essence of the infinite is invisible, we do not have to search out the divine Spirit, but, rather, we should recognize It as the center of all life. That which we see is merely a reflection of this invisible presence. The Spirit Itself cannot be seen, but It is felt. Just as we do not see the essence of beauty, but do feel its presence, so we do not see God but we do feel the Divine in everything. The Creator is revealed in His creation. The formless gives rise to the formed. We should consciously unite ourselves with this invisible essence which pervades everything, that which our lesson says is eternally unconditioned and undivided. To do this is to find wholeness.

TODAY I feel that I merge with the infinite. While there seems to be a beginning and an end to each particular experience, there is neither beginning nor end to myself. My real spirit is omnipresent in God, secure in good, and perfect in divine being.

January 10

I Have a Spiritual Vision Within Me Which Beholds a Perfect Universe

I am Alpha and Omega, the beginning and the ending, saith the Lord, which is, and which was, and which is to come, the Almighty.
Revelation 1:8

But verily thou art not able to behold Me with these thine eyes; the divine eye I give unto thee.
The Bhagavad-Gita

There is but one Brahma which is Truth's Self. It is from ignorance of that One that the god-heads have been conceived to be diverse.
Mahabharata

SPIRIT as absolute cause is the beginning and end of everything. If we place complete reliance upon this Spirit as being the adequate cause, then we may as certainly place complete reliance upon It as producing the desired effect. When we give a spiritual mind treatment we are using this absolute cause, which is the alpha. From it automatically proceeds the effect, which is the omega. Thus the treatment contains the potential possibility of its own answer. Jesus said, "The words that I speak unto you, they are spirit, and they are life." He knew that because he consciously dealt with first cause, there would be no question about the effect. Our lesson says that a lack of the realization that there is but one final power, has given rise to the belief in many gods. Some of these gods we call evil, lack, want, limitation, pain, death. These false gods must be deserted for there is but one, which is truth's self. We are told that while we cannot behold the invisible presence with these physical eyes, "The divine eye I give unto thee." This has an identical meaning with the saying of Jesus, that spiritual things must be spiritually discerned.

I HAVE a spiritual vision within me which beholds a perfect universe. Daily this vision guides me to success, happiness, prosperity, physical and mental well-being. My spiritual vision is open—I am awake to the greater possibility.

January 11

Today I Speak My Word, Knowing That It Will Not Return Unto Me Void

He is in one mind and who can turn him?
Job 23:13

Mind is Brahma; for from mind even are verily born these beings—
by mind, when born, they live;—mind they approach, [mind] they enter.
Taittariya Upanishad

The Mind, then, is not separated off from God's
essentiality, but is united unto it, as light to sun.
Thrice-Greatest Hermes

JOB tells us that God is of one mind, and Jesus clearly taught that this one Mind includes our own thinking. Emerson also tells us that "there is one mind common to all individual men." It is this eternal and perfect Mind which we use. "Let this mind be in you which was also in Christ Jesus." The Mind of God must be peace, joy and perfection. We enter into this divine state of being in such degree as our thoughts are peaceful, joyous and perfect. To practice the presence of God is to practice the presence of perfection, of wholeness. This perfection and this wholeness include joy, peace and the fulfillment of every legitimate desire. Hermes said that our mind is united to God's essence as light is united to the sun, that is, we are individualized rays of the universal light. And the Upanishad says that everything is born from Mind, lives in It and by It. "In Him we live and move and have our being." We live in Mind and our thoughts go out into Mind to be fulfilled. This is the principle of mind healing and demonstration. Each one individualizes this universal Mind in a peculiar, unique and personal way. This is our divine inheritance. But we have drawn too lightly upon it, not fully realizing as Jesus did the limitless significance of our relationship with the infinite. We should learn more fully to enter our divine companionship.

TODAY I make a greater claim upon good. Today I speak my word, knowing that it will not return unto me void. It must accomplish and prosper, not because of the power of my will, but because I am willing to let, to permit, to accept, guidance, power and peace.

January 12

I Know That the Truth Is in Me, Perfect and Complete

*I have not written unto you because ye know not the truth,
but because ye know it, and that no lie is of the truth.*
I John 2:21

*This is God your Lord; All power is His:
But the gods ye call on beside Him have no power over the husk of a date stone!*
The Koran

*However anxious you may be, you will not save [yourself].
The perfect men of old first had [what they wanted to do] in themselves,
and afterwards they found [the response to it] in others.*
The Texts of Taoism

THERE is no power, presence or person outside the Divine. God not only is, He is also one. Our lesson from the Koran says that a belief in any opposite to the one has no power, even as darkness has no power over light. God is light, and in Him there is no darkness. To believe in the light is to dispel the darkness. A knowledge of good overcomes evil. The consciousness of abundance dispels want and pours the contents of the horn of plenty into our uplifted bowl of acceptance. John tells us that there is no lie in the truth. The truth never contradicts itself; it never denies us our good; it evermore proclaims the divine presence in everything, through everything and around everything. If God is allness, then there is no otherness. Kwang-Tze tells us that anxiety will not save us, because anxiety is unbelief. Jesus also tells us to take no anxious thought for tomorrow. The Chinese sage said that perfected men find that they already have everything within themselves, after which they discover the same in others. This corresponds to the teaching of Jesus that the blind cannot lead the blind. We must know the truth about ourselves before we can know it about others. This is the lesson.

I KNOW that the truth is in me, perfect and complete. I know that I manifest the truth, the whole truth, and nothing but the truth. I know that the truth makes me free. Today it frees me from the burden of care and anxiety. Every form of fear, every sense of burden is dropped from my consciousness and I walk the way of truth lightly, joyously.

January 13

Today I Recognize That I Am a Perfect Being, Living Under Perfect Conditions

*All things were made by him; and without him
was not anything made that was made.*
John 1:3

His being is conceiving of all things and making [them]...He even makes all things, in heaven, in air, in earth, in deep, in all of cosmos, in every part that is and that is not of everything. For there is naught in all the world that is not He.
Thrice-Greatest Hermes

*There is naught whatsoever higher than I...
All this is threaded on Me, as rows of pearls on a string.*
The Bhagavad-Gita

ALL things are threaded on the Divine, "like rows of pearls on a string." Spiritual intuition tells us that beauty is at the root of everything. Ugliness is its suppositional opposite. We must sense not the opposite but the reality. "For there is naught in all the world that is not He." This means that God is in and through everything. It is this divine presence which we are to recognize. For every apparent opposite we are to supply a realization of the truth about that opposite. In this way we supply a spiritual sense that is transcendent of the form which the material sense has created. In this way one can look at, in and through a difficulty or a difficult situation, until he perceives the truth at the very center of its being. Thus the devil, that is, evil or false appearance, is transmuted into an angel of light, for there is naught beside Him. If everything enduring and true comes from God, the Creator, then we may be certain that no matter what the appearance is, the reality is always perfect. This is why Jesus tells us to judge not according to appearances, but to judge righteously. We shall always judge righteously when our knowledge is based upon the certainty of the divine presence, perfect at the center of everything.

TODAY I recognize that I am a perfect being, living under perfect conditions, knowing that the good alone is real. I shall also know that good is the only thing that has any power either to act or to react. Everything that I do, say or think today, shall be done, said or thought from the spiritual viewpoint of God in everything.

January 14

Today I Am Resolved to See Only the Good

*He brought them out of darkness and the shadow of death,
and brake their bands in sunder.*
Psalm 107:14

"Sin is an obstruction in the heart; an inability to feel and comprehend all that is noble, true and great, and to take part in the good." If man is to be free from sin, his mind and heart must be opened to the influence of enlightenment.
The Talmud

In the world there is nothing absolutely bad; Know, moreover, evil is only relative.
The Masnavi I Ma'Navi

WE all wish to be brought out of darkness into the light. To be free from the bondage of fear, superstition and want, the mind must be riveted on freedom. The thought must rise transcendent over bondage. If we do this, then we are brought from the shadow of darkness into the light of the glorious freedom of the sons of God. The Talmud tells us that if we would be free from sin (mistake) the mind and heart must be open to enlightenment. Ignorance of the truth is the great sin or mistake from which spiritual enlightenment alone can give freedom. But what is spiritual enlightenment other than an increasing capacity consciously to become aware of the divine presence as peace, joy and harmony. Our lesson tells us that "...evil is only relative." This is a blessed assurance that no matter what the so-called evil of limitation may look like, it is an effect, blown across the pathway of our experience by ignorance. If we are to know the truth that makes us free, we must first recognize the essential nonreality of evil as being a thing within itself; we must equally know the essential absolute reality of good, not only as the supreme beneficence, but as the absolute power.

THEREFORE, today I am resolved to see only the good; and whenever evil, in the form of lack, fear, pain or uncertainty, presents itself, I shall endeavor instantly to recognize its native nothingness; to know that it is entirely relative. I shall make every effort to see through this limitation to that which is boundless and free. I shall proclaim the glad tidings of the freedom of the kingdom of God in my experience, and in the experience of everyone I contact.

January 15

There Is a Subtle Power Within Me—
The Essence of Spirit

For, lo, he that formeth the mountains, and createth the wind, and declareth unto man what is his thought, that maketh the morning darkness, and treadeth upon the high places of the earth, The Lord, The God of hosts, is his name.
Amos 4:13

From Him is the seed of all things, and it is He that upholds the Earth with all her mobile and immobile creatures.
Mahabharata

The Atman [the real self] is permanent, eternal and therefore existence itself.
Raja Yoga

THE great prophet Amos tells us that the God of hosts is the name of the power that forms the mountains, creates the winds, and declares Its presence in the sanctuary of our own thought. This poetical description of Spirit brings a sense of lightness, of peace and of transcendent joy. He seems to have lifted the load of life in his declaration that the Spirit treads upon the high places of the earth. This transcendent thought of God should ever be with us, and, like Jesus, we should walk over the waves of human disturbance rather than being submerged by them. Again, our lesson tells us that the Atman, which means the real self, is eternal and permanent, and here the text swings into the profound observation that Spirit exists within Itself. This has a definite meaning in demonstration. Life does not depend upon something outside itself, but immediately precipitates itself in our experience when we recognize it. It is this divine recognition which gives us transcendent power and we may rely upon this law for it is absolute. "Look unto me, and be ye saved, all the ends of the earth."

THERE is a subtle power within me, the essence of Spirit. I am sustained. I am guided. I am kept in the way of peace, prosperity and joy. Every atom of my being is vibrant with life, alive with deathless self-existence. There is something within me today which sings a celestial song, which exalts. This song finds its echo in everything I do, causing the deaf to hear, the blind to see, and awakens the paralysis of fear into life and action.

January 16

The Peace and the Power of a Conscious Recognition of the Divine Presence is With Me Today

Now the Lord is that Spirit; and where the Spirit of the Lord is, there is liberty.
II Corinthians 3:17

There is an originating and all-comprehending [principle] in my words, and an authoritative law for the things [which I enforce].
The Texts of Taoism

My fifth name is All good things created by Mazda, the offsprings of the holy principle.
The Zend-Avesta

WE all desire to experience liberty, and to know that the all-comprehensive Mind and principle is in the very words we speak. The Zend-Avesta tells us that all good things are created by Mazda (the principle of light). Here we have a concept of liberty, of light and of freedom accompanying our words; a divine authority imparting a creativeness to our thought. The creative power of Spirit is in our word in such degree as we become conscious of Spirit. We know that words of love overcome thoughts of hate. We know that peace will heal confusion, and that a sense of power will overcome the belief of weakness. All our work should be built upon the supposition that good overcomes evil not by combating, but by transcending it. The noncombativeness of Spirit is the principle back of the law of nonresistance which Jesus so plainly taught. The Spirit has no opposites; It is always joyous, perfect and free. There is no difference in the essence between our spirit and the Spirit. The spirit of man is the Spirit of God in man—the two are one.

THE peace and the power of the divine presence is with me today. Therefore, I walk calmly, knowing that I am enveloped in the divine presence. I am fully conscious that my word liberates every bondage, whether it be in myself or in others. I know that my word is the law of good automatically executing itself, irresistibly proclaiming itself; inevitably fulfilling itself.

January 17

I Know That I Live in the Changeless Reality

And the world passeth away, and the lust thereof;
but he that doeth the will of God abideth forever.
I John 2:17

And the horde of evil passions cannot tarry there, even for a moment.
Hymns of Mahayana Faith

All that is with you passeth away, but that which is with God abideth.
The Koran

NEITHER the will of God nor the nature of God can change. Reality is the same "yesterday, today and forever." That which was is, and that which is, will remain. Man's nature is spiritual. The only thing about him that can change is that which ought not to be permanent. We are changeless beings living in a changing world. Thus all of our experiences are bound together on a thread of continuity which Lowell called "the thread of the All-Sustaining Beauty which runs through all and doth all unite." It is wonderful to know that something permanent, substantial and eternal stands in the midst of our being, and, I believe, watches with joy the eternal change taking place. To the Spirit these changes are merely variations of experience. The Spirit is never caught, tied or bound. Ugliness may seem to exist for a brief moment but beauty, like truth, endures forever. All that is evil passes; as our Hymns of Faith says, it cannot exist even for a moment when faced by the divine reality. Everything that we now experience objectively will change, as it ought to, "…but that which is with God [of good] abideth."

I KNOW that I live in a changeless reality. I am not disturbed by the passage of time, the movement around me, nor the variations of experience through which I go. Something within me remains immovable and says, "Be still, and know that I am God." This "I Am" which is God within me, is substantial, changeless and perfect.

January 18

I Know That I Understand
How to Speak the Word of Truth

It is the spirit that quickeneth; the flesh profiteth nothing; the words that I speak unto you, they are spirit, and they are life.
John 6:63

And where do name and form both cease, and turn to utter nothingness? And the answer is, "In consciousness invisible and infinite, of radiance bright."
Buddhism in Translations

All the objects in the world are of one and the same taste, are of one reality, have nothing to do with the modes of particularization, and are not of dualistic character.
The Awakening of Faith

THIS lesson tells us that the objective world is quickened by the indwelling Spirit. The words of truth are life unto every form which they animate. All words which are spoken in a realization of the divine nature, are words of truth, and all such words give life. "It is the spirit that quickeneth." Our lesson also tells us that all objects, that is, the entire objective universe, comes from one substance. This substance is differentiated, that is, manifest in many forms. It looks as though the cause were dual because the forms are all different, but our lesson clearly states that we must not fall under this delusion which is of a dualistic character, but, rather, penetrate the unity back of all form. In our text from Buddhism, we have the idea that there is a place where both the objective name and form cease to exist as things in themselves. There is an invisible consciousness which radiates all forms. This does not mean a denial of the objective world, but, rather, an affirmation that it is an effect projected from, by, and within a transcendent cause which has complete control over it.

I KNOW that I understand how to speak the word of truth. I know that the invisible power of the Spirit is with me. I know that my world is peopled with forms of light, with the divine radiance. I know that I am a perfect being, living under perfect conditions with other perfect beings in a perfect God.

January 19

I See God in Everything; Personified in All People; Manifest in Every Event

Look not every man on his own things, but every man also on the things of others.
Philippians 2:3,4

Theirs was the fullness of heaven and earth;
the more that they gave to others, the more they had.
Kwang-Tze

One is the Sense that's active through them—their passion for each other.
'Tis Love Himself who worketh the one harmony of all.
Thus, therefore, let us sing the praise of God.
Thrice-Greatest Hermes

JESUS said, "Give and to you shall be given." All the great scriptures have announced this central and transcendent truth, realizing that every act carries with it a sequence, bringing the result of this action back to the self. This is what is meant by karma, for karma means the fruit of action. Emerson called it the law of compensation, and Jesus proclaimed the same law in his teaching that as we sow, so shall we reap. This is why Kwang-Tze tells us that the more we give to others the more we have. Whitman also refers to this when he says, "The gift is most of the giver and comes back most to him." This all means the return of the self to itself. The great apostle did not tell us to forget the self, he merely told us to also remember everyone else. That is, we are to see ourselves each in the other and behold God in all. Hermes tells us that when we realize love as the great harmony, we shall all sing the praise of God. Before we can do this we must perceive this harmony in each other and in everything. Thus, everything separated is united at the root. "Over all, in all and through all," the "sustaining beauty" of the inevitable "seed of perfection" to which Browning referred as nestling at the center of our own being.

I SEE God in everything, personified in all people, manifest in every event. The Spirit is not separated from the person or the event; It unites each to Itself, vitalizing each with the energy of Its own being; creating each through Its own divine imagination. I, too, am an instrument of Its perfection, and today I recognize my union, which is perfect and complete.

January 20

Today I Uncover the Perfection Within Me in All its Fullness

Again, the kingdom of heaven is like unto treasure hid in a field; the which when a man hath found, he hideth, and for joy thereof goeth and selleth all that he hath, and buyeth that field.
Matthew 13:44

Success [in the attainment of objects] forsaketh the person whose heart is unsteady, or who hath no control over his mind, or who is a slave of his senses.
The Mahabharata

Without either hunger or thirst, beyond all grief [all] rejoice in the place of heaven.
Katha Upanishad

WHO would not be successful in the true sense of the term? For there is no success without happiness and a sense of certainty. There is something eternal about success. There is no grief in success, because one who is truly successful is no longer sad. He knows the things of this world are but temporary. His treasure is truly in heaven. Jesus likened it unto a treasure hid in the field, and he said he would sell everything we have in order that we might purchase this field and uncover this hidden treasure. This treasure, the Mahabharata tells us, cannot be found while the heart is unsteady, while one is a slave to objective appearances, or while he lacks control over his thought world. All of this means that success, even in our objective undertakings, depends, first of all, upon stability of mind, consistency of purpose and concentration of effort. The kingdom of heaven is already hidden within us. The field which contains this hidden treasure is our own soul. The priceless pearl is covered by the hardened shell of experience. We must learn to see God at the center of our being.

TODAY I uncover the perfection within me. In its fullness I reveal the indwelling kingdom. I look out upon the world of my affairs, knowing that the Spirit within me makes my way both immediate and easy, for I know that "it is not I, but the Father that dwelleth in me, he doeth the works."

January 21

Today I Enter Into the Limitless Variations Which the Divine Spirit Has Projected Into My Experience

For all flesh is as grass, and all glory of man as the flower of grass. The grass withereth, and the flower thereof falleth away: But the word of the Lord endureth forever.
I Peter 1:24-25

All products of Brahm, which is reality, are themselves real; and there is nothing different from it. Whoever says that there is [anything different], is not free from illusion but is like a man talking in his sleep.
Raja Yoga Philosophy

The unreal hath no being; the real never ceaseth to be.
The Bhagavad-Gita

THE Gita tells us that unreality has no existence, while reality cannot cease to be. Our lesson also states that all the effects of the Spirit are themselves real, and that there is nothing different from the divine Spirit. Jesus tells us to judge not according to appearances. However, he did not tell us that appearances are unreal. The unreality of appearances lies not in the thing itself, but rather in our interpretation of it. If we spiritually interpret the universe, we shall understand it, enter into it, become one with it. We shall see that the bird, the rock, the mountain and the river are spiritual manifestations of the joy of the divine Mind. The illusion is seeking to interpret them as being separate from the infinite. The blade of grass may wither and the petals fall from the flower, but the idea, "...the word of the Lord endureth forever." This is a very interesting lesson, since it teaches that there is not only a fundamental unity, there is also an eternal variety. Without this variety life would become stagnant.

TODAY I enter into the limitless variations which the divine Spirit has projected into my experience. I know that all things are good when rightly used. I perceive that all experience is a play of life upon itself. I enter into the game of living, then, with joyful anticipation, with spontaneous enthusiasm and with the determination to play the game well and to enjoy it.

January 22

I Am Alive, Awake and Aware, My Spiritual Eyes Are Open

For now we see through a glass, darkly; but then face to face: now I know in part; but then shall I know even as also I am known.
I Corinthians 13:12

O ye people, earth-born folk, ye who have given yourselves to drunkenness and sleep and ignorance of God, be sober now, cease from your surfeit, cease to be glamored by irrational sleep!
Thrice-Greatest Hermes

If ye knew God as He ought to be known, ye would walk on the seas, and the mountains would move at your call.
The Kashf Al-Mahjub

"FOR now we see through a glass, darkly;..." How familiar this passage is to all of us, but what does it mean other than our vision is clouded by a material sense of things? Hermes tells us that we are both drunk and asleep; that we are ignorant of God. Emerson tells us that once in a while we awake from our slumber and look about us to perceive the world of reality, but too soon sink back again into sleep. And from another ancient text, quoted above, we are told that if we knew God as we ought to, we would be able to walk on the seas, that the mountains would come at our call. All progress is an awakening. Every new scientific fact is a discovery. This also is an awakening. It is really true that we are largely asleep, dreaming away the hours. "Awake thou that sleepest, and arise from the dead, and Christ shall give you life." It is indeed "high time that we awake from this sleep." No one can awaken us but the self. Let us, then, make every endeavor to arouse the mind to reality and to penetrate the gloom of fear and superstition; to cast aside doubt and uncertainty; to behold the light which is eternal.

I AWAKE! I awake! I awake! I am alive, awake and aware. My spiritual eyes are open. As from a long night's sleep, I awake!

January 23

Today I Shall Walk in the Light, My Mind Shall Be Illumined

Thy sun shall no more go down; neither shall thy moon withdraw itself: for the Lord should be thine everlasting light, and the days of thy mourning shall be ended.
Isaiah 60:20

Who uses well his light, Reverting to its [source so] bright,
Will from his body ward all blight.
The Tao Te Ching

The virtuous and well-conducted man, your majesty, is like a medicine in destroying the poison of human corruption; is like a healing herb in quieting the disease of human corruption; is like water in removing dirt and defilement of human corruption; is like the magic jewel in giving all good fortune to men.
Buddhism in Translations

THERE are so many illustrations in the sacred texts of the world, relative to the light. The Spirit is thought of as being the essence of light. Man is spoken of as being the "candle of the Lord." "The light shines in the darkness and the darkness comprehendeth it not." That is, the darkness has no power over light; light will overcome darkness, but darkness cannot overcome light. When Isaiah said that "...the Lord shall be thy everlasting light..." he meant that there is a light within us, the light of truth, of Spirit, of God, which cannot become obliterated, cannot be blown out. The "candle of the Lord" burns forever because its wick is sunk deep in the wellsprings of reality—that light, that spring, that substance, to which Jesus referred when he told the woman at the well that if ever she drank from it she would never thirst again. It is no wonder that the woman asked him to give her of this water that she might no longer be compelled laboriously to draw from the fountain which can become depleted.

TODAY I shall walk in the light and my consciousness shall be illumined. My thoughts shall be guided and my way guarded, for I know that in my light there is no darkness. In this divine light there are no shadows.

January 24

Today I Bestow the Essence of Love Upon Everything

> *The law of the Lord is perfect, converting the soul... The statutes of the Lord are right, rejoicing the heart: the commandment of the Lord is pure, enlightening the eyes.*
> Psalm 19:7,9

> *For the Self-begotten One, the Father-Mind, perceiving His own Works, sowed into all Love's Bond...so that all might continue loving on for endless time, and that these Weavings of the Father's Light might never fail.*
> The Chaldean Oracles

> *But love will the God of Mercy vouchsafe to those who believe and do the things that be right.*
> The Koran

"THE law of the Lord is perfect" and the law of the Lord is love. We are made perfect in the law when we enter into the communion of love with one another and with the invisible essence of life. Love is the fulfillment of the law, that is, we never can make the most perfect use of the law unless that use is motivated by love, by a sincere desire to express unity, harmony and peace. As the true artist weds himself to the essence of beauty, imbibing her spirit that it may be transmitted to the canvas, or awaken a living form from cold marble, we so must wed ourselves to the essence of love that we may imbibe its spirit, and, transmitting it, give loveliness to all events. We should not hesitate to express our appreciation for people, things and events. There is too little enthusiasm about life. We sacrifice hope on the altar of unbelief and fail to extract the essence of reality from the invisible, because we refuse to rejoice in our apparently trivial relationships. Love will not remain abstract. Its power of transmutation in human events comes only as we catch its vision and mold it into human experience.

TODAY I bestow the essence of love upon everything. Everyone shall be lovely to me. My soul meets the soul of the universe in everyone. Nothing is dead; everything is alive. Nothing is ugly; everything is beautiful; everything is meaningful. This love is a healing power touching everything into wholeness; healing the wounds of experience with its divine balm.

January 25

Today I Walk in the Light of God's Love

God is a Spirit: and they that worship him must worship him in spirit and in truth.
John 4:24

I the Father of this universe, the Mother, the Supporter,
the Grandsire, the Holy One to be known, the Word of Power.
The Bhagavad-Gita

The Tao produced One; One produced Two;
Two produced Three; Three produced All things.
The Tao Te Ching, Part I

OUR lesson tells us that God is the Father, the mother, the supporter, and grandsire. It tells us that from the oneness of God proceeds the law, the essence and the word. Then it tells us that God is Spirit. Wonderful indeed is this conception of the union of all life, which Jesus proclaimed in the ecstasy of his illumination. "I and the Father are one." All cause and all effect proceed from the invisible Spirit. Man is one with this Spirit and cannot be separated from It. His word has power because his word is the action of God through his thought. Power is, we use it, we do not create it. Let us seek to use the power of this word more generously, with a greater idea of beneficence, its abundance and its availability. When we learn to believe, then our belief is increased. Receiving much, we shall receive, giving everything, we shall, in return, receive all. Let us be willing to die to the lesser in order to become resurrected into the greater. This is the true meaning of the thought that we must lose our lives in order to find them. Naturally we must let go of ignorance if we would gain knowledge; we must stop walking in darkness if we would walk in the light.

TODAY I walk in the light of God's love. Today I am guided and my guidance is multiplied. I know exactly what to do; exactly how to do it. There is an inspiration within me which governs every act, every thought, in certainty, with conviction and peace.

January 26

I Believe in Divine Guidance and I Know that Underneath Are the Everlasting Arms

The eternal God is thy refuge, and underneath are the everlasting arms.
Deuteronomy 33:27

*All this universe has the [Supreme] Deity for its life.
That Deity is Truth. He is the Universal Soul.*
Chhandogys Upanishad

But God will increase the guidance of the already guided.
The Koran

IF God is our refuge, why is it that we refuse to avail ourselves of this divine security? The psalmist tells us that "the Lord is nigh unto all them that call upon him...in truth." This can have but one meaning. We cannot call upon God in truth unless we enter into the divine nature in truth, that is, we cannot expect love to become hate, nor peace to enter into confusion. If we could call upon God in truth, we must become like the truth. This is the seemingly unfathomable mystery of the infinite, invisible essence which surrounds us. Jesus tells us that if we abide in Him, then His words will abide in us, and we shall ask for anything that we will and it shall be done unto us. The everlasting arms are beneath but they bear us up only when we enter into the truth. The Koran tells us that God increases our guidance once we have guidance. This is a mystical (mystical does not mean mysterious, it means an intuitive perception) way of saying that if we believe in divine guidance, then we will be divinely guided. "Act as though I am, and I will be." "Believe and it shall be done unto you."

TODAY I believe in divine guidance. Today I believe that underneath are the everlasting arms. Today I rest in this divine assurance and this divine security. I know that not only all is well with my soul, my spirit and my mind; all is well with my affairs.

January 27

I Bless Everything and Know that All Good Will Multiply in My Experience

But whoso looketh into the perfect law of liberty, and continueth therein, he being not a forgetful bearer, but a doer of the work, this man shall be blessed in his deed.
James 1:25

It [God] was not created in the past, nor is it to be annihilated in the future; it is eternal, permanent, absolute; and from all eternity it sufficiently embraces in its essence all possible merits.
The Mahayana

That itself on which all things depend, and from which every transformation arises!
Kwang-Tze

JAMES tells us that we should look to the perfect law of liberty, follow its precepts and then we shall be blessed in our deeds. This means to keep the eye single, or centered, on the presence, the power and the responsiveness of Spirit. The law of God would have to be a law of liberty, since bondage could not come from freedom any more than death could be born of the principle of life. We often wonder why we are so limited, and too frequently project the blame for our limitations upon the universe itself. This is a psychological trick which we play in ignorance of the true facts. Limitation is not imposed upon us by the universe, but through our own ignorance.

Every discovery in science tends to prove this. As Kwang-Tze says, all transformation, that is, every form, arises from the invisible and takes temporary form in our experience. Fortunately, none of these forms is permanent. We should look upon them as the play of life upon itself. In our own experience we are privileged by the creative to become co-creators in our personal affairs. As our lesson says, the divine creative Spirit embraces every possible action. No greater freedom could be found nor given, and we should daily open our consciousness to the divine influx, expecting greater wisdom, more definite guidance and more complete self-expression.

TODAY I lift up my consciousness and receive a more abundant expression. I bless everything and know that all good will multiply in my experience. I expect the good. I live in a state of joyous anticipation, as well as quiet realization.

January 28

Today My Heart Is Without Fear, I Have Implicit Confidence in the Good, the Enduring, and the True

> *Though an host should encamp against me, my heart shall not fear: though war should rise against me, in this will I be confident.*
> Psalm 27:1,3

> *When one cherishes no fear of anything, when one is not feared by anything, when one cherishes no desire, when one bears no hate, then is one said to have attained to the state of Brahma.*
> The Mahabharata

> *Holiness is the best of all good. Happy, Happy the man who is holy with perfect holiness!... The will of the Lord is the law of holiness.*
> The Zend-Avesta

FEAR is the only thing we shall be afraid of. It is not the host encamped against us, nor the confusion of war around us, that we need to fear; it is a lack of confidence in the good which alone should cause concern. Through inner spiritual vision we know that evil is transitory but good is permanent. We know that right finally dissolves everything opposed to it. In confidence, then, and with a calm of peace, we know that the truth never fails to win every issue. The power of good is with us. The power of the spirit is supreme over every antagonist. Then we should cherish no fear, and when we neither fear nor hate we come to understand the unity of life, and then, our lesson tells us, we have attained to the state of Brahma (conscious union with God). Thus the Zend-Avesta tells us that "holiness is the best of all good," and it hastens to add that there is no difference between the law of holiness (wholeness) and the divine will. In words, since the nature of God is peace, then the will of God is toward peace; since the nature of God is love, then the will of God is toward love—"Who knows not love, knows not God, for God is love."

TODAY my heart is without fear. I have implicit confidence in the good, the enduring and the true. I enter into conscious union with the Spirit. I am happy, whole and complete in my divine self. Therefore, with joy I enter into the activities of the day and with confidence I look forward to tomorrow.

January 29

I Shall See Him Reflected in Every Form, Back of Every Countenance, Moving in Every Act

The spirit of God hath made me, and the breath of the Almighty hath given me life.
Job 33:4

Thou hast begotten the Man in Thy self-born Mind, and in Thy Reflection and Conception. He is the man begotten of Mind, to whom Reflection gave form. Thou hast given all things to the Man.
Fragments of a Faith Forgotten

We created man: and we know what his soul whispereth to him, and we are closer to him than his neck-vein.
The Koran

AFTER long meditation and much deep reflection, having passed through the confusion of human experience, Job finally arrived at the conclusion that the spirit of God was within him, and that the breath of God was his life. We all have traveled this same pathway of experience; the journey of the soul to "the heights above," and always there has been a deep inquiry in our minds: What is it all about? Does life make sense? What is the meaning of birth, human experience, and the final transition from this plane, which we call death? Somewhere along the line we too must exclaim with Job, "The spirit of God hath made me and the breath of the Almighty hath given me life!" With the Koran we must realize that the Divine is closer to us even than our physical being. Nothing can be nearer to us than that which is the very essence of our own being. Our external search after reality culminates the greatest of all possible discoveries—reality is at the center of our own being. Life is from within out. We must no longer judge according to appearances, but, rather, base our judgments on the assumption that the God-Mind dwells within us; proclaims or reflects us into every act. Thus the search after reality culminates in the realization of the ever-present good. The search, at this point, should cease, and we should at once enter into our divine inheritance, no longer as searchers after, but now as users of, the highest gift of heaven.

I FEEL that my search is over. I feel that I have discovered the great reality, and today I shall speak this reality into every experience I have. I shall see Him reflected in every form, back of every countenance, moving in every act.

January 30

I Know That Every Apparent Death Is Resurrection, Therefore Gladly I Die to Everything That Is Unlike Good

Yea, though I walk through the valley of the shadow of death, I will fear no evil; for thou art with me; thy rod and thy staff they comfort me.
Psalm 23:4

Unhappy is he who mistakes the branch for the tree, the shadow for the substance.
The Talmud

Gain for yourselves, ye sons of Adam, by means of these transitory things which are not yours, that which is your own, and passeth not away.
Fragments of a Faith Forgotten

WE are told that we must gain a knowledge of that which cannot pass away. The Talmud says that unhappy conditions arise when we mistake shadow for substance. Even the valley of the shadow of death causes no fear when we arrive at the consciousness of the psalmist who, from the exaltation of his divine deliverance, proclaimed "...thy rod and thy staff they comfort me." The rod and the staff of truth is the realization of the substantiality and the permanence of that which cannot change. We are ever renewed by the passage of the divine light through our consciousness. "Behold, I make all things new." The revitalizing, regenerative power of Spirit flows from the consciousness of wholeness into our physical organism and into every objective act, when we give the realization of divine presence free passage through our thought. Emerson tells us that in these moments we are conscious that we as isolated beings are nothing, but that the light is all. Thus he admonishes us to get our "bloated nothingness" out of the way of the divine circuit. How wonderful to realize this possibility to which he refers—nonresistance and nonburden. Let us, then, learn to let the burden slip from the shoulders of personal responsibility and enter into our divine union with enthusiasm.

I KNOW that every apparent death is a resurrection. Therefore gladly, today, I die to everything that is unlike the good. Joyfully I am resurrected into that which is beautiful, enduring and true. Silently I pass from less to more; from isolation into inclusion; separation into oneness.

January 31

I Release Every Tension of Mind and Body

Release and ye shall be relaxed.
Luke 6:37

TODAY I release all thoughts of fear from my mind. Today I lay down the burden of carrying the load of responsibility for life for myself or for others. Today I relax all sense of strain. I remember that Emerson said "The universe remains to heart unhurt;" that Jesus said, "Let not your heart be troubled." Therefore, I lay all trouble aside, seeking to look through it, beyond it, above it; to detach it from the realm of reality, to separate it from any consciousness that it belongs to me or to anyone else, regardless of what any problem of the moment seems to be.

Today I proclaim my divine inheritance. I am rich with the riches of God. I am strong with the power of God. I am guided by the wisdom of God. I am held in the goodness of God, I arise and return unto my Father's house. Knowing that the law of good operates through my word, that is, through my thought or faith, upon my expectancy and acceptance I speak my word.

I align myself with the powers of goodness and of right action. I abide in perfect and complete faith in God as my ever-present good. I take up no arms to fight the negative. I merely turn from all fear; turn joyfully and resolutely to faith, realizing that light is immune to darkness, that the night has no power over the day, that dawn dissipates the shadows of midnight. I turn my attention to the light eternal, without struggle, realizing that that light, shining through the dark places of my consciousness, will dissipate them and that I shall walk in that light in which there is no darkness. Not only shall I walk in this light, I shall radiate it. I shall impart it to others.

I SHALL remember the saying, "Let your light so shine before men that they, seeing your good works, shall glorify your Father which art in heaven." I shall remember that the Father which art in heaven is in that heaven which is within me.

February 1

I Am Established in Right Thinking, and No One Can Confuse Me This Day

Blessed is the man that walketh not in the counsel of the ungodly.
Psalm 1:1

THE "ungodly" are those who perceive, accept and describe evil. Unfortunately there are many people whom we meet each day who are in such states of consciousness. Unless we are exceptionally careful of the ideas accepted by us, we shall let a few false ones slip into the back corners of our mind. Gradually this infiltration makes an impression, and we become discouraged and feel that all men are out to defraud us. As students of the Science of Mind, we *know* that this is not true, and that we must perceive the truth operating through our fellow man. We are faced with the necessity of finding God in man, for people around us are born of the same Mind and love of God that we are, and our knowledge of this will set us free from any negation that comes our way. Our offices, homes and activities are filled with the sons and daughters of God. We must do all that we can to actually know and experience this.

BECAUSE I believe that God is omnipresent as life, love and wisdom, I now see these spiritual qualities alive in everyone with whom I live and work. Every individual in my world is a son of God, a creative expression of divine love. Each one offers to me only that which is good, creative and true. All else is as nothing to me, for I know that I am established in a perfect Mind, where all is order, peace and right action. There is no confusion, for God is the eternal peace of my soul. I see this within myself, and I seek this same peace within my fellow man. God within me, God within each one I meet this day. All is good in my world.

February 2

I Give Thanks in Advance for the Answer to My Prayer

His delight is in the law of the Lord, and in his law doth he meditate day and night.
Psalm 1:2

THE law of Mind never fails. Even when it delivers to us the things and conditions we do not like, it has still functioned perfectly. Our use of it determines our experience, and wise is the man who only thinks rightly. Prayer, scientifically understood, is a statement of spiritual fact. It convinces us that good alone is true, and right alone is victorious. As we are convinced of these facts, the results are brought into our lives by the law of life. The psalmist advises us to delight in the law of the Lord, which is the law of Mind. He suggests that we think about this law both day and night. We may have what we want, but we must think it definitely and continuously, in order to have it made manifest. Thanksgiving in prayer is vital, for it makes us believe that we already have our good. When the idea is established within us, it then takes form around us.

I GIVE thanks that there is a perfect law of Mind, and that I am able to use it. God responds to me as I respond to Him. I now turn to the indwelling Spirit and affirm Its presence. I know that every true desire of my heart is being established unto me today. I place these desires in the law of good, and rejoice that its perfect action is now taking place in me, around me, and through me. All this day I remind myself that my demonstrations already are made. I give in advance for the answers to my prayers. My whole being is open and receptive to that good which is now arriving on my doorstep. I rest in the law and meditate upon its accuracy.

February 3

I Am Secure, for I Am in the Father and the Father Is in Me

He shall be like a tree planted by the rivers of water, that bringeth forth his fruit in his season; his leaf also shall not wither; and whatsoever he doeth shall prosper.
Psalm 1:3

THE omnipresence, omniscience, omnipotence and omniaction of God as infinite Mind are the security of man. These eternal verities sustain us at every instant and in every place. They are ours in days of good cheer, they are ours in times of despair. They are never lost, they are merely forgotten in our confusion. We are not under the law of material problems and world beliefs. We are under the law of the Spirit which maintains us in freedom and peace. All that God is, is around us and within us, and is eternally asking of us that we recognize It. Jesus had the capacity to recognize God where those around him were recognizing evil. We, too, must see the possibility of God, rather than the impossibilities that the world believes. Our security lies in this ability to know truth regardless of conditions, and love regardless of hurts.

ALL that God is, is now alive in my world, my body and my mind. This presence and power is real to me this day, and I rest in Its eternal embrace. I am secure, for His Mind thinks through me; and His love enfolds me. I am not afraid of any negative situation, for I know that I am in the Father and the Father is in me. Nothing can disturb me, for divine order is now established in my mind and perfect peace now fills my heart. There are no impossibilities today, for God is my eternal possibility of greater good, greater love and greater health.

February 4

I am Victorious Over All Difficulties, for I Have Faith in God, the Good, Omnipotent

The Lord knoweth the way of righteousness; but the way of the ungodly shall perish.
Psalm 1:6

THE victorious attitude is the one that recognizes the unlimited power of God. Without this awareness no one can be victorious over the negatives of life. Those who live without spiritual vision and understanding are forever trying to solve their problems by manipulating their human minds, and exerting their human wills. This exhausts them, frustrates them, and gives them no peace. The recognition of God as cause, and as the creative power of this world brings victory to the soul. It does this because all problems begin and end within the individual's own consciousness. As we realize that God's Mind is in us as the basis of our individual consciousness, we begin to solve our problems at their point of origin, which is within ourselves. We find the inner security which comes from knowing that God's ideas in us are now giving us correct instruction in the way we should go.

I HAVE faith that within me is the presence of God as pure Mind. I have faith that this inner Christ is now victorious over all the problems facing me this day and this week. I let go of all human will. I believe that God has prepared for me increased good in every department of my life. I accept this good, and rejoice in it. I am victorious, undaunted. I go forth to handle the affairs of my life with wisdom and love. Nothing can stop the action of God from taking place in my experience, for I love God and know His inner presence. I am poised, confident and sure, for I am established in unlimited good. This is the truth and I declare it.

February 5

The Father in Me Doeth the Work, and I Let His Mind Bring Forth Perfect Results

O Lord, our Lord, how excellent is thy name in all the earth.
Psalm 8:1

TODAY we are labor conscious, and it is essential for us to have a correct understanding of the spiritual nature of our work. Whether this work is in the home or in the commercial world, it is the same. The spiritual idea behind all work is the individualizing of the universal action of infinite Mind. Our jobs, regardless of location or income level, are the places where we individualize the eternal activity of God. It is that point where we "let" God unfold through us. Jesus did his mighty works because he was able to let God flow through him. We are trying to do the same, and this requires a constant reminder to our outer minds that the inner intelligence, born of God, will work through us as we let it. The work of the Lord through man is always toward perfection, and that is why the psalmist praises the excellency of the name of the Lord. This name is infinite Mind forever unfolding through man.

THE unlimited business of God is taking place through me and giving me ease and comfort in my daily work. God is never fatigued, and His action taking place in me is one of ceaseless energy, vitality and joy. I rest in the consciousness of God, and know that at every instant I am sustained, directed and prospered by the unlimited action of the indwelling Father. All resistance to employment is gone, I love to express the creative activity of God in my work this day. I work with joy, I accomplish with ease and I fulfill this day with good results.

February 6

I Am the Creation of God, Therefore, I Have Nothing to Fear

What is man, that thou art mindful of him? And the son of man, that thou visiteth him? For thou hast made him a little lower than the angels, and hast crowned him with glory and honor.
Psalm 8:4,5

THERE seem to be strange quirks in the human mind. It has the ability to remember so much that is not good, and to remember so little that is good. Whenever we look to the past, we almost always remember the great hurts, and fail to recall the great joys and blessings we have once experienced. Memory, in its true spiritual sense, is the capacity to remember our origin in God and the steady unfoldment of our nature through experience. It is the ability to know again that we are created by an infinite Mind and prospered in all our ways by an infinite love. It reminds us of our divine destiny to overcome all evil, and to abide in all that is true and good. As we do this, all fear is removed from our thought, for there is an inner uprising of faith in ourselves and in our fellowmen. The Mind that created us sustains us, unfolds our good before us, and leads us in pleasant ways.

TODAY, there is nothing to fear, for I remember that I am a spiritual being, and nothing can touch me, save that which is good. No material belief or situation has power over me, for "He that sent me is with me." My own divine nature repels and destroys the untruths of negation. They never have been a part of the real self which I am. I have faith in only that which is of good report. I love God and believe in God. I recognize the divine idea which I am in the Father's Mind. I am the creation of perfect God and I fear nothing, for God is all.

February 7

I Take Dominion Over My World Today and Handle It Rightly

Thou madest him to have dominion over the works of thy hands: thou hast put all things under his feet.
Psalm 8:6

TIMIDITY has never been a virtue, and modern psychology has proved that it is a definite indication of a wrong habit pattern in the unconscious. Many people who never give the impression of being timid, fail to really take dominion over their own thought and organize it into efficient patterns. As metaphysicians, we know that until we control our thinking, we shall never control the conditions of our environment, business and personal health. The point of control is always within, and the wise person starts to assume dominion over his disorganized thinking. This is easier to accomplish when we realize that Spirit within us is urging us in this direction. God wants us to control ourselves, and not other people. We are spiritually equipped to do this.

BY the power of God in the midst of me, I now take dominion over my own thinking. I know that peace in my mind means peace in my world. I recognize that within myself this day the Mind of God is in full control of my every activity. I am poised and centered in God's eternal peace. I meet every situation as it arises with confidence, for I have faith that the right idea will emerge out of God's Mind for me to use at every instant. I refuse to let fear control me, and I joyously let God have dominion in my affairs. I accept each idea as it comes to me, knowing that God's ideas answer every question and solve every problem. I am in control.

February 8

Today I Praise the Health of God in My Body

I will praise thee, O Lord, with my whole heart;
I will shew forth all thy marvelous works.
Psalm 9:1

THE law of response is the law of praise. Whatever we bless increases, and whatever we curse decreases. The key to the use of this law is to watch our ideas and note the ones we are praising. This is easy to do, as the ideas we talk about the most are the ones we are praising. Like all laws it is impersonal. When we constantly discuss disease, we are actually praising its power in our lives, and the law produces further illness and discomfort. Likewise, when we are not at our best physically, we can praise the health of God in our bodies, and the law will bring forth greater ease, vitality and strength. Those who are sick need to praise the health of God within them to be healed. Those who are in perfect health should praise this same divine health, as it will then be maintained and made permanent. Health is a part of our spiritual inheritance and we bless the one Mind for it.

I BELIEVE that God is the health of my body. I recognize this great spiritual gift in every part of me. I have faith in its healing, restoring, refreshing power. It fills me now with perfect life, energy and strength. I praise and bless this great inner action of God. I dedicate myself to the right use of this health. No fatigue, strain nor illness can touch me this day, for God is my perfect health. My work is easy, and my body responds to every action necessary to my work today. All is ease, comfort and joy. I respond to the health and vitality of my fellowman. All whom I contact are equally alive with God's radiant health, for God is the health of His people.

February 9

I Make Right Decisions, for the Judgment of God Within Tells Me What to Do and When to Do It

> *The Lord is known by the judgment he executeth:*
> *the wicked is snared in the work of his own hands.*
> Psalm 9:16

PEOPLE come to the doors of professional consultants with the query "What shall I do about this?" Apparently, we have lost the knack of finding the answers to our questions from our own inner resources. Yet, the prophets of every faith have told us of the inner capacity, born of God, to set ourselves straight and to know what to do. The quandaries of the human mind are amazing in their complexities, and the wisdom of the divine Mind is amazing in Its simplicities. God in the midst of us knows what to do and is seeking to impel us toward right decisions. Whenever we do not know what to do and when to do it, we turn to that one in the midst of us and affirm its capacity to give us the clue. Infinite wisdom never fails to respond to the receptive mind and the loving heart. Divine ideas appear in our consciousness and we make right decisions with ease.

EVERY question in my life has an answer, and every problem has a solution. I turn in thought from that which seems to be, to that which really is. Divine intelligence working in my mind now knows exactly what to do. I accept this inner guidance, and follow its instructions. Every moment of this day I make wise and loving decisions which bless and benefit my fellowman as well as myself. I judge not by appearances, I know they are often incorrect and false. I have faith that God's Mind now decides every issue, selects every right idea, and gives me true accomplishment with ease. My thought is clear and strong, for God's ideas are mine today.

February 10

No Confusion Can Exist for Me, for I Am Established in Peace

He hath said in his heart, I shall not be moved; for I shall never be in adversity.
Psalm 10:6

WE are established eternally in a peace which has never been disturbed. When the appearances of adversity and confusion confound us, it is indicative that definite meditation is needed to restore our thought in the peace that forever abides in fullness. God is never disturbed, hurt or aware of adversity. The universal Mind only knows the peace, order and harmony of Itself. Within us this same Spirit knows these things for us in our individual worlds. As we remember this and affirm this, we are moved out of adversity into prosperity, out of error into truth. No confusion can exist in the mind of him whose thought is stayed on God. Our homes and business will take on this same harmony, for these are merely the extensions of our thinking and respond to each mood of our consciousness. We then abide in peace and work in order.

TO every inharmonious and disturbing idea in my mind I say "Get thee behind me Satan," for I refuse to be disturbed today. I dedicate myself to twenty-four hours of peace, order and constructive thinking. God's presence in my world guarantees my peace. The adversities of material thought and situations cannot come nigh me, for God's inner love maintains me in divine accord with all that is good and true. Nothing can confuse me, for I know that his Mind in me is always calm, poised and sure, and this Mind is my mind now. I use each hour to demonstrate the peace of being. I work in peace. I walk in peace, for God is the peace of my soul.

February 11

I Dedicate My Speech to That Which Is True, Just and Loving

The Lord shall cut off all flattering lips, and the tongue that speaketh proud things.
Psalm 12:3

HONEST people speak truthfully and wisely. It takes greater wisdom to know when to be silent, than when to speak. Most of us talk far too much, and our effusiveness bears witness to our undisciplined minds. We flatter people and while doing it know that the words are not true, but we also know the person to whom they are addressed will probably hope they are true. True religion should produce a race of honest people who say only what they mean. Too often we are weighed in the balances of life and found wanting, because we have made extravagant and incorrect statements. The law of Mind gives us back our words in form, and this is not always a pleasant experience. Students of the Science of Mind should make an honest attempt to control their speech, watch their words and always say that which is loving and wise, not always easy to do.

MY words shall not return unto me void and they shall accomplish whereunto they are sent; therefore, I dedicate my speech to truth. I speak that which is loving and wise in the sight of God and of man. I know that God speaks through me, when I am at one with his Mind in the midst of me. I let every word of my mouth be one of true appraisal based on the way the situation is in God. Thus, only that which is constructive, valuable and just comes forth from my lips today. I speak the truth, and the truth is that which is true of God in man. I praise the good, and I deny the evil. I love to speak the loving word unto my fellowman.

February 12

God's Activity in Me Maintains Me in Prosperity

I will sing unto the Lord, because he hath dealt bountifully with me.
Psalm 13:6

THE recognition that prosperity is born of God, and is the rightful experience for all who are spiritually minded, is necessary if we are to evolve according to God's idea of man. Too long has money been the symbol of evil. The very people who proclaim against prosperity are merely giving emphasis to their state of mind which prevents them from having it in their own lives. We need to love the wealth of God as well as the wisdom of God. His eternal abundance surrounds us at every instant, but we can partake of it only as we accept it as our own. We do this by acknowledging that all creation is the manifestation of God's Mind, and that we are the sons of God equipped to receive and dispense the universal goodness. It flows to us and operates through us as we accept it as our own. Rather, as we demonstrate prosperity we can share it with those who do not yet know its divine source.

THE abundance of all good surrounds me and operates through me this day. I have faith in God's prosperity for me, and I accept it now as mine. Like Jesus, I say "all that the Father hath is mine." I accept it with joy and use it with wisdom. I realize that I am responsible for the right use of God's money in my life. I have no fear of lack, and do not believe that lack can affect me. I know that I am the inlet and the outlet to all that God is and has. I lovingly share my good with my fellowman, for it is not mine, but of Him that made me. I affirm abundance, talk abundance and expect abundance. I look out upon my world and see the bounty of God made manifest, and I love it.

February 13

There Is No Resistance in Me—I Let God Act

Lord, who shall abide in thy tabernacle, who shall dwell in thy holy hill? He that walketh uprightly, and worketh righteousness, and speaketh the truth in his heart.
Psalm 15:1, 2

IF the power of God is greater than the assumed power of evil, then it is up to us to prove it. Too many people say they believe that God is omnipotent, and continue to demonstrate unhappiness, illness and lack. The fact is that if they really believed it, they would prove it in their own experience. One of the reasons for failure in proving our principle is an unconscious resistance to spiritual things. Often we are unaware we have this resistance, and thus seek alibis for our lack of good. There is a simple way of removing this block to spiritual demonstration. It is the affirming that God in man doeth the work. It is the knowing that infinite Mind thinks through our minds at every instant, and Its ideas are flowing through us into form. The "righteous" are those who let God work through them for the accomplishment of good.

I BELIEVE that this is God's universe and that His Mind releases through me its perfect ideas at every instant. I believe that I am the creation of infinite Mind, and therefore I am open and receptive to all ideas born of God. There is nothing in my consciousness which refutes the things of the Spirit. There is no resistance to God and His good. I am now consciously receptive to the divine inflow of truth. I accept it, I assimilate it, and I pass it on to my fellow-man in joy and delight. I let God work in my mind, my heart and my affairs.

February 14

I Accept All Changes on My Pathway and Find God In Them

I have set the Lord always before me; because he is at my right hand, I shall not be moved.
Psalm 16:8

THE pure in heart see God. All others see a material world filled with problems. Thomas Troward says that the higher intelligence always controls the lower. As we develop spiritually, we move to higher levels of intelligence and begin to control the lower ones. When our world pushes us around, it is indicative that we are not in control of our consciousness. We have not realized that Mind is supreme, and we are the directors of Its law. As we take control over our thinking and direct it toward that which is good, we are the sons of God. This is the aim of this teaching, and these daily lessons are awakening within us the higher intelligence and projecting it through dynamic right thinking into the world. As we do this we become the "pure in heart" and our world becomes radiant with God.

TO every problem in my world, I now speak the truth. I say of these, that they are insults to the God-given intelligence within me. I now take dominion over my consciousness. I believe that God dwells in me and operates through me as I think. I now declare that God is on every step of my pathway. Whatever needs to be done, is being done now by the action of infinite Mind. Therefore, I accept every change that appears on my pathway, and I find God in it. Every problem is now disappearing, for God is increasing in my world all the time. I see God everywhere, and where God is, no evil endures. I am in control of my world, and I release God into it, until there is nothing to see there but good.

February 15

The Joy of the Lord Is Mine Today

*Thou wilt shew me the path of life; in thy presence is fullness of joy;
at thy right hand there are pleasures forevermore.*
Psalm 16:11

SELF-PITY is the indication of an egocentric mind. This common error should be treated as definitely as we would treat a disease. Actually, it is a temporary illness of the consciousness. Its cure is to realize that the only way the joy of the Spirit can function in our world is by functioning from a point within us. We cannot experience joy around us, until we have created it within us. God is the joy and zest of life. His presence within and around us is forever calling our attention to the happiness of living the abundant life. Too much thinking in personal terms causes us to start sympathizing with ourselves. It is easy to describe the hurts and offenses that are offered us, and to inwardly build them into false judgments of people and conditions. But no one destroys our joy but ourselves, and no one creates our joy for us. God's Spirit within is the cause and the producer of our happiness.

THE fullness of joy is for me this day, because I love God and appreciate His Spirit in my fellowman. There is no self-pity in my consciousness. I believe that the joy of the Lord is within me, and I saturate my thinking with it this day. I have happiness in my heart and joy in my soul. I laugh and live in peace. I give joy to all whom I meet. I speak only of those things which bring joy to my friends and happiness to myself. I see my present world as heaven. I see my present family, friends and coworkers as spiritual beings. I see God everywhere, and my joy is full. I give thanks to the unfailing presence of God for this joy in my life.

February 16

God Made This World and I Find It Good Today

The heavens declare the glory of God; and the firmament sheweth his handiwork.
Psalm 19:1

OUR only contact with the world is through our five senses. Each of us reacts to the impressions that come to us from them in different ways. When we make judgments of the world, and of our particular situations in the world, we are actually stating our own limited viewpoints. We are the only thinkers in our individual worlds. We alone decide and evaluate the impressions that come in to us. No matter what negative reactions appeared in the mind of Jesus, he cleared them out and saw the goodness of God in his world. He was able to heal, prosper and free those around him, because he kept his thought cleared of the false judgments which his senses told him were seemingly true. We can face the negatives of the universe and see through them to the divine world made by the one perfect Mind.

TODAY, I dedicate my five senses to the presence of God. Whatever my senses tell me about myself, my fellowman or my world, I shall question. I shall see if it is in accord with God's idea of man and his world. I shall see if it accords with a perfect God, creating a perfect man, and maintaining that man in a perfect world of order and love. I refuse to accept any judgment based upon the false standards of illness, fatigue, lack and inharmony. These are not of God, and they cannot be true of my world, myself or my fellowman. I affirm that God is perfect, He made me perfect, and He made this world a heavenly place. I know this is the truth. Only God I see, taste, touch, smell and hear, for God is all there really is.

February 17

I Stop Dreaming of Good and Start Producing Good

> *The law of the Lord is perfect, converting the soul;*
> *the testimony of the Lord is sure, making wise the simple.*
> Psalm 19:7

WE are the producers of the works of God. Mind's only conscious outlet is through man, and this means definite, specific work on our part. Dreams and visions are of little value unless brought forth into visibility in this world. Ideas without forms through which to operate are inconceivable to those who know the law of Mind. Nebulous thinking produces nebulous results. Generalizations may sound well to the ear, but not until practical application has been made do they help to lift the race of men. God as our inner life, love, intelligence and capacity to produce is an actual God. Our lips may declare our belief in God, but our bodies and affairs show the proof of what we really know. We may glibly talk metaphysics and remain sick, unhappy and limited. When we practice metaphysics we demonstrate that we really know the one Mind and Its processes, and good is produced.

TODAY I am going to prove my beliefs in the supremacy of Spirit, and of Its indwelling action as life, health, power and beauty. I am showing to the world my true understanding of truth. I state that God is my life, and I prove it by speaking and doing only those things which are wise and true. I affirm spiritual prosperity, and refuse to discuss, envision or fear lack. I believe God's presence is in all men, and I shall find some good in each person I meet. When night comes, I shall go to sleep knowing that to my best knowledge, I have been faithful to Him in whom I have believed.

February 18

Divine Intelligence Is in Control and
I Am Victorious in Everything I Do This Day

Wait on the Lord: be of good courage, and he shall strengthen thine heart: wait, I say, on the Lord.
Psalm 27:14

THE secret of self-mastery is a simple one. It is the clear concept that creation begins and ends within the consciousness of the individual experiencing it. Mind is the only cause and law is the only process. The law does not work with our dreams and visions, the law works with what we really are. It brings forth into visibility our real understanding of ourselves. We are in control of our worlds only when we are definitely watching our thought and directing it into the law. We are always the centers of our universe. God never looks down upon us, for good is looking out from the midst of us. The psalmist reminds us to wait on the Lord. This means to stop a moment and decide whether the idea you are giving the law is a good one, a divine one. God strengthens the good ones, and ignores the others, for they are not of His eternal comprehension.

THERE is only one Mind, so my mind is a function in that one Mind. God's Mind expresses intelligence, love and perfect right action. These activities are now in me and are now working through me. I let these spiritual ideas have full control of my thinking and my feeling today. I set aside all my personal opinions based upon the questionable appearances of evil. Divine intelligence in me guides me to right and loving decisions. God's love in me causes me to speak well of my fellowman. God's life in me maintains me in perfect health. These are statements of truth and I accept them. There is nothing in me to oppose them, for God is in control of my thinking today.

February 19

Every Negative Is Destroyed by My Knowledge of Truth

I will extol thee, O Lord: for thou hast lifted me up, and hast not made my foes to rejoice over me.
Psalm 30:1

EVERY negative condition that stands on our pathway is a test of how much we know about God and His Mind. If we agree with evil, we are the victims of evil. If we agree with good, we are demonstrating the power of God. This day, like all others, will offer us many opportunities to give evidence of our ability to overcome evil with good. To the extent that we accomplish this we are worthy of the name "the sons of God." Like David, we must affirm that "The Lord is my shepherd; I shall not want." The hidden enemies of our own consciousness need to be revealed and destroyed by such affirmations of what God really is. They wither under prayer and flourish under worry. Consistent right thinking of ourselves as creative outlets for the infinite Mind and Its infinite love guarantees their demise.

GOD is truth, and I am the expression of truth. Only the truth functions in my thought today. To every negative I say "begone." I am willing that every destructive idea in my unconscious mind now be revealed to me, and I now dismiss it. God fills my whole area of consciousness with His unlimited power of good. I am cleansed of all error, and filled with all truth. My mind and God's Mind are one and no evil can exist in me, happen to me nor proceed forth from me. I am a son of God releasing good into my world, and offering good to everyone with whom I live, work and have fellowship. God speaks through me His truth and I live in a perfect world right now.

February 20

Nothing Can Prevent Increased Abundance from Appearing in My Life Today

And in my prosperity I said, I shall never be moved.
Psalm 30:6

PROSPERITY is the presence of God as ease. It is the ability to do whatever needs to be done at the instant of time that it needs to be done. We must realize that prosperity is a larger term than just money. Money is the symbol of the exchange of ideas in mind, and as such it is good and necessary. Numberless people demonstrate prosperity without using much money. They always have what they need and want at the time they need it and want it. Most families have a "poor relation," someone who has never worked in his life, but has always managed to get along comfortably. Such people are clear in their thought regarding prosperity, but are not clear regarding money. So, they demonstrate ease and freedom without actual money in their hands. We want to make a complete demonstration, and have both money and freedom, and this can be accomplished by scientific prayer, which is the disciplining of consciousness.

THERE is only one power, the power of God. This power is the only power at work in my affairs, and it is always working for increase. I am now under the law of addition and multiplication. Never again will the law of subtraction and division operate in me. I fill my mind with God's ideas of abundance, and nothing can prevent their full demonstration in my affairs. There is no evil to stop this from taking place, as God is all there is in my world. I praise prosperity. I talk prosperity. I love prosperity, for God is my prosperity. I accept it with joy, use it with wisdom and release it again into my world with love. My world is easy, and increased good is appearing.

February 21

God Is Never Late, Mind Is Always on Time, and So Am I

I will instruct thee, and teach thee in the way which thou shalt go.
Psalm 32:8

THE accuracy of nature is apparent to all. The universe is an orderly system of intelligence, and we exist in it as orderly spiritual beings. Procrastination and delay are unknown to the divine presence, and should be unknown to us. Time, spiritually understood, is an orderly method of living easily. Its sole value is measurement. Many people develop an unconscious resistance to time, and are habitually late for appointments. These same people usually find their demonstrations delayed, because they are in a consciousness of delay. If we are often late in our daily schedules, we can hardly expect the law of Mind to deliver our demonstrations at the instant we think they should appear, because the law can only deal with our own thought. Students of this teaching would do well to think deeply on this idea. Ideas appear on time. Nature is orderly and accurate. We can easily discipline ourselves to new habits of time which agree with God's.

I LIVE in the presence of God, where all is accurate, orderly and right. There is no delay in God's response to me, as I now clear my thought of every belief of delay. I do whatever needs to be done on time and in order. I refuse to believe that I am under any pressures of time and space. Every idea I need appears in my consciousness on time and in right sequence. I see my watch as a friendly means of being prompt in every engagement this day. I arrive on time with ease and peace of mind. I am accurate, prompt and orderly in everything I do. As the Father in me doeth the work, it is easy and light. God is never late, Mind is always on time, and so am I.

February 22

I Receive Divine Inspiration and Know Just What to Do

The counsel of the Lord standeth forever, the thoughts of his heart to all generations.
Psalm 33:11

TRUE prayer is the correction of a belief in separation. We forget that man and God are one, and in our confusions troubles are born out of duality. All demonstrations are the result of unity. Our method of accepting these ideas is to believe that we are receiving them and then to act upon their guidance. As we affirm that we are divinely inspired to right action, we receive the idea that is born of the Spirit to meet the need of the moment. We must constantly remind ourselves that God is no respecter of persons, that to all is given the divine possibility, but only those who know that they are one with His Mind shall receive it. We pray to erase duality and to realize unity. We are one with Mind and Its ideas. All indecision is erased and the decisions of truth and love are made. The way is easy and the burden is light for the inspired and illumined who have found their oneness with God.

TODAY is the day of the Lord. Today is the day of salvation. Each hour is alive with inspiration, guidance and vision. God's pure ideas are now functioning in my consciousness. They lead me into pleasant ways, and I work in peace and joy. I know exactly what to do, how to do it, and I follow through with accomplishment. All indecision is forever dissipated, and divine inspiration is mine now and forevermore. God and I are one, not two. God's Mind and my mind are one, not two. There is only this one source delivering to me what I need to know at the time I need to know it. I act with authority, exactness and love, for God is my inspiration now.

February 23

I Have Faith in the Father of God and the Brotherhood of Man, and My Actions Show This to Be True

Blessed is the nation whose God is the Lord:
and the people whom he hath chosen for his own inheritance.
Psalm 33:12

THOSE whom the earth has labeled great have been people who extended their thinking to include all nations and all races. Only people with petty minds indulge in racial hatreds and distinctions. God's perfect idea of man is the basis for every living soul, and we must believe this and act as though it were so. When we dislike people and groups, we are bearing witness to our small and limited viewpoints. The people in whom we fail to find good are born of the same Mind, operate under the same law, and express the same life as we do. Our inability to see their divine origin is our self-created stumbling block. Often, we are held back by our petty dislikes of other people. Jesus could include the whole world in his thought because he believed in a God who was in all and acting through all. The "chosen people" are those who have chosen to love their fellowman and find good in him.

I BELIEVE in the Fatherhood of God and the brotherhood of man. No one is better than myself, no one is less good than myself. I live in God's universe filled with God's beloved people and I cooperate with them in love. I hate no man, and dislike no man. I love the truth that expresses in every nationality, every race and every creed. I extend my thinking to include them all in universal blessing. I know that every person is unfolding in spiritual understanding and growing in wisdom. Every person I meet today brings more of God to my remembrance. They bless me in interesting and loving ways. They enrich me with ideas of value.

February 24

I Am Making God Visible on Earth

I will bless the Lord at all times: his praise shall continually be in my mouth.
Psalm 34:1

MAN is the image and likeness of God. Man is the means which infinite Mind has of self-expression. If we know this, then we shall act in accordance with it, and cease from that which is foolish and negative. Through us the action of God is taking place; through us God is making Himself visible. Truly, we are blessed and a blessing, as we so live that all who contact us find God. Our only means of blessing the Lord is by releasing His thoughts through our minds and His love through our hearts. Our friends and coworkers are seeking to find God expressing in us and through us. We are advised to let our light shine, to heal the sick, prosper the poor and bring peace to the unhappy. Only as we see ourselves as the activity of Spirit is this possible. To all is given the opportunity to be the radiant expressions of God, and the wise accept it, the others take the harder pathway.

MAY I so live in the Christ Spirit, that all who contact me this day shall be healed; that all who contact my thought shall be blessed. Wherever I go, I spread abroad the good news that God is in man and is the true self of man. I release only that which is true of God and His perfect Mind. My lips are dedicated to speaking truth, and my heart is dedicated to loving all whom I meet on my pathway. God is my mind, my life, my all. I am the visible representative of God on earth and I walk my way in dignity, poise and peace. Beauty surrounds me, peace is within me, for God is all there really is in my world. This is the truth of this day, and I bear witness of it.

February 25

I Forgive Myself for All My Mistakes

O taste and see that the Lord is good: blessed is the man that trusteth in him.
Psalm 34:8

THE Bible stresses the necessity of forgiveness. This key idea is necessary to a fully developed and well-balanced viewpoint. We cannot go ahead while looking backward. Those who have offended us are merely the symbols of our own inner mistakes. They bear witness to the times wherein we have failed to remember God in our fellowman. The truly spiritual person is never hurt by others, so there is no forgiveness necessary for him. Only those who are still on the pathway from matter to Mind need to learn how to forgive. The true metaphysician has erased the possibility of seeing evil in his fellowman, and has gone beyond forgiveness into complete spiritual understanding. We can do this today. It may not be easy, and it may not be quick, but it can be done if we see God and His Christ in every man we see. This is the forward look; this is the upward reach. It lifts us to the very hills of the Lord.

MY consciousness is governed and controlled by a law of Mind. Through this law I am able to destroy evil and establish all good. I now think deeply of all who have hurt, annoyed or confused me. To them I say that I am sorry that I failed to see God in them and around them. I release freely from my mind all thought against any man. I behold each one in my world as the son of God, expressing the truth of life. I am forgiven, for I have forgiven my neighbor, and I have found God where I formerly believed error to exist. I praise and bless the good of all whom I know. Divine love in me reaches out and enfolds them in understanding and peace. I now am at peace with God and man.

February 26

What I Give to My World, I Receive from My World

Depart from evil, and do good: seek peace, and pursue it.
Psalm 34:14

THE universe is not to blame for our success or our failure. Too often, we use it as our alibi for failing to attain our goals. The wise have always known that they alone determined their good or their evil. The universe is a plastic, impersonal substance forever taking form according to the patterns which we give to it. Each of us is what he is because of what he conceives himself to be. Each of us is where he is because of his general state of consciousness. Metaphysics without teaching a law would not be a science. We are constantly thinking something, and the sum-total of our thinking comprises our mental attitude, our consciousness. This is what we give to the world and on the basis of what we give, the world responds in return. Its sole purpose is to respond to us and create forms for us. Knowing this, we stop our stupidities and hold fast to our right thinking.

I STOP blaming the conditions of my world and the people around me for my failure to demonstrate truth. I look squarely and frankly at myself, and see that which no other man can ever know about me, my real inner thinking. To every negative in my consciousness I say "Begone. You have no part of me. You never did have and you never will have." I am a spiritual expression of life, and I am now determined to offer to my world only that which is true of God and of God's creation. All else is dissolved and gone. The Lord is with me, His Mind indwells me, and His plan for me is now in full action establishing me in peace, success and permanent health. I cooperate fully with God today.

February 27

There Is No Death, and I Will Never Die, for I am Spirit

*How excellent is thy loving kindness, O God!
therefore the children of men put their trust under the shadow of thy wings.*
Psalm 36:7

ONE of the greatest, if not the greatest, delusions that pursue the human mind is the idea of death. Yet, this idea is contrary to all nature and to all reason and logic. It is inconceivable that a just God would create a temporary man to flourish and then to wither. If God is an eternal, creative presence and Mind, then His creation must be equally eternal. We should constantly deny the possibility of extinction or of a supernatural future heaven and hell. God is the life of man, and His idea of life can only include progression, unfoldment and evolution. If the universe is evolving, then we must be evolving also. We are consciousness living in Mind, and our bodies are secondary. At the right time we release our bodies and move on into larger realms of mental experience. All mourning is self-pity, and all belief in death is contrary to God and God's idea of man.

MY mind is an eternal function of the one Mind, God. It never started and it will never stop. I am a spiritual being, born of the Spirit, living as the Spirit, and moving on to larger activities of the Spirit. There is no belief of death in my consciousness. I know that I shall always be an individualized expression of God, forever expanding in wisdom and love. I give thanks for my present world and its vital activities, but I know that I shall always have a similar world with equally similar activities. I have no fear of change, I trust in God, the good, to move me forward at the right time and in the right way. I greet the future with confidence, and I work this day with joy and freedom.

February 28

Life Moves Me into Ever-Increasing Good Today

For with thee is the fountain of life: in thy light shall we see light.
Psalm 36:9

THE universe is pushing us forward. It does this because it must. There is no retrogression in God. Mind is forever evolving new ideas and these ideas are forever urging us on to greater good. Only those who look backward grow feeble. Their disintegration touches our sympathy, but wisdom tells us to release them to their own stagnation, and catch up with those in the vanguard of advancing souls, who let God work through them. To the alert, God speaks. Mind reveals Its ideas and good appears everywhere. The law of life is the law of growth, expansion and increase. We must accept this, for it has been given unto us freely, and all that it asks is that we follow its instructions. As we look ahead and behold the ideas of God unfolding within us and projecting themselves into form through us, we see our increased good.

I MOVE forward in the divine design of my life, and find the future pregnant with good. The Christ Mind is within me, and I follow Its urges toward a richer and fuller life. There is no bondage to the past, for today I am free in God to express all His ideas fully. I see ahead on my pathway with faith, vision and love. I accept the great and true experience which my God has prepared for me because I love Him, His Mind and His truth. The life of the Spirit within me compels me to move on from the past, do my best in the present, and envision good in the future. No evil can stop me, no wrong thinking can hold me back, for I know that His plan for me is undefeatable. I give thanks that life moves me forward into greater good today.

February 29

There Are No Accidents, There Is Only the Eternal Protection of God

Trust on the Lord, and do good: so shalt thou dwell in the land, and verily shalt thou be fed.
Psalm 37:3

RIGHT thinking and living is spiritual life insurance. We are secure from all evil when we view life as it is in God. This establishes us in law and order, and no accident can befall us. Disorderly thinkers have disorderly experiences. Those who sense and assimilate the law of the universe rise into a way of life that is one of order. The presence of God enfolds us, indwells us and operates through us, but unless we know this we experience fear. As fear ensnares us in its false conclusions, we become accident prone. As faith takes hold of us, we become poised and established in order. There are no accidents, for God is law, and law bespeaks order. Each accident is merely the effect of a hidden cause within the one experiencing it. As we trust in the Lord and His law of cause and effect, we set up only positive causes and receive only positive effects. Thus, we are set free from the belief in accidents, and God's presence is our security.

TODAY law and order are the basis of my living. I refuse to believe that I can be the victim of circumstances. Nothing can happen to me that is not caused by me. I now dedicate my thinking to the perfect ideas of the Spirit, and I do not set up any disorderly causes which will produce disorderly effects. I live in God. I think with the Mind of God. I am secure in the divine protection of an unfailing presence and an unlimited power. I give orderly thinking to my world and receive orderly results from my world. My knowledge of the truth has set me free from the confusions of false thinking. I know that only good will happen to me today.

March 1

I Am Strong With the Power of God

Let every soul be subject unto the higher powers.
For there is no power but of God: the powers that be are ordained of God.
Romans 13:1

THE Bible tells us that the powers that be are ordained of God. And since God exists everywhere, the power of God is wherever we recognize it—not only all the presence, but all the power. We have no power of ourselves, as though we were separate entities, therefore we say with the psalmist that our strength cometh from the Lord who made heaven and earth. What we really do is to use a power greater than we are, which power is our strength, but we ourselves are not the power. Of ourselves we can do nothing, nor of ourselves do we even hold our bodies in place; rather, we rely on the power of gravitational force which operates upon us. In just such a manner we are operated upon by spiritual powers which become our strength when we use them. It is in this sense that we are strong with the power of God, the only power there is.

MY strength cometh from the Lord who made heaven and earth. Recognizing this strength which is perfect, complete and everpresent with me, I have implicit trust and confidence not only in its availability right where I am, but in its action in and through everything I am doing. There is a power behind my every thought and word. There is a power upholding and sustaining me in everything I do. There is a power going before me and preparing my way. I rest in this power in calm and serene confidence, with perfect trust and faith. I know that this power is good, it is constructive, it is activated by love, it is directed by divine intelligence, and I use it even in the simplest things in my life. Today, then, I accept that all the power there is belongs to me. In joy and in gladness I recognize and use this power. Therefore, today I am sustained and upheld by it, in peace, in joy and in wholeness.

March 2

I Am Guided by the Wisdom of God

Thus saith the Lord, Let not the wise man glory in his wisdom....
But let him that glorieth, glory in this, that he understandeth and knoweth me.
Jeremiah 9:23-24

SOME universal and infinite intelligence governs everything, holds everything in place, and directs the course of everything. The intelligence that governs the planets in their course is the same wisdom that is in the anthill or the beehive; this same wisdom is in the bird that flies north in summer and south in winter and knows where to find its food. But that which is blind or instinctive knowing in the animal, should become conscious knowing and will in the human. In the animal kingdom it works as a blind force; in the human kingdom it works through blind force only in the automatic reactions of nature such as the involuntary functions of the human body. But the more personal use of it—whether or not we shall call upon the one Mind and Spirit to direct and govern our affairs—this depends upon our personal choice. This is what freedom and individuality mean.

TODAY I am guided by the wisdom of God in everything I do, say or think. Since there is nothing large or small in the infinite and divine Mind, I know that the same wisdom that governs everything in the universe is brought to bear upon the little things in my personal life. I permit this wisdom to direct me. I affirm the presence of this wisdom and acknowledge its action in everything in my life. Therefore I know what to do under every circumstance. I know how to plan my life and direct my path because I recognize the infinite wisdom is doing this for me by doing it through me. There is no uncertainty nor confusion in my life. The divine Spirit always knows what to do, therefore I am never without guidance. There is one wisdom, one intelligence, one Mind. I live and move and have my being in this one. My every act, thought and purpose is guided by this wisdom.

March 3

I Am Held in the Goodness of God

...and God, even our Father, which hath loved us...
comfort your hearts, and establish you in every good word and work.
II Thessalonians 2:16-17

IF we assume an all-powerful or infinite presence and power back of, within and through everything—as we must—then we should realize that this power or presence, which is God, could not possibly operate against itself without destroying itself. We know of no energy in nature that can destroy itself. This means that the power back of everything actually is good, or, as Jesus said, "There is none good save one, which is God." We need not worry about this or wonder about it or ask questions about it. It is self-evident that goodness alone can endure forever. Good is a synonym for God. Good and God mean the same thing. Therefore, the final truth and absolute reality about all things is that God is good. And since God is the divine presence right where we are, good is right where we are and ever available to us. But we must recognize and claim this good if we are to use it.

TODAY I know that my good is at hand. I see this good in persons and places and things. Nothing but goodness can go from me, and nothing but goodness can return to me. There is nothing unlike goodness in my experience. There is nothing but kindness, nothing but generosity. My whole inner being responds to this goodness, recognizes it everywhere. Feeling it everywhere, seeing it everywhere, I am enveloped in it. And even as I draw this goodness to me and become saturated with it, it flows out in every direction, blessing everything it touches, helping everyone, bringing wholeness and happiness to everyone. "His goodness endureth forever," and I endure forever. In joy, then, I awake to every new day; in joy I rest in the eternal goodness, and evermore there is a song in my heart as it overflows with the acknowledgment of good.

March 4

I Am Free With the Freedom of God

Stand fast therefore in the liberty wherewith Christ hath made us free.
Galatians 5:1

WE all wish to be free, but at the same time we should realize that liberty is not license. To say that we are free with the freedom of God does not mean that we are free to do that which contradicts the divine nature. We are free only in that freedom which God is—the freedom to be alive, to enjoy living, to enter into the activities of everyday living with enthusiasm and interest. We are free to love and be loved. We are free to give full and complete expression to every capacity we possess, provided this freedom harms no one and hurts no thing. This is freedom enough because if we were free to do that which is destructive we should ultimately destroy ourselves. And, in so doing, we would not only deny but would defame the nature of divinity itself. Therefore we always pray, "Thy will be done," but within this will we know there is scope enough for self-expression—plenty of room to move around and express life to its fullest.

I AM free with the freedom of God. Today I manifest this freedom in joy. I think of it with deep gratitude to the giver of all life and with a deep inward sense of my union with the whole. In my own will and imagination I see myself free, complete and perfect. I feel back to the center of my being, which is God, and affirm that His freedom is my freedom. And I include my own physical body in this freedom as well as every activity in which I am engaged. I expand my consciousness and invite new experiences, knowing that they shall be created for me by the same power that makes everything. I enter into this freedom with complete abandonment, with the feeling that all things are working out well, and with the deep and sincere desire to so live that my freedom shall be imparted to others, that we all may feel that we are in partnership with the infinite.

March 5

I Share the Gifts of God

...I will give unto him that is athirst of the fountain of the water of life freely.
Revelation 21:6

WHAT a wonderful thought this is, that the very fountain of life flows open and free; that the gifts of heaven and earth are so bountifully bestowed upon all who receive them. But there is another thought for us to consider. If God, or life, has already made the gift, then even God, the supreme and perfect one, must wait our acceptance of this gift. Perhaps we err in that we do not expect to share the gifts of God. Perhaps we are bound by the thought that we are not yet good enough to accept the gifts of the kingdom of good, or that we have not developed spiritually enough to appreciate them. Too often we feel that these gifts are withheld and so we do not live in an enthusiastic and confident expectation of sharing with the infinite. What a wonderful thought this is to actually share with the infinite in the boundless gifts of life!

TODAY I consciously share in the gifts of life. I open my whole thought and my whole being to the divine influx. I empty myself of everything that denies this good I so fervently desire. I establish my mind in expectancy, a feeling that all the good there is must belong to everyone who will take it. I am receiving the divine gift right now. I am entering into the spiritual inheritance which life has willed that every person should possess. Today I am seeing the gift of life coming to me from every source, and even as it comes into my outstretched hands, uplifted to receive it, I enjoy the gift and pass it on. Freely I give everything I have, blessing the gift as it passes through me to others, that it may be multiplied in their experience and in God's good way come back again to me.

March 6

I Am Comforted by the Promises of God

Blessed be the Lord...there hath not failed one word of his good promise.
I Kings 8:56

THE Bible is filled with divine promises, revealed through the spiritual intuition of great souls. We are promised long life and happiness, riches and abundance, health and success. The Bible contains more promises than any other book ever written and tells us to accept the fact that these promises are not vague, uncertain things. More particularly it tells us that these promises are fulfilled right now, in the day in which we live. "Beloved, now are we the sons of God." We need not wait to enter into the fulfillment of these promises. They are eternally given and wait only on our acceptance. This acceptance is a mental as well as a spiritual act; it is the mind accepting its highest hope in complete confidence, placing its entire reliance on a power greater than itself.

TODAY I accept the divine promises. I accept them with the simplicity of a child, with the joy of one who receives his good in grateful acknowledgment of "the all-sustaining beauty." I accept divine guidance watching over me. I accept the enveloping presence of the life that sustains me. I accept the beauty and the peace of this presence. I accept happiness and success. I accept health and wholeness. I accept love and friendship. I realize that what rightfully belongs to me as rightfully belongs to everyone else. Therefore I promise myself and all others to live as though the kingdom of God were at hand for all people. I accept a good beyond my fondest imagination, beyond my greatest dream, knowing that this good which I accept will flow through me into complete expression. He shall give to me even more abundantly than I have asked, for the promises of God are as certain as life, as immutable as law, as personal as the air I breathe. Today I accept my good.

March 7

I Am Rich With the Richness of God

...every beast of the forest is mine.. and the cattle on a thousand hills...
for the world is mine, and the fulness thereof.
Psalm 50:10,12

HOW beautiful was the thought of Jesus when he told us to "consider the lilies of the field, how they grow; they toil not, neither do they spin; And yet I say unto you, That even Solomon in all his glory was not arrayed like one of these." Jesus was telling us to identify ourselves with the abundance of nature, the constant outpouring of the divine life in goodness, in riches, in everything that makes for happiness and wholeness and success. God cannot fail. The Divine will never fail us if we have implicit confidence in It. But we are so caught with fear and doubt and uncertainty that it becomes necessary for us to take time every day to reaffirm our union with the great out-flowing givingness of life. This is the purpose of prayer and meditation. It is natural that we should wish the more abundant life. It is right that we should accept it. God has already made the gift; it is up to us to receive it.

TODAY I receive this goodness. Today everything that I am and have is increased by it. I identify everything I do with success. I think affirmatively, and in all my prayers I accept abundance. Whatever I need, whenever I need it, wherever I need it, for as long as I need it, will always be at hand. I no longer see negation or delay or stagnation in my affairs, but rather, claim that the action of the living Spirit prospers everything I do, increases every good I possess, and through me brings gladness and joy, happiness and success to everyone I meet. Everything I think about shall be animated by the divine presence, sustained by the infinite power, and multiplied by the divine goodness.

March 8

I Speak the Truth of God

He that speaketh truth sheweth forth righteousness...
the lip of truth shall be established forever.
Proverbs 12:17-19

WE all wish to speak the truth, but have we realized that every time we make a claim about ourselves that is different from the claim we would make about God, we are falling into the error of denying the divine presence in our experience? God is truth and truth is God. We also are included in this divine and perfect unity. Therefore, every claim we make about God, the living spirit, should equally be made about ourselves because we live and move and have our being in this infinite truth or presence. To say that we are poor or sick or weak or unhappy, is to deny God. God is not poor, God is not sick, God is not weak, God is not unhappy. We must, then, make every endeavor, in simplicity and in truth, to identify our personal lives with that one life which forever more proclaims: "I am that I am," or, "I am and that and this and everything else I also am." There is nothing separate from this one I Am.

TODAY I say to myself: I am one with the truth of God. I speak this truth and proclaim it to be the reality of my experience in what I call "little" and in what I call "big." In the simplest and the most complex things I recognize the one truth—changeless, permanent and eternally manifesting Itself. Therefore I know the truth about myself. I know the truth about everything I do. I know the truth about everyone I meet. I know the truth about every situation I find myself in. This truth is not only perfection, it is also power. It is not only presence, it is also action. Therefore, the truth and the power and the presence and the action of the living Spirit flow through everything I do, say and think. I do know the truth, and the truth I know frees me and keeps me free.

March 9

I Witness Everywhere the Beauty of God

And let the beauty of the Lord our God be upon us...
Psalm 90:17

I BELIEVE it was Plato who said that God is love, truth and beauty. It has always seemed wonderful to me that one of the world's greatest thinkers should have included beauty as a necessary part of the divine nature. How evident this beauty is everywhere we look! How wonderful is the landscape, the sunset or the color of the desert at dawn. How beautiful is the daffodil in its sweet simplicity. And what majestic beauty and strength in the mountain and the wave. Everything is rooted in beauty. Beauty is harmony and right proportion. It is symmetry and charm and grace and loveliness. Surely we should identity ourselves with this terrific beauty that pours its warmth and color over everything and seems to be at the very root of our being.

RECOGNIZING beauty in everything and knowing that God is the very essence of this beauty, I include myself, my personality, my individuality, my whole being, in this beauty. I am some part of an infinite harmony, a terrific loveliness, a universal flow of warmth and color and givingness. I claim all this as my own, not because of any particular merits I personally possess, but rather, because of the necessity of its being true. I shall no longer think of myself as separate from this beauty or different from it. Therefore today, to law, to order, to love, to power, I shall add this other thought—divine beauty is everywhere. In this beauty I am beautiful. In this infinite warmth and color I live and have my being. Its beauty flows through every act, its charm and grace manifest in every movement, in every thought, imparting itself in love to everyone I meet. Today I see beauty in others—the charm, the grace, the presence of the living Spirit.

March 10

I Give Thanks for the Blessings of God

And he...took the five loaves, and two fishes, and looking up to heaven, he blessed, and brake, and gave the loaves to his disciples, and the disciples to the multitude.
Matthew 14:19

HAVE you and I had the faith to bless that which perhaps seemed so very small—a loaf of bread and a fish—and to expect it to become multiplied in our experience to such an extent that it would not only bless us but also bless everyone around us? We cannot help but believe that as Jesus broke the bread and blessed it, in his own mind he saw it multiplied and growing and flowing out to those around him. This is an example we should follow—to bless what we have, recognizing that it flows from a limitless source; we are merely using it and distributing it. There is always more. The limitless resources of the Spirit are at our command. The power of the infinite is at our disposal. We have as much to use as we know how to take. But the taking is a thing of the thought, the will, the imagination. It is a thing of an inward feeling or interior awareness in that place where the mind has unified itself with the living Spirit.

TODAY I bless everything I have. I bless everyone around me; I bless the events that transpire in my life, the conditions and situations with which I am surrounded. I bless everything that goes out and everything that comes in. I acknowledge an increase of right action in everything I do, say or think. I bless myself and others, for we are all partakers of the same divine nature, all living in the one Mind, all animated by the same presence, all sustained by the one power. "Bless the Lord, O my soul: and all that is within me, bless his holy name." In joy and in love my blessing rests on everything. In confidence and in peace the blessing of God rests upon me.

March 11

I Am Radiant With the Health of God

*Then shall thy light break forth as the morning,
and thine health shall spring forth speedily...*
Isaiah 58:8

WHATEVER we identify ourselves with we tend to become. Whatever we think about gradually becomes a subconscious pattern, always tending to manifest itself in our experience. Therefore we should endeavor to identify our physical bodies with the spiritual reality which is the very substance and essence of the physical being. We do not deny the physical body, but rather, affirm that every organ and action and function of the body is radiant with the perfection of God. There is an inner life of complete perfection which exists at the center of everything; otherwise, nothing could be. We should identify ourselves with this perfect pattern of our being, claiming its reality in our experience, and continuously knowing that we are animated by the living Spirit.

TODAY I identify my body with the action of God, the radiant life of the divine being. Today I identify my physical body with my spiritual body, claiming that they are one and the same. Therefore I see that every organ, every action and every function of my body belongs to the rhythm of life, is a part of the radiant presence of the living Spirit. There is one divine circulation flowing through everything—flowing through me right now. There is one infinite rhythm at the center of everything. I am a part of this perfect whole. There is perfect circulation, perfect assimilation and perfect elimination. There is perfection in every part of my being, and wholeness and completeness. This physical body is a temple of the living Spirit which animates it, sustains it, rebuilds it, after the image of Its own perfection, and keeps it in perfect health, in perfect harmony, in perfect wholeness.

March 12

I Express the Glory of God

Now is the Son of man glorified, and God is glorified in him.
If God be glorified in him, God shall also glorify him in himself...
John 13:31-32

PERHAPS this is one of the most profound thoughts Jesus ever gave to the world, for it really tells us that when man is glorified in God, then God is glorified in man. And it means exactly this: Life is a mirror to each one of us, and as we see the glory of God in this mirror, so shall this mirror reflect back to us that same glory. For Jesus says that if God be glorified in him, God shall also glorify him in Himself. So shall the image and its reflection become one even as the Father and the Son are one, in glory, in honor and in majesty and might. No more exalted concept of divine union could possibly be given than this.

TODAY, then, I glorify myself in God and I glorify God in me. For I am in Him and He is in me. And as He is glorified in me, so am I glorified in Him. I do give thanks for this intimate and complete union of my soul with its center and its source. And I do recognize in myself and in others the glory of the incarnated God. Realizing the one life without and within, consciously uniting with it, I proclaim its presence in everything. Knowing that there is no great and no small, I proclaim its presence in the smallest as well as the greatest. All my affairs shall reflect the glory and the power and the majesty and the might of the infinite Spirit. And all that I do shall proclaim His love, His life, and His light. "Now is the Son of man glorified, and God is glorified in him." I am that Son, and God is glorified in me today.

March 13

I Judge, and Am Judged, With the Justice of God

*...my judgment is just; because I seek not mine own will,
but the will of the Father which hath sent me.*
John 5:30

JESUS, the greatest of all the illumined, said, "Judge not that ye be not judged, for with what judgment ye judge ye shall be judged," by which he meant that we cannot judge others harshly without receiving back into our own consciousness and experience the very things we claim for others. While Jesus was the most compassionate of all men, he was also the most just, for he knew that our lives are governed by an exact and immutable law of cause and effect. He knew, and we all must learn, that it is impossible to wish something for someone else without at the same time willing it for ourselves. If we all were to follow this rule we should become kinder, if only for the purpose of self-preservation and personal happiness, for no one wishes to injure himself. Always, then, we are placed in this position—we dare not wish anything for anyone that we would be unwilling to accept for ourselves. If everyone were to live by this rule there would be no injustice in the world.

INFINITE Spirit within me, which is God, causes me to think and act kindly; constrains my mind to gentleness and peace; guides my thoughts into loving kindness and eternal forgiveness, and causes me in all my ways to follow the path of truth and justice. I judge no man and am judged by none. It is my sincere desire that everything I do or say or think shall come into harmony with universal truth and peace, with love and joy. Consciously I let go of everything that is unkind and seek to so enter into communion with the eternal Spirit that I shall reflect to my environment and manifest in all that I do, the spirit of kindness, of justice and compassion.

March 14

I Enjoy the Companionship of God

And I will pray the Father, and he shall give you another Comforter, that he may abide with you forever.
John 14:16

COMMUNION with the Spirit is one of the greatest privileges of life. By communion with God we do not mean telling the infinite what to do or how to do it, for that is talking at God rather than communing with Him. By communion we mean silently entering into divine harmony and beauty until we feel that harmony and beauty in our own souls, in our own minds. For instance, if one finds himself distraught and mentally upset, and he follows the simple practice of communing with peace, he will find that peace enters into him. He does this by dropping all confusion from his mind and thinking about peace; he dwells on its meaning and feels that he is breathing it into himself until it floods his whole being with harmony. This is real communion—not telling peace what it ought to do or be, but entering into its spirit, silently, quietly and alone. And so it is with love or joy or any other attribute of the Divine—we must commune by listening and feeling this presence until the presence is real to us. This is the very essence of communion.

GOD is my companion. It is impossible for me to be lonely or alone, for wherever I go the one presence will accompany me. I have an infinite companion who goes with me wherever I go. I have partnership with the infinite which is steady and strong and certain. This same presence I feel in everyone else—the one companion of all. I am guided by this presence, I am guarded by it, I am kept in the shadow of its strength. I am fed by the bounty of its love. I am guided by its wisdom. This presence is closer to me than my breath, nearer to me than my hands and feet. Therefore, I have no sense of aloneness, no feeling of isolation, because all the presence there is, is my companion. In this companionship there is love and beauty, there is peace and joy, there is happiness and success, today and forevermore.

March 15

I Am Supplied from the Substance of God

The Father loveth the Son, and hath given all things into his hand.
John 3:35

WE all have need of many things. We cannot believe that the divine Spirit wishes to withhold any good from us. It is the nature of God to give, and it is our nature to receive. Back of every idea of supply, every need in our human lives, there is something which forevermore gives of itself and takes the form of our experiences when we permit it to. Whether it be a house to live in, money that we have need of, or employment that furnishes the gratification of adequate self-expression—always there is the giver flowing into these things. But the Divine has already given Its entire being to us. God has not failed humanity. But humanity has failed to accept the gift. It has failed to enter into the spirit and the nature of the giver. It has even refused to believe that there is such a gift or such a giver. How, then, can even God really give us what we refuse to accept? This is why Jesus told us we must believe that we have really received the gift before we see its evidence. This is an active faith but it should be a faith built on the sure knowledge, the certain foundation, the positive conviction, that there is something that responds to us, gladly, readily, willingly, joyously and without limit.

TODAY I am living in the quiet and joyous expectation of good. God is not only my life, He is substance taking form in everything I do. God is not only the actor, He is acting through me now. God is not only the giver, He is also the gift. This gift I receive in joy, with gratitude, and with a complete sense of security. I expect everything I do to prosper. I expect new and wonderful experiences to come to me. I am living in complete confidence that the kingdom of heaven is here and now that I am prospered in everything I do.

March 16

I Am Endowed With the Perfection of God

Be ye therefore perfect, even as your Father which is in heaven is perfect.
Matthew 5:48

WHEN Jesus said, "Be ye therefore perfect, even as your Father which is in heaven (within you) is perfect," he was telling us that there is a perfection at the center of all things, which, recognized, will spring into being. We must learn to identify ourselves with this perfection, to so accept it that it is real to us, and to so live that it may be expressed through us. Every organ, action and function of our physical body is rooted in spiritual perfection, from which it draws its life. If this were not true we could not be here. No matter how imperfect the appearance may be, or painful or discordant, there is still an underlying perfection, an inner wholeness, a complete and perfect life, which is God.

THEREFORE I say to my physical body: "Be ye therefore perfect because you already are perfect in the divine sight. There is one life, that life is God, that life is your life now. This life circulates through you. It animates your whole being. You are one with its peace and wholeness. There is no inaction in this divine life. There is no stoppage nor hindrance nor obstruction to it. And whatever may seem to be to the contrary is false, for I am identifying my physical body with the body of pure Spirit. I am opening my mind as a channel for the realization of the divine presence. I affirm it and accept it. There is nothing in me that can deny or reject it. Because God is perfect, I am perfect." Quietly I affirm and reaffirm these simple statements until they sink into my consciousness and become a habit pattern of thought which is no longer rejected. With complete conviction I accept the wholeness of the Spirit and as I do so I identify myself and everything that I am with the harmony and the perfection and the wholeness of the life of God.

March 17

I See With the Eyes of God

...one thing I know, that, whereas I was blind, now I see.
John 9:25

THE ancients said that there is an "all-seeing eye" and that if we could cause our physical eyes to see with its vision we should be looking at things as they really are. But is it not true that too often we see with a blurred vision because we are so confused mentally? The all-seeing eye of God, by its very nature, being one and only, must forever see things as they really are. This is why Jesus said to judge not according to appearances but to judge righteously. We cannot expect to draw a pattern of this right seeing from the objective world of confusion or our inner thoughts of doubt and fear. Therefore we are told to see and act according to "the pattern shewed to thee in the mount," that is, we are to look and think independently of the confusion around us. We are to view everything as we feel the divine, infinite and perfect being must know and understand its own creation to be. This is seeing with the eyes of God.

TODAY I am seeing with the eyes of the Divine. I am looking at things in a perfect and direct way. I am seeing through confusion to peace, through doubt to certainty, through fear to faith. Quietly, then, I review myself, those around me, and everything that occupies my attention, bringing to them all a broader vision, a deeper insight, a more complete perspective of the infinite harmony which I know is back of, in and through everything that God has made. I am keeping my eye single to this one truth—what God has done is good, therefore my experiences are good. What God has created is wonderful, therefore I am surrounded with good. In calm judgment, then, I sit quietly within myself and in my imagination look around and see everything according to the divine pattern. As I do this everything I look upon shall become transformed and reborn.

March 18

I Am Warmed By the Love of God

Behold, what manner of love the Father hath bestowed upon us, that we should be called the sons of God...
I John 3:1

IT has been truly said that love is the loadstone of life, the treasure of earth and the highest gift of heaven. We all wish to feel that we are kept in the arms of love, protected by its shelter and warmed by its feeling. But someone might ask, "How do we really know that 'the universe rests on the shoulders of love?'" The answer is more simple than it might appear. For instance, no one is ever harmed by love. The more love there is in one's life, the better off he is; while the opposite to love, which is hate and dislike, can actually consume a person mentally and destroy his health physically. If, then, love tends to build up while the opposite tends to destroy, we may be certain that there is a universal reality to it; that we actually are immersed in an infinite love as well as a divine wisdom. And we must learn to feel the presence of this love and rely on it. Therefore, let each say to himself, daily:

I AM one with the love of God. I am one in the love of God with all people. My love goes out to everyone and I know that it is returned from everyone. Overlooking everything that might seem to deny this divine beneficence, I trust that infinite love will guide and protect me in everything. And I counsel my own soul to show forth this love in such a manner that it shall embrace and warm the heart of humanity, bringing confidence and trust and faith and hope to everyone it touches. Daily I affirm that love governs all of humanity into pathways of peace and joy. Daily I affirm that love goes before and makes the way plain and happy. And daily I affirm that my own love is renewed and rekindled by that great and vast love in which I am immersed, that love which is God.

March 19

I Am Governed by the Law of God

For I delight in the law of God, after the inward man...
Romans 7:22

THIS scriptural passage tells us first of all that we should have delight in living. All creation is a manifestation of the delight of God—God seeing Himself in form, God experiencing Himself in His own actions, and God knowing Himself in us *as* us. For the highest God and the innermost God is one God, and not two. But the passage also suggests that in addition to delight, the enjoyment of realizing that we are alive and awake and aware, we are also subject to the exact law that must govern everything—the law of the Lord that is perfect. We are, then, to combine our idea of delight with the concept of law, for love and law are the two great realities of life—love as the outpouring of the Spirit; law as divine government. Let us, then, find delight in the law of the Lord which is perfect, as we say daily to ourselves:

I AM one with the infinite Spirit of love, one with the outpouring of the divine life. I am governed by the perfect law of the inward man, made in the image and likeness of that which is pure, whole and perfect. My whole life finds its impulsion in love and all my actions are governed by the law of good. As I meditate upon this perfect law of God, I realize that it is operating in my affairs, in my body, in my mind and in my spirit. I know that the law of good is absolute; it is complete; it is operating in and through me now, bringing about everything that is good, everything that is right, everything that is happy. And since this law must be perfect as well as exact, and since it must know how to bring everything about that is necessary to my good, I place my whole trust in it. And so I say today, and every day: The perfect law of good is governing everything I think or do and all my relationships with others. I delight in this law and I delight in the divinity within myself and all people.

March 20

I Honor the Presence of God

...If I honor myself, my honor is nothing: it is my Father that honoreth me...
John 8:54

IF I honor myself alone, not realizing that I am one with the divine presence, then I shall quickly exhaust the small portion of good that I, as a human being, can at any one moment contain. But if I honor the presence of God in me, of God around and through me, of God in and through everything, then I am indeed honoring the presence of God, for one Spirit is over all, in all and through all, and one presence *is* all. There can be no separation from this presence, no apartness, no division. It is one, complete and total, equally distributed and everywhere available. To feel this presence in things, in people and in human events, and to sense that it is all-inclusive, really is to honor God and to provide in one's own self a place where the Divine can go forth anew into creation.

TODAY I am honoring the presence of God. I feel His beauty in the rose-tinted dawn and in the glow of the evening sunset. In the rose I find the loveliness of His beauty. In the mountains I see His strength. In the quiet of evening time I feel His presence. And throughout the night I know that this presence overshadows me, therefore I sleep in peace and wake in joy and live in a consciousness of good. Seeing God in others, I enter into companionship with the divinity in all people. In the outstretched hand, in the smile of recognition, and in the warm embrace of friends, I feel the one presence, the one power and the one life. And so I give thanks—with a song in my heart and with a joy unspeakable I give thanks to this presence. May I evermore embrace and be embraced by the love, the beauty and the goodness of God.

March 21

I Relax in the Peace of God

And the peace of God, which passeth all understanding, shall keep your hearts and minds through Christ Jesus.
Philippians 4:7

WE often wonder if peace really exists anywhere. In a world distraught with so much confusion and chaos we deeply need an inner, abiding sense of calm and tranquility. Peace of mind really is what the world is searching after because without it we have only a sense of insecurity and loneliness. Without peace, deep and abiding, there can be no happiness nor contentment, no sense of security, no confidence. And yet, Jesus said, "My peace I give unto you," and the Apostle said, "The peace of God, which passeth all understanding, shall keep your hearts and minds through Christ Jesus." This means that in such degree as we attain peace, Christ, or the anointed of heaven, the true and divine Sonship, makes itself known to us. For He is not met through confusion, but only when the mind is tranquil, and, like an unruffled body of water, reflects the Divine images of peace and perfection.

TODAY I enter into the peace of God. My mind is stilled from all confusion, and I feel a deep and abiding inward poise. Christ, the Son of the living God, the one Son begotten of the only God, is real to me. I keep my mind stayed on this divine inner presence, and, letting every thought of discord slip away, I meet the reality of myself, the eternal and changeless truth about me, which is that I am the Son of God, I am one with Him forevermore, there is no separation, there is no apartness. Here and now, within me, there is a voice that says: "Peace. Be still and know that I am his God; God in me, around me and through me, the divine Son forever incarnated and forever kept in the bosom of the Father." I glorify the name of this Son; I exalt his presence. "I am that which thou art; thou art that which I am." And that which I am, and that which Thou art, is one and the same.

March 22

I Partake of the Nature of God

The Spirit of God hath made me, and the breath of the Almighty hath given me life.
Job 33:4

NO one can doubt that God is perfect. But Jesus said, "Be ye therefore perfect, even as your Father which is in heaven is perfect." And he had already located heaven within. He also said, "Thy kingdom come, Thy will be done, in earth as it is in heaven," by which he meant that when we do the will of God, earth will be like heaven, that is, the without will be like the within, for the two really are one. Therefore our claim, our affirmation, our prayer and our acceptance, our communion with the infinite, should always be based on the realization that God is in and through His creation as well as around and about it. When we make this claim we are not speaking from the standpoint of the little, isolated ego that we appear to be, but rather, we are acknowledging, accepting and agreeing with a perfection that already exists. You and I had nothing to do with the creation of this perfection—we did not think it up or plan it out or cause it to be. For this we should be profoundly grateful. For the human mind is finite and limited. Our claim, rather, is one of identifying ourselves with the Divine, recognizing its presence, and accepting its action in our lives.

REALIZING that God is all there is, that God is perfect, and that God is right where I am, I gratefully acknowledge and accept my own perfection. Seeing and knowing myself as God must see and know me, I boldly claim the perfection of God to be my own perfection. There is nothing separate from the Divine. I am one with It. I am one in It. I am one of It. It flows through me and is my life. I am rooted in Its completion, Its wholeness. God is my life and my life is God—there is nothing else. Therefore anything that claims to be something else I repudiate, I deny. I separate myself from everything that contradicts the nature of my being, and simply and sincerely, and with complete relaxation, accept that which God has given—myself.

March 23

I Am Happy in the Harmony of God

Now there are diversities of gifts, but the same Spirit....And there are diversities of operation, but it is the same God which worketh all in all.
I Corinthians 12:4,6

WE do not all have the same gifts because no two people are ever alike. Nature never reproduces anything identically. And there are diversities of operations. We are all engaged in different types and sorts of activities which express the unique individualization which each one of us is. But it is the same God working in all of us. This is one of the most terrific concepts we could entertain—that out of all the variations of life, the infinite variety of color and form and people— the rosebud, the elephant, the snow-capped mountain, the tiny mouse in the field—one power is working, one life is expressing, one energy is animating, one presence flowing through and one law controlling. The one Mind is working in and through us now, not as big or little, or hard or easy, but merely as spontaneous self-expression. Back of our smallest act is the strength of the universe. Behind all our thoughts is the infinite thinker. Diffused through every human activity is the divine presence.

TODAY I am realizing that all my thoughts are formulated in the divine Mind; all my actions are sustained by the infinite energy; all the power there is and all the presence there is, is right where I am. Therefore I open the channels of my thought to the influx of this divine presence which is now doing something unique and different through me. I feel the impact of this presence in my own mind. I sense its feeling and imagination in my own thinking. I see it operating through all my actions. And since there is no big nor little, everything becomes important because everything is the self-expression of that within me which doeth all things well. Therefore I surrender myself completely to that one power, that one all-knowing Mind, that one presence, which is beauty and love and peace and joy.

March 24

I Am Secure in the Everlasting Arms of God

The eternal God is thy refuge, and underneath are the everlasting arms.
Deuteronomy 33:27

THE everlasting arms suggest divine protection, complete certainty, and the assurance that all is well with the soul. And how could it be otherwise since the spirit of man is God. Therefore, when we say that we are secure in the everlasting arms of God, we are realizing that our spirit, being one with His, and never separated from its source, must be, and is, as secure as God. It is this inward sense of our union with the whole that binds us back to the eternal presence and gives us the joy of knowing that there is nothing to be afraid of, either out of the past, from the present, or in the future.

I AM secure in the everlasting arms of God. I feel the divine presence in, around and through me, and all people. A great sense of calm and peace flows through my whole being, in confidence and in light. Realizing that there is no separation between the Spirit within me and the Spirit which God is, and knowing that there is but one Spirit, which is God-in-me and God-in-everything, I feel confidence and safety and security in that presence which evermore wraps itself around me and flows through me. I am indeed secure today in the everlasting arms of good, of peace, of joy and of life. I am secure in the consciousness that today, and every day, I shall be guided and guarded and protected. And I am secure in the consciousness that all people are protected by the same divine presence, governed by the same law of good, and guided by the same infinite love. I am one with all, both visible and invisible; one with the seen and the unseen; one with God and one with man. I bless this unity.

March 25

I Am Cleansed by the Purity of God

Thou art of purer eyes than to behold evil, and canst not look on iniquity...
Habakkuk 1:13

WHEN the prophet said that God is of too pure eye to behold evil and cannot look on iniquity, he was proclaiming one of the most profound concepts the human mind has ever entertained. For he was really saying that God, who is the originator of all things and the first principle of all life, can never experience evil, nor see it, nor know it. "Thou art of purer eyes than to behold evil, and canst not look on iniquity." What could be plainer or more evident than that he was saying that God neither creates nor experiences evil; that we are cleansed by the purity of that which has never entered into impurity—we are cleansed by the purity of God. Suppose we liken this purity of God to a clear stream of water which knows no impurity and in which we bathe. The very act of our entering the stream purifies us without contaminating the stream itself. And so it is in our relationship with the Divine, who is free from all evil, and the law of good that knows no limitation.

TODAY I enter into the stream of pure life, knowing that as I bathe in the spiritual waters of perfection, my whole being is cleansed, purified and made whole. Today I turn from all evil, from every sense of limitation, of fear or uncertainty, and bathe in the waters of freedom, purifying myself from the belief or experience of want or need. Today, as I bathe in the waters of pure Spirit, I loose every negation of the past. I am cleansed of all fear of the future. I am purified from all uncertainty in the present. I enter a new, a complete and a perfect life, here and now. Today is God's day. I shall rejoice in it. I shall sing a song unto that which is beyond all evil.

March 26

I Live in the Life of God

...as the Father hath life in himself, so hath he given to the Son to have life in himself.
John 5:26

ALL life is one life. Just as every physical substance known derives from one universal energy, so there is but one life principle, which is God, in which we all live and from which infinite source our individual lives are drawn. If this one life is present everywhere, it is also within us. To say that the life of God is the only life there is, means that my life is not only in God and of God and from God—it *is* God, in and through me. If this were not true I would have a life separate from God, which is unthinkable and impossible. But if it is true that the life of God is my life now, how wrongly I must have been thinking about this life. I have judged it falsely and condemned it unnecessarily and in every way, shape and manner, in my ignorance, have denied the very thing I should be affirming.

THERE is one life, that life is God, that life is my life now. In Him I live and move and have my being, and He lives in me and moves through me. I deny, then, that there is any life separate from good, and I affirm that every organ, action and function of my physical body is animated by the divine life which created and sustains it. It is this life that is circulating through me now, in happiness, in harmony and with perfect rhythm. I am one with the whole, therefore I say to my mind: "You are to live and think and feel this truth until it is spontaneous and natural. And when you say, 'God is my life,' you are to know that the entire life of the divine and perfect presence is now flowing through you." I affirm this today—the life of God is the only life there is; that life is my life now, complete and perfect.

March 27

I Experience the Wholeness of God

For we know in part, and we prophesy in part. But when that which is perfect is come, then that which is in part shall be done away.
I Corinthians 13:9-10

HOW true it is that we do see as through a glass, darkly, or only in part. But to all of us there come fleeting moments when our inward vision is opened and we seem to look out upon a newer and broader horizon. The apostle tells us that when that which is perfect shall come, then that which is in part shall be done away. What he really is saying is that we are all at a certain place in our evolution but that there is a complete certainty before us. We shall continuously expand and experience more and more of that life which already is perfect. But there is no reason why this awakening shall not come now. For we are not really waiting on God—God is waiting on us. "Behold, I stand at the door and knock." All nature waits our recognition and even the divine Spirit must wait our cooperation with It.

TODAY my eyes are open more widely and I look out upon a broader horizon. Across all the experiences I may have had which were limited or unpleasant, I now see the rosy hue of a new dawn. Letting go of that which is little, I now enter into a larger concept of life. Dropping all fear, I entertain faith. Realizing that every form of uncertainty is seeing only in part, I open my spiritual eyes to that which is wholeness. And even as I do this, the limitation, the fear and the doubt slip away from my experience, taking their departure in quietness and in peace as I turn to that which is greater and better and fuller of eternal life, of happiness and of peace. Today my eyes are open to the breadth and the height and the depth of that life which is God, that life which is good, and the law which is perfect.

March 28

I Imbibe New Ideas from the Creativity of God

> ...*The Son can do nothing of himself, but what he seeth the Father do: for what things soever he doeth, these also doeth the Son likewise.*
> John 5:19

EMERSON tells us that the Ancient of Days is in the latest invention. In other words, since God is all there is, the only presence, the only power and the only Mind or intelligence, when we conceive a new idea we are thinking directly from the creativity of God. It is not our isolated, limited human personality that projects this new idea. We are merely the instrument through which this projection takes place. But we are in partnership with the projector. God really is in the latest invention, in the newest song, in the latest novel, in the last picture that was painted, and in that feeling which we have of new and greater and better things to come. For God is all there is—there is nothing else besides. God is both the inventor of the game and those who play in it, the author and actor, the singer and the song.

TODAY I imbibe new ideas from the creativity of God. My whole consciousness is alive and awake and aware. It is impregnated with divine ideas and shall bear fruit after the image of the impression conceived within it and the divine imprint made upon it. Today, then, I expect new ways of doing things; I expect to meet new people, form new friendships; I expect everything in my experience to enlarge and deepen and broaden. I expect more good than I have ever experienced before, and today I expect to give out more, to increase my love for others. Today I expect from myself a more gentle approach to life, a more kindly feeling, a more beneficent impulse. New thoughts, new ideas, new people, new situations, new ways of doing things and a new influx of the Divine shall make this day perfect, glad and an expression of limitless bounty from the storehouse of the infinite good.

March 29

I Am Vitalized by the Strength of God

I shall be glorious in the eyes of the Lord, and my God shall be my strength.
Isaiah 49:5

IF God is all the life that there is, then this life contains the only energy there is. If we are really hooked up with the eternal, everlasting and perfect energy, then we should never become weary at all. And when we have an enthusiastic and glad outlook on life we seldom do become weary. Therefore we must convince ourselves that we are vitalized by the strength of God and we must do something to ourselves which makes it certain that this infinite energy shall increasingly flow through us. It is up to us to make the decision, to follow the course of affirmative thinking, prayer and meditation which shall continually keep this stream of divine energy flowing through our minds, our bodies and our affairs, animating everything we do with the vitality that knows no weariness.

TODAY I am energized by the vitality of the living Spirit. All the power that there is, all the energy and vitality that there is, is mine, and all the enthusiasm for life, the glad expectation of the more yet to be, and all the gratitude for what has been and now is. Every weight or burden of thought or feeling falls from me and I am lifted up into the atmosphere of that energy, that vitality which knows only the joy of its own being and the strength of its own being. I am one with all this—vitalized, energized and magnetized by the living Spirit. This energy is never depleted, it is never lessened. All of it is present right where I am; all the enthusiasm for life is right where I am, and all the joy in living is right where I am. Everything within me, then, today and every day, responds to the thought that "I shall be glorious in the eyes of the Lord, and my God shall be my strength."

March 30

I Am Enriched by the Abundance of God

> ... *prove me now herewith, saith the Lord of hosts,*
> *if I will not open you the windows of heaven, and pour you out a blessing,*
> *that there shall not be room enough to receive it.*
> Malachi 3:10

WHAT a promise this is! As though the Divine were issuing a challenge to the human and saying, "Perhaps things are better than they appear to be. Have you ever really tried having confidence in the Spirit? Have you ever experimented with your own mind to see if you could come to a place where you really believe there is good enough to go around?" It is as though the prophet were telling us that even the divine bounty itself, lavish and extravagant as it must be, waits our acceptance. Possibly we have been holding our bowl of acceptance and our chalice of life upside down so that even the fruit and the wine of the Spirit cannot be poured into it. Yet the windows of heaven must forever be open.

TODAY I open the windows of my own soul that the windows of heaven may pour into my experience a blessing greater than I am able to receive. Nor would I withhold this blessing from others, for as surely as it comes to me, just so surely shall it go forth multiplied and increased to heal and help, to bless and enrich and gladden others. Today my faith, my hope, my expectancy, look up and out and behold a limitless abundance present everywhere, flowing through all things; a limitless love giving of itself to everything; an infinite peace enveloping all. And behind it all, and around it and through it, a joy forever singing a song of happiness and fulfillment. This is my day, this is my heaven, this is my life, this is my God. In Him will I put my trust.

March 31

I Am Joyful in the Joy of God

*Thou hast made known to me the ways of life;
thou shalt make me full of joy with thy countenance.*
Acts 2:28

EMERSON says that prayer is the proclamation of a joyful and a beholding soul. And throughout the Bible we find so many references to the joy of God and the gladness that we should have in His presence. How can we help being glad and filled with joy if we believe that the presence and the power back of everything is one perfect life, forever giving of itself, forever flowing through us in wondrous light and power. Jesus said that if the multitude did not break forth in song, the very stones would be compelled to, by which he meant that all nature is alive and awake and aware with the divine presence, and that all nature and everything in life responds to the song of the heart.

THEREFORE, today I am filled with joy. Let every sense of depression or heaviness depart from my mind, and let my soul be lifted up in song to the giver of all life and to the joy of living. Joy shall accompany me like a companion and happiness shall be to me as a comrade. There is a song in my heart, singing unto the Creator of all things, and there is an invisible chorus responding through everything in nature, through every person I meet, for today I am meeting everything with joy and happiness, with song and laughter, with the gladness of the heart. I proclaim this day to be one of happiness, of thanksgiving and of praise to the most high God, to the divine presence that inhabits eternity and finds a dwelling place in my own soul. Today I express joy and gratitude to this inner presence, and this presence in which I am enveloped is one living Spirit of color and responsiveness—my Father, in my heaven, and my Father in every other person's heaven—the author of joy, of peace and wholeness.

April 1

I Am Divinely Guided to Right Action

The Lord is my shepherd...
Psalm 23:1

I AM divinely guided to right action in every experience of this day. I know that true wisdom is of God, and that it uses my consciousness as its seat of operation. God is the "shepherd" of my life; and this inner Mind and love guide me into paths of perfection and ways of joy. God's perfect action can never cease and can never be delayed. Always, it guides me. Always, it inspires me. Always, it blesses and benefits me.

I rejoice in my inner source of truth, for it never fails me. Each hour I am sustained by truth. Each moment I am led into right thinking. Each instant I am inspired to do the loving thing, to speak the loving word. Because I follow the guidance of the Spirit within me, I am a blessing to my fellowman.

Infinite Mind sustains me at every moment. I never fear indecision, for divine ideas lead me aright. There is a power born of God which indwells me, upholds me, and guides me. I am receptive to it and am blessed and benefited by it. Divine inspiration is upon me, and I rejoice in its wise instruction. I am powerful in my decisions; and the law produces my good.

God in me knows what to do, how to do it, and when to do it. I am now one with God, and this full knowledge is now mine. I am free from all uncertainty, for my God delivers every idea to me at the instant of time that I need it. "The Lord is my shepherd" and I let my inner Lord control my mind, discipline my emotions and keep straight my affairs. All doubt is destroyed; all truth is revealed.

April 2

Today I Live in Abundance, for God Supports Me in Every Way

...I shall not want.
Psalm 23:1

I LIVE in a universe that is God-created and God-sustained, and I shall never lack any good thing. The intelligence that brought forth this universe is the intelligence of my mind today. The lavishness of nature is proof to me that my own personal life can be filled with an abundance beyond the limits of my present belief. I now accept this lavish good which God is pouring into my world by means of my consciousness.

I destroy every fear of lack and limitation, and I know that God in me has already given to me more than I shall ever be able to use. I am fully receptive to the good which my Father has planned for me. I accept it in every form, whether money, friends, gifts or opportunities. I seek the prosperous ways of life, for I know that I am God-ordained to experience their good.

His power is my power, and His love is mine to distribute in my world. My riches are of the mind and spirit, and they demonstrate for me all that I need or shall ever want. I refute all belief that I cannot afford the best. His desire for me is my everlasting good. I accept prosperity. I accept money as God in action. I accept myself as prosperity.

I saturate my mind with God's prosperous ideas, and I give them full authority in my thinking to act through me. I know that I subjectively accept and that the law of Mind has already moved into action, and their acceptance is immediate. Today I live in abundance, for God supports me in every way. I appreciate the action of prosperity in all my affairs.

April 3

Today I Am Living in Heaven, Working With Joy and Sharing My Good

He maketh me to lie down in green pastures...
Psalm 23:2

MY present world is heaven, for my thought is centered on God. I am already in my good, and I now search for my present world and find it. On every side the blessings of Almighty God are awaiting my recognition. They crowd upon me with their infinite possibilities of love, joy and growth. I find them in every moment of this day. I see them in the face of every friend, coworker and stranger. God appears to me through my church, my home and my loved ones.

God's presence in me looks out through my eyes and sees His own glory about me. My world is alive with beauty, for love is established on every hand. Nothing but good surrounds me; nothing but Spirit acts through me; and nothing but constructive words speak from me. My present experience is alive with God, and my future is secure, for only "green pastures" can be mine, now and forevermore.

I dwell in God's perfect and complete creation. Nothing can be taken from it, and nothing can be added to it. All that I will ever need is where I am. All that I have sought is at hand. I gladly accept the good, and I hold my thought in line to see it as it happens to me. I do not waver from my faith in God, and my faith in His promises of my present glory.

I love to love with the love of God. I love to live in a world of order. I love to let divine ideas sustain me. God never fails me, and I never fail God. Today I am living in heaven, working with joy and sharing my good with each one I meet. I am enfolded in God, expressing God, for all is God.

April 4

In the Midst of Me Is the Stillness of God

...he leadeth me beside the still waters.
Psalm 23:2

I AM poised and established in God's perfect peace. No longer can the world confuse me, for now I am secure in truth. This day I dedicate myself to peace, order and harmony. I have faith that the action of God in my mind is one of peace. I truly know the "still waters" that are deep within me, and I am refreshed as I draw from them.

In the midst of me is the stillness of God, where all ideas await my acceptance. Calmly and quietly I take from this inner Spirit of good. God's healing peace flows through me as I accept it, and I am healed. I feel this inner peace, not only in my body, but flowing through my mind. I know that whoever contacts me senses this peace, and knows that it is from God. I have peace in my life this day, and I give peace to my world this day.

There is nothing to disrupt, confuse or annoy. Order reigns in my experience, and law brings forth my every thought. The holy Spirit of right action dominates my thinking, and I am poised in perfect results. No matter what tries to disturb me, I see it as nothing. I am peace, and I radiate peace. My subconscious accepts this demand I make upon it, and brings it forth.

Nothing can enter my experience except those situations which bring me peace. All men offer me peace, and I accept it. Every word spoken to me is peaceful, and every word I speak brings healing to my fellowman. I think rightly and peacefully about all whom I know, and thus they, too, are led "beside the still waters" for my thought enriches their lives with peace. Peace, being the action of God, is omnipotent in my world today.

April 5

I Relax and Allow the Action of God to Move Through Me

He restoreth my soul...
Psalm 23:3

I KNOW that within me God is now in full action and I am made whole. God created me, God maintains me, and when I need help His Mind restores me to wholeness. Never for a single moment does the indwelling Spirit cease Its perfect action. Always, It flows through my mind as right thinking, through my body as health, and through my world as order. I recognize this perfect divine activity and allow it to restore me to wholeness.

In the divine Mind there is a perfect pattern of my true self, and of my true self-expression. This spiritual design restores my soul, heals my body and prospers my affairs. I have complete faith in God's plan for my life. I give it my full thought and know that it is now blessing and benefiting me. God's life is my life now and forevermore. God's peace is mine now and forevermore. I relax and allow the action of God to move through me.

I am free of all frustration, for divine intelligence uses my mind as an open channel. There is nothing in me to oppose the good which God has already created for me. I let it happen. I am balanced and poised in the one Mind, and there are no impediments to the divine action. There is within me that which impels me to right decision. God moves me forward with ease.

The joy of the Lord is my joy this day, for I am restored in all my ways. Strength, power and wisdom act within me. I am renewed and all is well. I let go of yesterday, and I have no fear of tomorrow, for this day is God's day in my life and affairs. I am a whole person, expressing all that God is and has.

April 6

Love and Wisdom Are Balanced in Me

...he leadeth me in the paths of righteousness...
Psalm 23:3

THE righteousness of God is my righteousness now. Today I offer to my world only the right action of a wise mind and a loving heart. I do this because my inner self impels me to do it. It leads me into right activities, right decisions and right associations. I love to let out more and more of God into my world through my right thinking and wise behavior.

The naturalness of God fills my mind, and I am free and natural as I express His life, love and wisdom. I have no false piety, only the knowledge that God loves to act through me and I let Him. I am expressing my real inner and perfect self in all I do, say or think. I am established in true righteousness, and this inner sense of balance and normalcy leads me into increased good.

All inner confusions are now erased. My subconscious is completely receptive to the good, the potent and the right. Deep within me God's ideas are accepted with joy and demonstrated with ease. My true divinity awakens and I walk free of all that would limit me. The royal road to true success is before me, and I walk it with power and ease.

In me love and wisdom are balanced, for God is my source of love and wisdom. I release these great qualities of life with joy and ease. I rightly use my mind for positive thinking. I rightly use my love for lifting my fellowman. All who contact me this day sense my inner right-mindedness and are benefited. My mind is centered in Spirit, my body is centered in health, and my life is divinely directed in all its ways.

April 7

In the Midst of Me Is the Light of My World and I Let That Light Shine

> *...for his name's sake.*
> Psalm 23:3

I ACCEPT my divine destiny. I accept that which God has planned for me. I know that there is a pattern of good for my life. This is true because the infinite Mind has arranged it this way. God acts by means of man. God knows what man should be, and I am that man whom God has made in His own image and likeness. Unto me is given the unlimited possibilities of good, because the divine Mind acts through me.

As I live rightly, think greatly and love largely, I am a joy to God and a blessing to man. I do this "for his name's sake." I realize that to this end was I born, for this cause came I into the world—to bear witness to the truth. God in me is impelling me to right action. God in me is inspiring my mind with right ideas. I am alive with this holy presence.

I refuse to believe that I am flesh and blood subject to the whims of fate. I arise in my divine selfhood and see that God alone rules my mind and heart. The one Mind thinks as me; the one love loves by means of me. I am the spiritual activity of a power which knows what it is doing and knows how to do it. In the hands of omniscience I rest in the full assurance of my eternal good.

In the midst of me is the light of my world, and I let that light shine. It created me in order to act through me. I recognize my responsibility to do this for God today. I know that as I do it the whole of God is backing me up, and the law of God is producing my good. My present is filled with good; my future is secure in greater good; for God is on my pathway and I cannot fail.

April 8

I Believe That God Is the Only Reality of My Life

Yea, though I walk through the valley of the shadow of death...
Psalm 23:4

I AM secure in God. Nothing can withstand truth, and I am knowing the truth of my being today. I realize that evil is neither person, place nor thing. I believe that God is the only reality of my life. There is nothing to prevent my good from appearing in my life right now, for I am open to the ways of the Spirit. I face my problems with an inspired mind, and a faith that good alone can triumph, for good is God in action.

Within me is an intelligence greater than anything the material world can devise. I turn to this inner Christ center and know that "greater is He that is within me, than he that is within the world." Nothing can stop the onward action of truth in my soul. I am undaunted by negatives, for I know that my God is with me and His Mind is leading me.

My world must respond to my thought, for that is the law of Mind. I now declare the peace, love and beauty of God as my true environment, and these now bless me. God surrounds me, infolds me and upholds me at every moment. My word is the law unto the thing to which it is directed. I speak the truth, and the truth is all that I can experience.

I stand in the midst of a flexible universe that responds to my thought and acts upon it. I, alone, am the creator of good in my world. I handle my thought rightly in order to bring this good forth into my experience. I am free of all problems, all fear and all possibilities of failure. I know with certainty that God is for me. I say "no" to all evil; I say "yes" to all good.

April 9

I Am Surrounded and Upheld by Almighty God, and My Soul is Filled With Peace

> ...*I will fear no evil*...
> Psalm 23:4

GOD is where I am, and in this presence I am secure today. I will fear no evil, for I understand truth. Sustained by the Mind of God I live fearlessly, joyously and freely. Nothing can stop the right action of God in my life. At every instant God acts, and I know this action is around me, within me and upon me. There is nothing to fear; there is only God to know.

The power of the Spirit is my protection from all that is unlike God. This power is working for me and is working through me. It makes my way easy and my burden light. It goes before me and eliminates every obstacle that would confound me. Immersed in the divine presence I am now experiencing its good, its peace and its love. I am surrounded and upheld by Almighty God, and my soul is filled with peace.

God is all there is, and there is nothing to believe except this eternal goodness. Evil is a lie, and departs from me now forevermore. I cannot believe in sickness, lack or unhappiness. I know that there is no power, no authority and no continuity of negation. My world, being the presence of God, is aware only of truth and beauty. All other does not exist.

Regardless of circumstances, I keep my mind free of worry and doubt, for I know that Spirit is the only cause and love is the only effect. I have complete faith in God and His law of right action. Radiant with love, no one can hurt me. Inspired by divine intelligence, nothing can confuse me. Filled with the perfect peace, nothing can disturb me. I meet life this day with ease and the expectancy of increased blessings.

April 10

I Build Wisely, for the Mind That Created Me Is With Me and Working Through Me

...for thou art with me...
Psalm 23:4

I AM always sustained by a perfect God. I am never alone, and never lonely, for the universe is my friend. It was created by a loving intelligence to serve me. All people bring me a touch of God. All circumstances are impressing me with good. Where I am, God is, and that is all I need to be happy. Around me at every instant is divine companionship and divine love. God looks at me through every face; God blesses me through every situation.

The law of good is working for me, and I give it full power in my life now. There is no law of evil to oppose it, for God is one. I know that I am held lovingly and firmly in the law of good. The peace that passeth all understanding is mine, for I let God do the work. I set aside all my human opinions and material belief and give God a chance to act through me. I know that the only result of this decision will be increased blessings in my life.

I construct new forms based on new ideas. I let the old patterns fall away, and I rejoice in a new heaven and a new earth. Letting go of the past I press forward to new and greater ideas of truth. New foundations appear, new temples are built and new good happens. I build on the sure knowledge of the goodness of life, and the permanence of love.

Within me now is the power of God fulfilling all my desires. With me now is divine love making lovely and gracious my way. Within me now is God's intelligence making every right decision. I lack for nothing, for the Mind which created me is in me and working through me.

April 11

I Work With the Power, Intelligence and Joy of Divine Mind

...thy rod and thy staff they comfort me.
Psalm 23:4

SURROUNDED by good, I walk this day in peace. The Mind and love of God support me in every decision I make and in everything I do. It is impossible to escape from the presence of God, so it is impossible to lack for any good thing. All that God is, is mine this day. It supports me; it enfolds me. I feel this eternal presence of love.

Like David, the psalmist, I know that the rod and the staff of Spirit are bringing forth my demonstrations of truth. The Mind and the law are mine to use today. They will produce for me my sincere desires, for they must create what I choose to think. I turn in thought to God, knowing that His instant response is assured. I give thanks in advance for my healing. I accept my good from God.

There is joy in my heart and hope in my thinking. I shall never again be blocked in my roadway of expanding understanding. I am joyous, for I know that I am never defeated and never repulsed. God's action through me is victorious, and my demonstrations come to pass on time and in order. This is the joy of living according to truth.

I am encircled with the armor of truth. I walk through the presence of God. I work with the power, intelligence and joy of divine Mind. Everything blesses me, and I bless everything. I cannot fail, for God Himself created me and acts through me. My word is the law unto my universe, and I speak words of truth. Sustained at every moment by love, I live in peace, work in joy and relax in beauty. All is well with my soul.

April 12

Joyously, I Accept the Good Which God Is Distributing in My Life

Thou preparest a table before me in the presence of mine enemies...
Psalm 23:5

AT every moment of this day I am surrounded by good. This is true, because God is always omnipresent, omnipotent and omniscient. There is nothing to confuse me, for God is the order of my life. All good flows to me; all good flows from me. Where I am, God is and all is well. Knowing this I walk serenely through my day with complete assurance that divine Mind is my mind now. Only that which is true belongs to me and operates through me.

The table of the Lord is prepared for me and I eat therefrom. All the ideas of infinite Mind are being offered to me now. These nourish and sustain me, as I accept and assimilate them. They are inspiration to my mind. They are wisdom in handling my emotions. They are beauty and peace to my soul. Joyously, I accept the good which God is distributing in my life.

I am subject to the divine distribution of love. It showers affection upon me and love upsurges within me. It beckons me to move on to my demonstration. It bids me welcome in the heaven that is here and now. Unto me is given the full kingdom, and I accept it as a child accepts his security. My true dwelling place is in God right where I am at this moment.

Because I am established in right thinking, no evil can befall me. Because I am established in love and wisdom, no man can dislike me. Because I know that God is the only power, no situation can hurt me. These things I know, because I know and understand God and my eternal place in His plan. I am the beloved son of a perfect Father. My security is in Him who brought me forth to express His nature.

April 13

I Am a Radiating Center of Joyous Activity

...thou anointest my head with oil...
Psalm 23:5

I AM filled with the joy of living, for I know that I am created of the Spirit to express the Spirit. Therefore, I am a channel for joy, and I let it flow from God through me into my world. I am a radiating center of joyous activity, and today I offer this to my world. My business is joyous; my home is joyous; my whole being is joyous. I thank God for life and for the zest of living victoriously in His perfect universe.

My head is anointed with the joy of the Lord. It flows through my body as healing. It pours into my consciousness as unending inspiration. I relax and let this inner joy of the Spirit take over my life and all its affairs. I rest in the assurance that this is my day of demonstration, for my heart is glad and my whole soul is at peace. I am glad to be living in these times.

There is a permanence to all good feelings when they are recognized as God in action. The zest of living is mine, because I know that life flows through me with a joyous purpose. Within me is the good shepherd, the Christ, and He gives me joy that will not pass away. I enjoy life, and I enjoy my relationships with people. God brings me a happy experience through every person I meet. I am glad to be alive as a spiritual being.

Thinking of God as the source of my joy, my way is now easy and my burden is light. I know, as did Jesus, that "He that sent me is with me." Mind directs me, love upholds me, power acts through me. Steadfastly thinking of truth, I walk forward in life knowing that all things work together for my good.

April 14

I Know That God Is Blessing Me Now With His Whole Spirit

...my cup runneth over.
Psalm 23:5

I ALERT my mind to every blessing in my life this day. I know that I abide in the omnipresence of good, and that around me on all sides God is pressing upon me as good. "My cup runneth over." There is no limitation to the amount of God in my world, and I let this great presence flood me with blessings. Unlimited health is mine; uncountable prosperity is mine; eternal peace is mine.

I drop out of my consciousness every contracting thought of limitation. I know only the expanding truth of life, and I become a greater person, a rarer soul and a more loving companion today. I know that God is blessing me now with His whole Spirit. I have faith in the Christ that abides in me in fullness. I have faith in the overflowing cup of truth, and I drink therefrom of the living waters, and I shall never thirst again.

The holy Spirit of life, love and wisdom is upsurging within me to make me a greater person. Unto me there comes the guidance of a Mind supreme. I know that more good is within me than I can now sense and appreciate. All that is of truth pours itself into my consciousness, and I freely accept all its bounty. The richness of the universe is mine to use and to enjoy.

Knowing that abundance is mine, I also know this for my friends, my coworkers and my family. Theirs, also, is a cup that runneth over. To them also is given the richness of the Spirit. We are all living together in a spiritual universe, that is forever showering us with blessings. For all those blessings that appear on my pathway, I rejoice and give thanks.

April 15

I Am Impelled to Count My Blessings, and To See God Everywhere

Surely goodness and mercy shall follow me all the days of my life...
Psalm 23:6

PERMANENT good is now mine, for I am established in the Mind of God. Never again shall temporary good be mine. This day, I am in my eternal good, because I know that I am in God forevermore. My security is in Him who is the author and finisher of my faith. Though the world may change about me, yet within I am at peace for I know God, love God and appreciate God. Good never begins and never ceases. This constant flow of God through me is my life and my eternal hope.

I am free in the belief of time and space. I use both of these for my convenience, but they never limit me. I know that eternity and infinity are mine, and I enlarge my consciousness daily. I look at my changing world and see the permanence of heaven. I look at my own calendar years and see eternity unfold. All sense of age leaves me, and I let God's eternal life be mine. I am living the life of God. I am in God's perfect heaven right now.

Mind outpours Its rich treasures of truth to me. I am receptive to them, and my subconscious establishes them. I accept myself as an unlimited creation of a perfect Mind. I assimilate God's ideas and they transform me into a new and greater person. God uses me as His open channel for the production of beauty, peace and power. I am a blessed outlet of an infinite Mind.

I am impelled to count my blessings, and to see God everywhere. Surrounding me is His presence, within me is His Mind. I abide at every instant in a holy peace, an unending security and a love divine.

April 16

I Steadfastly Increase My Awareness of God in My Present World

...and I will dwell in the house of the Lord forever.
Psalm 23:6

I LIVE in an expanding universe that is potent with divine possibilities. On every hand the presence of God is beckoning to me, inviting my growth. Truly, I dwell in the house of the Lord today. There is nothing to hold me back, for His Mind in me presses me forward into larger living and greater thinking. I steadfastly increase my awareness of God in my present world. Right here and now I make my demonstration. I joyously accept an expanding, unfolding life of true service to God and to my fellowman.

I live in an evolving universe that bids me to grow in the ways of the Spirit. God is seeking to make me a greater person, and a more useful citizen of His good heaven on earth. I seek out larger ideas of truth. I keep the windows of my soul open to new and fresh ways of knowing truth. I evolve into that "image and likeness" which is already my inner pattern. I let go of the "little" to accept the "more." I grow in wisdom, in spiritual stature, in favor with God and with man.

Where I am, I shall make my demonstration of truth. I no longer wait for the future to solve my problems. Today, I live in omnipresence, and right now my good is at hand. What I seek is seeking me. The idea I need is now in my consciousness, and the law of Mind is producing it. I relax and realize that today is good, tomorrow will be better, and each day is God's day.

I live in a loving universe, where God's friendliness is on every hand. Divine love enfolds me and flows from me. I love the love of God in everyone I know. I am loved by the love of God in everyone I know. I dwell in love this day.

April 17

Today Is a Day of Results As I Let God Think in My Consciousness

Our Father...
Matthew 6:9

ONE God, one presence, one Mind, one law and this is my divine heritage, for It created me out of Itself. All this surrounds me, dwells in me and acts through me. "I stand in the Great Forever, I live in the ocean of Truth." I am the beloved Son of the Father, and I do that which pleases Him today. With eyes uplifted unto the hills of truth, I walk my pathway in wisdom and love.

I have divine integrity. I know that with His Wisdom inspiring me I can never make a mistake. The world cannot fool me, and my fellowman cannot confuse me. I am a spiritual being in a spiritual experience right now. Ideas are coming to me at every instant, and they offer me a greater portion of life than I now have. I accept them, and increase my good.

Unto me is given the truth, for all that the Father hath is mine. God presents Himself to His universe by means of me. "He that seeth me, seeth Him who sent me." I accept this divine inheritance and fulfill my true place in the Father's plan. I am the child of a king, who rules in grace and truth. Knowing this, I dedicate my life to expressing the attributes of God.

I am an ever-unfolding expression of infinite Mind. This Mind indwells me and leads me into health, prosperity and peace. I let God think in my consciousness. I let divine love be my expression and my joy. I know that He who made me will never fail me. I give thanks that I am a spiritual being living in God's universe of order. The benediction of the Almighty is upon me, and today is filled with good.

April 18

I Accomplish Great Things Today, for I Am Established in Righteousness

...which art in heaven...
Matthew 6:9

IN God I live and move and have my being. In me God lives and moves and has expression. All that God is, I am. All that God is, is where I am, for this world is heaven when I see it rightly. I cannot escape God and, therefore, I cannot escape my good. There is a divine inevitableness to my life. I cannot be held in limitation, for my divine self impels me to right solutions. No error can long endure, for God alone lives forevermore.

Established in the conviction that God is my only experience, I am now open to spiritual ideas. I welcome them, for they reveal to me the true riches of the kingdom of heaven. I enjoy every attempt to solve my problems through right thinking, for I know I am developing spiritually. I know that my thinking is based on truth and that all doors are open to me, and that all limitations have ceased. I know this because every prophet, savior, teacher and Bible, has assured me that it is so.

The God which has inspired every great man, is the same God who is the true essence of my consciousness. One Mind rules and governs all. This Mind in me is authority over all that is unlike itself. Evil is erased by my recognition of the power and the presence of God. I walk with the great, the true and the mighty. Before me is the pathway of greatness.

Today, I have faith in God's universe, His heaven is my present abode. Unto me is given the fullness of truth, the everlasting joy and the hope eternal. I am a true citizen of the kingdom of God, and I am established in His righteousness. I accomplish great things today.

April 19

Knowing What God Is, I Now Express All That God Is

...hallowed be thy name...
Matthew 6:9

I HONOR my Creator by living in justice today. I give full credit to the infinite Mind that thinks through me. I know that as I let God govern my thought and control my emotions I will be successful. I cannot make a mistake for I affirm that God indwells me, acts through, and acts for me. This I do, for I believe that true wisdom is not of man but of God. This wisdom is now mine, and it directs the affairs of my life.

I am indebted to God for His patience, His love and His wisdom. I pay my debt by living according to His laws. I forgive myself my own wrong conclusions, and free myself from the past. Today is alive with truth, and I know truth now. I believe in my own divinity and give all honor to Him who brought me forth out of His own substance of love. I act with wisdom worthy of the Mind which created me. I forgive and forget all evil, and hold fast to that which is good. I am conscious of God at this instant.

The wholeness of God is seeking expression through me. Mind never does things in parts, It always fulfills its ideas. Spiritually I am a whole person. This means I am not frustrated, not unhappy and not limited. All that the infinite is, individualizes itself through me. This wholeness is my real satisfaction. I am now happy with a permanent happiness.

To me is given the joy of knowing God and knowing him aright. Knowing what God is, I now express all that God is. I so live that all men shall call me blessed. I am a credit to God and a joy to my fellowman.

April 20

I Am True to the Kingdom of Heaven in My Thought This Day

...thy Kingdom come...
Matthew 6:10

I LET the kingdom of God be my basis this day. I know that this kingdom is one of righteousness and truth. I know that it is already here, and that I am already in it. I open my eyes to see God where I am. I open my consciousness to the inflow of spiritual ideas. I open my heart to the divine love of God. Into me now pours the living stream of truth, and I give it full power to act by means of me.

I am willing to set aside my personal opinions, prejudices and will, for "greater is He that is within me than he that is within the world." Divine intelligence now governs my thinking. I let God take over the operation of my life. I have absolute faith that increased good is the only result of God's activity. I believe that God's will for me is good and it is working for me now. Perfect Mind inspires me; perfect love upholds me.

I am a thinker in a divine law of Mind action. What I think causes something to happen. I gear my thinking to the Divine, and all that happens to me is good. I am cause to my world, and my thinking is based on right motives. My right causation necessitates my right experience. It is easy to prove God where I am, and in what I do. I now do this.

The kingdom of God is within me, and I now release it into my world. Through my mind, heart and hands God works, thinks and loves. Through my voice the word of truth is spoken. All who contact me are healed, blessed and prospered, for I am true to the kingdom of heaven in my thought this day.

April 21

I Let God's Perfect Will Be Mine This Day

...thy will be done...
Matthew 6:10

I AM the agent of the eternal. I am an ambassador at large for God. His will is that I shall express all His attributes, and I do this with joy. In me the will of God is accomplished by my right thinking, right loving and right action. I love to do the will of my Father, for as I do it, I have increased good in my life. I let my light shine before men, that they seeing that light shall glorify my Father.

I am aware of a divine purpose and a divine plan. God knows what he is doing, and in me God always knows what to do. I am a part of His plan, and I play this part with my whole being. In me the Mind of God is in full control, and this is my security. Knowing that the will of God is for greater good, I let that will be mine now. I cooperate fully with the indwelling Spirit. I turn within to this Spirit for the answer to every question, and the solution of every problem.

I accept the divine design of my life. Ahead of me is a planned road of ever-unfolding good. Each day brings added power. Each hour brings new and greater possibilities for my advancement. I look ahead and see my spiritual destiny evolve with ease. There is nothing to cause fear, worry or discontent, for God's will is my certainty of good.

I rest in the complete assurance that God's idea of me is perfect. God only knows that I am alive with His life, radiant with His health and expressing fully His purpose. All of this I now know for myself. I let God's perfect will be mine this day.

April 22

I Think Rightly and Lovingly This Day, and the Law Produces This in My Affairs

...in earth as it is in heaven.
Matthew 6:10

I BELIEVE that my life is governed by a divine law. I believe that this law is the way God acts in my experience. I know that I can use this law to demonstrate any good thing. All of God's ideas are available to me, and I now accept them, and give them to the law of Mind to demonstrate. I use this law rightly, because I give it only ideas of good.

I know that what I think and feel, I bring forth into my experience. I think rightly and lovingly this day, and the law produces this in my affairs. My "earth" is my world in which I live. My "heaven" is my consciousness, when it is thinking rightly. The law of Mind is the link between my thinking and my experiencing. Always, I demonstrate my thought, because the law never fails. No treatment is ever lost, no God-given idea which I assimilate will ever fail to materialize.

Divine Mind and its ideas are my heaven, and I am a transmitter for them. I turn my every experience into a heavenly one. I look out and see the glories of perfection around me. I look within and behold God's truth offering itself to me. I make heaven happen through my right thinking. My heaven demonstrated shows other people the way to theirs.

"The earth is the Lord's and the fullness thereof" and the kingdom of heaven is within me. Linking these two great ideas together assures me of heaven in earth today. I deliberately think of good. I deliberately discipline my emotions to that which is Godlike. I have faith in the law, and my prosperity this day is assured.

April 23

I Think of the Abundance That Is Now Mine, and Thank God for It

Give us this day our daily bread.
Matthew 6:11

GOD gives to me all that I am capable of receiving. My consciousness alone determines the richness or the poverty of my thinking. I am the recipient of all that God is, and today I increase my knowledge of God. Into my thought God pours all of His Ideas. I do not live by labor alone, but by every idea in the Mind of God. This is my true source of supply. Knowing this, I open my mind to receive the inflow of spiritual inspiration which the infinite is forever showering upon me. I love to think with the ideas of Spirit.

I accept the bounty of God, for I know that His Mind has planned it for me. My God is a rich Mind that knows only abundance, health and peace. These are mine today, for I am the beloved son of the Father. The Lord giveth, but does not take away. I eat of the bread of the Spirit. I am nourished in consciousness by the living truth. I hunger and thirst after righteousness, and I am filled, for God is within me sustaining my every right action.

My mental food determines the kind of world in which I live. I now choose my mental nourishment as wisely as I do the physical. If my body needs a balanced diet, so does my soul. As all of truth is offered to me, I have a perfect repast from which to select. I now balance wisdom with love, joy with creative work and power with true authority. My mind is well fed with truth.

Every channel of my thinking is now open and receptive to the ideas of truth, which are the true living bread. I feast upon the goodness of God. I think of the abundance that is now mine and thank God for it.

April 24

I Am an Heir to the Kingdom and I Now Dedicate Myself to Unselfish Living

And forgive us our debts, as we forgive our debtors.
Matthew 6:12

I LIVE in a universe of divine order. This universe expects me to live in it with wisdom and love, and this I do. I know that with creative thinking, premised upon good, there are no impossibilities for me. I know that God wants me to have all the good that I can mentally appropriate. I now dedicate myself to unselfish living.

I forgive myself for all my errors of omission and commission. I let God's healing currents of love cleanse my consciousness. I honestly seek to love my fellowman, for in him God abides. I see him as God sees him, and I bless him in thought and action. I release every unkind thought, motive and feeling from my mind. I take my true place as a spiritual being and let God alone rule and govern my life. I release love to every person, place and thing.

Having forgiven and released the mistakes others have made, I know that my own are equally dismissed. Therefore, all guilt is erased from my mind, and all past fear from my heart. I face today with a cleansed mind and a free spirit. No man sits in judgment upon me, and I judge no man. I am a free soul in a spiritual universe thinking God's thoughts.

Today, I honestly seek to live by the Sermon on the Mount. I will go twice the mile, and forgive seventy times seven. I will see the good in my coworkers, my family, my friends. I know that nothing can disturb me unless I let it, and I now close my mind to all evil. God in me is the only presence and the only power. God in me makes every decision, and renders every judgment. I love all people and am loved by all.

April 25

I Am Established in Right Thinking, and I Cannot Be Moved

And lead us not into temptation...
Matthew 6:13

I AM an outlet for the Mind of God. This eternal Spirit is always thinking rightly through me, and I rejoice in its perfect action in my consciousness. I am never tempted to think evil, for God is in me as my defense and my deliverance. Knowing that Spirit is the cause of my being, I cannot be led into temptation. I am strong in the Lord and the power of His right thinking. To every negative that appears in my thought, I am inviolate. Nothing but God and His perfect ideas have power in me, nor can act through me.

I stand firmly for the truth. I believe that this is God's universe, and I am willing that God should run His universe. I cease my human opinions and human judgments. I let God act through me. I let His Mind make every decision. I let divine love handle all my personal relationships. I relax and let infinite truth reveal itself in my life and affairs. I have faith that the holy Spirit of right action is now in full dominion in my consciousness.

I am not led into the temptation to believe that a power opposes me. I know that Mind alone is power, and all of Mind is for me. I decide whether my world shall be heaven or hell. My thinking and feeling alone determine my experience. Therefore, never again will I be tempted to blame outer circumstances and other people for my own wrong thinking. I think rightly always. I am permanently established in right thinking, and I cannot be moved. I leave the old patterns of thought, and I now think God's ideas with Him. My life is rich in love, and all my ways are peace, for I am an expression of a Mind that never wavers.

April 26

Peace Is Mine This Day, for There Is Nothing to Fight: There is Only God to Realize

...but deliver us from evil.
Matthew 6:13

I AM delivered from all my difficulties, for God in me is my deliverance. Infinite Mind knows no restrictions, and I, as Its representative on earth, am now free, whole and at peace. My consciousness controls my world, and I refuse to think evil. I think truth, and thus truth controls my world. Peace is mine this day, for in my thought there is nothing to fight, there is only God to realize. I love to contemplate the things of the Spirit.

As I steadfastly think of God and His heaven, I forget that evil has ever been, is now, or ever could be. I see that truth alone prevails, and love alone heals. I speak the truth and am healed by divine love. I am radiant with joy, for never again shall error fool me, nor human opinion ensnare me. I am Spirit, and I think in spiritual terms. I am the expression of divine intelligence, and all my thinking is geared to this premise.

The unreality of evil is true, and I accept this. I no longer seek it, or use it as an excuse for my own failure to see the good. God didn't make evil, and I refuse to believe in it, or in any power ascribed to it. The whole world is my friend. Cooperation greets me wherever I go. All people help me, and all situations bless me. I am delivered from all negation.

The action of God taking place in my affairs today eliminates and prevents evil from appearing. It has no power and no reality, and I see only God in myself and my affairs. My salvation is of God, for His Mind is mine to use for the glory of good and the furtherance of peace. I walk in wisdom, born of the Spirit, forevermore.

April 27

Victory for Me Is Certain, for God Permeates My World

For thine is the kingdom, and the power; and the glory forever. Amen.
Matthew 6:13

ESTABLISHED in truth, I see God everywhere. Around me, within me, beneath me, above me—God is the reality of my being. I live in a perfect presence. I am acted upon by a perfect power. I am living a life divine. The glory of the Lord is upon me, and I appreciate my blessings. In my experience today the kingdom, the power and the glory of truth are dominant. Victory for me is certain, for God permeates my world.

This victory is easy, for within me there is a divine center that knows no evil, and cannot accept evil. As I relax from all tension and let His Mind rule my thinking, I find that all things work together for good. There is no battle to be fought, for life moves through me with direction and purpose, and I let my good happen.

I speak with the voice of truth, and my words establish good. I hear only the truth, and my mind is centered in peace. I feel the encircling presence of love. I know that life is worthwhile, and I enjoy every moment of it. Unceasing joy is my lot, for I am finding God everywhere. My present world is heaven, and I live in it as a spiritual being.

I delight in finding good everywhere I look. I enjoy the feeling of spiritual security. I am free of fear, and strong in faith. I know that only God acts in my life today. Unto me is revealed the riches of the kingdom of heaven. All power is given unto me to use rightly. Glorious opportunities unfold before me. The eternal Mind whispers in my ear the sweet ideas of truth. I am free of the past, at peace in the present and secure in the future.

April 28

I Glorify God by Thinking Rightly and Loving Greatly

Now is the son of man glorified, and God is glorified in him.
John 13:31

THE glory of the Lord is upon me, and I am a son of the most high. I glorify God by thinking rightly and loving greatly. God glorifies me by becoming the thing I need at the instant I need it. I know no delay, for God's instantaneous results are assured. My universe is redolent with beauty. My life is filled with good. My mind is saturated with love and I see the face of God in every face I see. In the one Mind I think, and in me the one Mind prevails.

There isn't God and man, there is only God as man, and I am that man now. God and I are one, and God is that one. As I willingly let go of fear, faith appears. As I willingly let go of the belief in duality, oneness appears. As I realize that God is my Father and I am His son, the law establishes me in perfect results. I declare that I am the perfect creation of an unlimited God, and act to prove this statement.

I glory in the expanding ideas which God delivers to my consciousness. He never fails to offer me something greater than that which has gone before. His omniscience is within me, and I regulate all my thinking to its standards and its processes. Right thinking becomes natural to me, and right loving releases itself through me. The divine release through me is normal and easy.

I begin this day with the feeling that it will be good. God works in me and through me with ease. I know that good has been accomplished yesterday; and that even greater things are before me today. I give thanks for the good of my life, and I dedicate myself to the "greater works" which I shall do, and have started to do even today.

April 29

I Fulfill My Destiny Now

If ye know these things, happy are ye if ye do them.
John 13:17

I KNOW, beyond the shadow of a doubt, that God supports me in every right action. I feel the sustaining power of Spirit flowing through me, and I act with authority. I do those things which are pleasing to God and helpful to man. The joy of true accomplishment is mine today. I believe that God loves me, and His approval is all I need. I am glad to be an outlet for the perfect action of a perfect Mind.

I have a purpose in living. I was created to be a witness to the truth, and I fulfill my destiny now. Aware of God within me, aware of God around me, I act as a son of God should act. I do those things which are constructive and valuable. I not only know the truth, I act as the truth. I speak truth, think truth and radiate truth. My world reacts to my consciousness and truth appears on all sides. My way is easy and my problems are as nothing, for the truth makes glad my way.

My destiny is to be a creative person in a universe which responds to my thought. As a result of my conscious deliberations new and greater forms of good should and do appear. My right thinking produces experiences that lift and heal my fellowman. This I do, for it is my destiny to be a bringer of good tidings of great joy.

I delight in the magnificence of God's universe. I am glad that His Mind fashioned me out of Its own substance of good. I realize that I must live in accordance with God and His perfect law of mind action. I do this, for it is the only permanent way of peace and true accomplishment.

April 30

My Life Is Easy, for God Is Ruling My Day

Let not your heart be troubled, neither let it be afraid.
John 14:27

I HAVE faith in the eternal goodness of God and of man. I know that never again will fear distort my thinking, for I now am sure of my divine security. The Lord is with me wheresoever I go. Divine intelligence guides me, whatsoever I do. Divine love flows through me to whomsoever I meet. This is the truth of this day, and I am established in it.

I am unafraid and untroubled, because I know that I walk in omnipresence, think with omniscience and act with omnipotence. Order, harmony and peace abide in me and flow from me. New ideas come to me; old ideas are released from me. Having no fear, I meet every situation with poise. There is calm, beauty and joy on every hand, God's perfect world is my world, and God's perfect people are my only contacts. My life is easy, for God is ruling my day.

Every hour of this day is alive with God. His Mind never lets me go for even a split second. Divine guidance is forever in me, seeking to lead me into greater accomplishments. Turning within to Spirit, all pressure is taken from me. I no longer need to assert myself, for now the truth flows out from me and its divine assertion delivers me from all problems.

Peace fills my mind; love fills my heart and God is always where I am. I discard doubt, for I know that the one Mind knows what to think in me, and what to produce through me. Lovingly and trustingly, I let my God-self express. I declare the glad tidings of great joy to my fellowman. I thank God for life, and I live this life fearlessly, wisely and lovingly.

May 1

Today I Permit the Power Greater Than I Am to Flow into Newness of Life Through Every Thought and Action

...I will lead them in paths that they have not known...
Isaiah 52:16

SOMETIMES we are confronted with problems which we do not seem able to solve and right here is the place to prove to ourselves that there is an intelligence which knows how to bring things to pass for us. In doing this we should shut everything else out of the mind and rest quietly for a few moments while we confidently affirm the divine presence and actually believe that it is guiding us. Now think of your problem and consciously take it into your thought, not as a problem, but as though you were receiving the answer, as you meditate:

I AM bringing all my problems to the altar of faith and I know that every true desire of my heart will be fulfilled through the power of love. My first desire is that all my thoughts and all my acts shall give joy and gladness to everyone around me. I wish the healing power of love to flow through me to everyone.

I believe that divine intelligence, which is the Mind of God, is guiding, guarding and directing my thoughts and acts. I believe that God already knows the answer to this problem; therefore I am letting go of the problem, as though it were difficult, and I am listening to the answer, as though it were sure. The answer to this problem not only exists in the Mind of God; I affirm that it is in my mind now, that something in me does know what to do. I joyfully accept divine guidance. I am open to new ideas, to new thoughts, new hopes, and aspirations. This which so recently seemed a problem, no longer exists for the Mind of God, which knows the answer, is quietly flowing through my thought and feeling. A great peace and joy come over me as I accept this answer from the giver of all life.

May 2

Today I Am Conscious That My Body Is Vitalized By the Living Currents of Life

And the prayer of faith shall save the sick, and the Lord shall raise him up.
James 5:15

WHEN we say that the body is spiritual we are not denying the physical body. The physical is included within the spiritual. If the Spirit, or divine intelligence, has seen fit to give us a physical body it would be absurd to think of the body as an illusion unworthy of our attention. Rather, we should think of the body as a spiritual instrument now. Every statement we make about the body, or belief we hold about it, which causes the mind to accept Spirit as the substance of the body, tends to heal.

MY body is the temple of the living Spirit. It is spiritual substance now. Every part of my body is in harmony with the living Spirit within me. The life of the divine Spirit flows through every atom of my being, vitalizing, invigorating and renewing every particle of my physical body. There is a pattern of perfection at the center of my being which is now operating through every organ, function, action and reaction. My body is forever renewed by the Spirit.

I am now made vigorous and whole. I possess the vitality of the infinite. I am strong and well. The life of the Spirit is my life. All Its strength is my strength. Its power is my power. I feel that my whole being is renewed, invigorated and made alive. There is complete stillness and perfect peace at the center of my being as I wait on that presence which makes all things perfect. Every breath I draw is a breath of perfection, vitalizing, upbuilding and renewing every cell of my body. I am born of the Spirit. I am in the Spirit. I am the Spirit made manifest.

May 3

Today I Seek and Find New Opportunities for Self-Expression Through My Faith in the Power of God

> ...*the darkness hideth not from thee...*
> *the darkness and the light are both alike to thee.*
> Psalm 139:12

TO be effective, prayer must be affirmative, but it is not enough merely to affirm the presence of God. We must add to this realization the thought that divine intelligence is acting in and through us now. Prayer is not a wishful or wistful wishing, nor is it an escape from objective reality. To be lost merely in our prayers might terminate in an unconscious desire to escape the activities of life. Therefore we affirm that divine intelligence not only knows what to do, it impels us to act on its knowing.

I AM handing my life and affairs over to divine intelligence, to the power that knows how to do anything. I am doing this in complete acceptance. Gratefully, and with deep peace, with complete conviction, I am receiving the all-good into my experience. I know there is nothing in me that can doubt either this divine goodness or the operation of its law in my affairs. I believe that everything necessary to the fulfillment of every good desire is now in full operation, that all the circumstances in my life are tending to bring it about.

If there is anything I ought to do about this I shall receive the impression to act. I shall receive guidance, and I shall be impelled to act intelligently. Therefore, I have a complete sense of ease and assurance. I look forward joyfully as I anticipate the good which is to come into my life. I believe that all who are now praying with me will receive the answer to their desires from the same source. My faith goes out to them even as their faith reaches back to me. For I believe that out of the great good in which we all live there will surely come to each one of us an answer to his particular need.

May 4

Today, As a Child, I Enter Into the Gladness of Living, Trusting in the Eternal Goodness

*Give, and it shall be given unto you; good measure, pressed down...
and running over, shall men give into your bosom...*
Luke 6:38

WHO would not be as a child again? Who would not again have the simple faith and childlike trust that somehow or other we seem to lose on the pathway of human experience? Things crowd in upon us until we lose one of the greatest of all gifts—the simple, spontaneous joy of living and a trust in the power of good which alone is able, ready and willing to meet all our needs. Let us, then, again return to the place of assurance that comes with the simplicity of faith.

I NOW command the multitude of doubts and fears that crowd into my mind to be quiet, while the divine miracle takes place in my life. I let every good I possess become multiplied as divine love acts upon my faith to bring into my experience everything necessary to my well-being. I know that this divine good includes all things that are necessary—food and shelter, love and friendship, and the accomplishment of every right purpose.

And so my faith, the faith of the little child in me, rises with expectancy to meet the new day, comes in joy to accept the bounty of heaven. With the faith of a little child I place my human hand in the invisible hand of the all-sustaining good, and I let the miracle of life and love take place. I break my bread, with thanks, and distribute such good as I have to everyone I meet. I say of my own household, and the households of all others: "God bless the four corners of this house, and be the lintel blest, and bless the bed and bless the board, and bless each place of rest. And bless the door that opens wide to stranger as to kin, and bless each crystal windowpane that lets the sunlight in."

May 5

I Am at Home in the Universe Wherever I May Be— One With God, One With People, One With That Abiding Faith That Knows No Fear

And all things that are mine are thine, and thine are mine; and I am glorified in them.
John 17:10 (E.R.V.)

THIS meditation is an all-inclusive prayer because it includes ourselves and others. It is truly doing unto others what we would they should do unto us and establishes a unity between ourselves and those around us, a feeling that we all are some part of the kingdom of good. This all-inclusive prayer, then, is one which expands our consciousness of the true self and at the same time blesses those around us.

BELIEVING that there is a divine presence closer to me than my very breath, and realizing that I live in the one perfect Spirit, and knowing that the God around and the God within me is one God, I say: My Father, which art in heaven within me, hallowed be Thy name. Thy kingdom is come now, and I accept it. Looking about me, I say to all people: Your Father, which is in your heaven within you, hallowed be His name, for you are one with Him forevermore. There is one life, that life is God, that life is your life now—and that life is perfect.

Looking upon the circumstances which surround me, I bless them even as Jesus blessed the bread and broke it, and even as the loaves and fishes multiplied in the outstretched and upturned hand of his love, so I know that everything in my experience that is good is multiplied and increased. Even as I feel the increase pressing into my own experience, I give it out, with no thought of return, that it may feed and bless and multiply the good of others, these others who are some part of me because God is in them and in me, and we are in each other.

May 6

I Am Aware That God Recognizes Me as the Divine Person He Intended Me to Be and I Accept My Inheritance of Wholeness Today

Ye shall have a song, as in the night... and gladness of heart as when one goeth with a pipe... into the mountain of the Lord...
Isaiah 30:29

LET us see if we cannot take the pipe of faith and go into the mountain of the Lord, which is the secret place of the most high within us, and let the whole pipeline of our lives flow from that perfect Spirit which is at the center of everything.

I AM one with the infinite and perfect Spirit, the giver of all good and perfect gifts. I open my mind and my heart, and, indeed, my whole body, to the inflow of this divine presence. I know that this living presence is in every cell of my body and every function of my being. I now accept this divine presence as the health of my body, here and now. I accept it as that which looses from me all that is unlike the perfect expression of life. There is no doubt or fear in my mind that rejects in any way all that God is, right here and right now.

My conscious acceptance of the fullness of the presence of God, through joy and love, flows out to bless those whom I would help, those with whom I would share this inner joy. I decree that whomsoever I would bring into the scope of my thought is now blessed and healed through the presence of good which is within. The radiance of joy in my own heart brings happiness into the lives of those about me. The abundance which prospers me supplies everyone around me with the good things of life. The light which warms the center of my own being so shines forth that all may find guidance and warmth and comfort in its rays. This is the light that lighteth every man that cometh into the world. This is the fount from which spring the living waters. I drink, and shall not thirst again. And even as I drink, I hand the chalice of my faith to all.

May 7

Today I Feel the Certainty of Faith Coming Into Action in Everything I Do, Say or Think

Thou shalt also decree a thing, and it shall be established unto thee.
Job 22:28

FAITH acts like a law because it is a law. It is the law of spiritual Mind in action. When we realize this we no longer feel that we must have faith in ourselves as isolated human beings, but rather, as human beings included in the great law of life. Then we can rest in complete confidence that our words are the presence and the power and the activity of the Spirit in us. All sense of making things happen, holding thoughts or concentration of the mind are put aside, and with quiet, childlike acceptance we make known our requests with thanksgiving.

GOD and I are one. Nothing can separate me from the Father. All that I am, and all that I do, is the divine presence expressing itself through me. The thoughts I think and the words I speak are life and truth. They are life and truth because God speaks them through me. Of myself I give no authority to my prayer, but the child of God in me knows that the authority of the Father brings the words that I speak to pass.

I speak the word of health for my body, my feelings and my thoughts, knowing that the Father within is the power which brings this wholeness into complete being. I speak the word of divine guidance and the wisdom of the universe wells up as a beacon to lead me into paths of right-use-ness, to make straight and clear my everyday paths. I speak the word of joy and the Father within frees me from loneliness and sadness. I speak the word of peace to the world and know that the peace of God reaches into the hearts and minds of the people of all nations.

May 8

A Great Peace of Mind, a Deep Sense of Belonging, a Complete Realization That God Is Right Where I Am, Fills My Mind Today

Her ways are ways of pleasantness, and all her paths are peace.
Proverbs 3:17

WHEN we meditate on spiritual thoughts we are affirming the presence of God in, around and through us. It is this close and immediate feeling of the divine presence, actively stated, that gives power to our words. The words of themselves would have no power without this deep feeling back of them. It is because we do believe in a power greater than we are that we can have this feeling, this inner conviction, this sense of certainty which all spiritual teachers have told us is necessary to effective prayer. Effective prayer is an acknowledgment of the presence and the power of good. It is an acknowledgment of this presence as close to us and this power as acting on our acceptance.

I KNOW that there is a power greater than I am. I know that there is a love that casts out all fear. I know that there is a faith which overcomes all obstructions. I am now entering into this love. I am now using this faith. I now have complete confidence in God, the living, loving Spirit.

I believe that the Spirit within me, which is God, makes perfect and happy the way before me. I enter into conscious union with everything that lives. I commune with the Spirit in all people and in all things. I feel an intimate relationship to the presence and the power which controls everything. I put my whole trust in God. I know that the Spirit will gently lead me, wisely counsel me. I know that the love which envelops everything flows through me to everyone, and with it there goes a confidence, a sense of joy and freedom, a buoyant enthusiasm for living, a zest for life. And there back to me today everything that makes life worthwhile—everything that is good, beautiful and true.

May 9

Today I Am Filled With Confidence and a Sense of Security Because I Am Actively Aware of the Presence of Spirit Within Me

For he shall give his angels charge over thee, to keep thee in all thy ways.
Psalm 91:11

DEEP within each of us there is a place of calm, of peace and security, where trouble and accidents do not occur, where truth and love reign supreme and good is the only power. It is to this place that daily we go in the silence of our own minds to commune with the Spirit that is both around us and within us. Truly this is our Father within, our heaven immediately available and always responsive to our approach. In our meditation we seek to make the presence of this Spirit more real to us, more immediate and more personal. And as we do this an inward sense of calm comes over the mind, a feeling of security and safety which every human being needs.

I KNOW that all the power there is and all the presence there is, is love, the living Spirit Almighty. I know that love is divine protection and I know that I am governed, guided and guarded into the pathways of peace and joy, and security. I know that this is true of all people. This is what I believe about everyone. This is what exists for the whole world. This is my prayer of acceptance today, and every day. I feel myself safe in the keeping of divine love and infinite power. I feel the soft enveloping presence of the living Spirit.

I know there is no confusion or doubt in the Mind of God. God's Mind is the only mind there is. This mind is my mind now, directing everything I do, guarding every movement I make. For all my ways are ways of blessedness, and all my paths are peace. I trust, I rest, I live and move and have my being in that which is complete, perfect, divine, whole and happy.

May 10

Good Is Forever Expressing Itself to Me As I Seek and Find the Best in Life

...thou art ever with me; and all that I have is thine.
Luke 15:18

REALIZING that we are in the midst of an ever-present good, and believing that there is a law that brings everything good into our lives, we should learn to think and act as though every wrong condition of yesterday were converted into something new and better today.

I BELIEVE that all the mistakes I have ever made are swallowed up in a love, in a peace and a life greater than I am. Therefore, I surrender all past mistakes into the keeping of this ever-present, divine, and perfect life. I affirm that love is guiding me into a real and deep cooperation with life and into a sincere affection for everyone.

Today is a fresh beginning, a new start, a joyous adventure on the pathway of eternal progress. Today is bright with hope and happy with fulfillment. Therefore, I affirm that this is the day that God has made, that it is good, and that I find fulfillment in it. There is something that is making everything in my life simple, effective and whole. There is something that is arranging every circumstance so that success and happiness will come from it. There is something in me that goes out in love and confidence to everyone I meet, something that blesses everything I touch, something that brings peace and comfort and joy to my world. In every thought, in every deed, in every act, I am sustained by an infinite power and guided gently into an increasing good, for myself and for others.

May 11

I Cleanse the Window of My Mind That It May Become A Mirror Reflecting Inspiration From the Most High

...and prove me now herewith, saith the Lord of hosts, if I will not open you the windows of heaven, and pour you out a blessing, that there shall not be room enough to receive it...
Malachi 3:10

WE should believe that God is the invisible partner in our lives and affirm that divine love goes before us and prepares the way. We should permit ourselves to be guided for there is something within us, deep at the center of our being, which knows what we ought to do and how we ought to do it.

I AM listening to the divine presence and permitting it to direct my path. Thoughts and ideas will come to me and I shall be led to follow them out in my everyday life. I shall be impelled into right action. I know how to meet every situation in calm trust and with the complete conviction that divine intelligence is guiding me. I wish to do only that which is constructive and life-giving; therefore I know that everything I do is prospered. Everything I touch shall be quickened into a newness of life and action. Every constructive purpose in my life will be fulfilled.

I have a deep sense of inner calm, a complete assurance that all is well. The same intelligence that governs the planets in their course is now acting as a law of good in my personal experience and in the experiences of everyone around me. I do thank God for this increase that is mine. I do accept divine guidance. I do believe that I am in silent partnership with all the power, all the presence and all the love there is. I place my life entirely and completely under the protection and guidance of this power, and I rest in complete assurance that everything I do is prospered.

May 12

Today I Receive the Inheritance Which God Has Given Me

...thou shalt rejoice... in all that thou puttest thine hands unto...
Deuteronomy 12:18

AFFIRMATIVE prayer means that we clear the mind of all doubt and fear and turn in faith to the great giver of life. It means that we become aware of the presence of God within and around us, here and now. It means that we affirm this presence and accept it, quietly, calmly and peacefully, in all its fullness.

I NOW let go of every anxious thought. I now surrender any doubt or fear into the great heart of love. I look out upon the world and say: "This is my world because it is God's world." I think of all people: "These are my friends because they live and move and have their being in the Father of us all." I now receive confidence and inspiration from the source of all life. I believe that love is guiding me. I believe there is a divine power that goes before me and makes perfect my ways in joys and happiness. I believe this power is flowing through me to the joy and happiness of those around me.

I have a faith, a conviction, and assurance at the center of my being. I have a love which envelops everything I contact and every person I meet. I have a friend within me who knows all my needs. I accept the kingdom which God has given. I accept the life which He has implanted in me, and this life reaches out to everything around me, in joy and gladness, with the blessed assurance that all is well. Believing that God is love, I affirm that there is nothing in me that could hurt or harm or hinder those around me from entering into the fullness of their own joy, into the completeness of their self-expression, into the perfection of their own being.

May 13

Today I Acknowledge the Outpouring of the Spirit Everywhere

God so loved the world, that he gave...
John 3:16

HOW could we better explain this than to use the words of Browning where he said: "'Tis Thou, God, who giveth, 'tis I who receive"? Or Emerson who said that we are "beneficiaries of the Divine fact"? The thoughts of both Emerson and Browning were thoughts of acceptance and recognition. Like all men of great spiritual insight, they knew that the gift of life is an eternal reality, that it is our office to accept it.

"GOD so loved the world that he gave..." Today I accept this gift of divine love which God has eternally given to me and to everyone. With deep gratitude and a childlike simplicity I enter into the joy and the peace which come from the realization of divine guidance. I know that love guides my thoughts even as it guards my life and action. I know that the eternal presence is really embracing everything. In this presence I serenely and confidently rest, placing all my hope and aspiration in its loving care. In this love I embrace the world and affirm that peace shall come on earth and good will among men.

I also realize that I belong to the universe in which I live, and it belongs to me. It is the gift of God. I am one with everyone I shall ever meet, and they are one with me. For we all are manifestations of the one divine presence.

Gratefully acknowledging and gladly receiving this benediction from heaven, I live and love and accept life in its fullness. "God so loved...that he gave..." I accept the gift.

May 14

I Place My Affairs in the Hands of Divine Goodness and Enter Into the Fullness of Life

Thy kingdom come. Thy will be done in earth as it is in heaven.
Matthew 6:10

WHEN Jesus said, "Thy kingdom come. Thy will be done in earth as it is in heaven," he was affirming that there is a perfection at the center of everything. He was telling us that when we reach this inward perfection it will be revealed to ourselves and others, and that it must finally establish the kingdom of God on earth, as it most certainly will.

REALIZING that the kingdom of God is a kingdom of joy and that the heart of the eternal is most wonderfully kind, I place my affairs in the keeping of divine love and I permit my thoughts to be directed by divine wisdom. The Spirit within me guides and directs my path, guides me into peace, prosperity and happiness.

God's perfect kingdom is established in me today. The Fatherhood of God is revealed through me as the brotherhood of man. This brotherhood I help to establish on earth today, for I know that it is within all people. This kingdom of oneness and love and peace draws me close to everyone I meet, in joy and in friendship. Therefore, my prayer for the kingdom of God on earth is a communion of my own soul with that one universal soul which overshadows and indwells everything. This is the kingdom I am recognizing as I affirm: "Thy kingdom come. Thy will be done in earth as it is in heaven."

May 15

I Know That the Life of the Spirit Is My Daily Life

The Lord is my shepherd...He restoreth my soul...
Psalm 23:1, 2

AS we take this thought for our meditation today: "The Lord is my shepherd ... He restoreth my soul," let us feel that we are one with the divine presence, and enter into conscious communion with it. This is affirmative prayer and spiritual meditation. It is through spiritual meditation that we reach out, or in, to that divine presence which fills all space and also finds its dwelling place in the sanctuary of our own hearts.

"THE Lord is my shepherd...He restoreth my soul." Believing that God is everywhere, and knowing that the divine life can and does restore my soul, I now affirm and deeply accept divine guidance. I believe that I am sustained by an infinite power, guided by an infinite intelligence and guarded by an infinite love. I feel this presence in, around and through me, and through all people. There is a power greater than I am upon which I may rely. I am relying on this power and I am letting its intelligence govern and guide me. I am fully aware of divine love and protection.

I lay aside every doubt or fear and gladly enter into a newness of life. I do believe that the Lord is my shepherd. I do believe that He restoreth my soul. I am lovingly aware that the divine presence is not only close to me, it is not only right where I am; it is also within me and what I am. It is this inner "I Am," this Spirit of God within me, that is my shepherd. I not only shall not want—my cup shall run over. A table is prepared before me. This is the table that God has spread and I gratefully acknowledge this divine bounty, this feast of life. For God's abundance is my abundance, His good is my good, and His life is my life now.

May 16

My Life Shows Forth the Spirit That Never Fails and Constructive Action Fills My Day

And I, if I be lifted up from the earth shall draw all men unto me.
John 12:32

WHEN Jesus spoke of being "lifted up from the earth" he meant that that which is human about us must consciously become united with the Divine. In ancient writings the earth stood for the lowest form of life while heaven represented the highest. Therefore, being lifted up from the earth means uniting earth with heaven. This daily lifting up of our thought is necessary if we wish to so unite ourselves and everything we are doing with the Divine, the spiritual power that flows through us and into all our acts.

I AM now waiting upon the Spirit within me. I know that It is close to me and that It governs my life in harmony and peace. And I know that through me It brings joy and happiness to everyone I meet. Through the power of this indwelling Spirit I am a blessing to myself and to others.

I am lifting up my whole mind in faith to the realization that the Spirit of God is within me and that this perfect Spirit is my real self. I invite the Spirit to direct my thoughts and acts, and I believe that It is doing so. I expect new ideas, new thoughts and new ways of doing things to stimulate my imagination into action. I invite and expect new circumstances and situations.

I know that as they present themselves, the intelligence within me will accept them and act upon them. I know that the divine presence within me will make itself known to every person I meet, to every situation I contact. I know that it will bring life and joy to everything and everyone.

May 17

The Spirit in Me Is Alive, Awake and Aware, Flowing Ever Through Me in Perfect Life

The Spirit of God hath made me, and the breath of the Almighty hath given me life.
Job 33:4

MAN is a spirit but he seldom recognizes this greatest of all truths about himself. Seldom does he invite the Spirit into his mind or open all the doorways of his thought in complete acceptance. The Bible tells us to let that mind be in us which was in Christ, which, of course, is the Mind of God and the invisible guest in every person.

I KNOW that this invisible guest within me, the angel of God's presence, is counseling me wisely, leading me unerringly, directing my thoughts and actions in harmony, in peace, in poise, in love and in cooperation. Because God cannot fail, and because the divine presence within me is God as my real self, I know that there is a power flowing through my word of faith which makes straight the way before me. I know that the great giver of life is giving through me that gift which is gladly made and which returns multiplied, only to go out again to increase its blessing and to multiply its own good as it blesses others.

I know there is a presence that came with me when I entered this life, and I know that this same presence will go with me when I leave this physical form, for it is the presence of eternal life, the life that cannot die. I have no fear of the past, the present or the future, for I am living today as though God really were all-in-all, over all and through all. I feel this presence in love, life and goodness. I feel it in action, power and certainty. It is with me today, making my life whole and complete.

May 18

My Mind Is Receptive to New Ideas and My Thought Is Centered on New Beginnings

For behold, I create new heavens and a new earth:
and the former shall not be remembered nor come into mind.
Isaiah 65:17

NOTHING is ever twice alike. It is said that the physical body is never more than a year old, that we discard many bodies through life. Everything is continuously being re-created and it literally is true that the divine creative Spirit is forever making a new heaven and a new earth. We must permit It to make a new one for us.

THERE is no judgment, no condemnation, no fear and no doubt in my mind. I condemn no one and no thing, not even myself. Forgetting that which is past and having no fear of the future, I live today as though the new heaven and the new earth were already an accomplished fact in my experience. I live in harmony with people and with all the situations that surround me. I see and feel the presence of good running through everything. I have complete faith that this divine presence will reveal itself to me in every thought, in every word, and in every act.

There is nothing in my past experience and nothing in my thought about the future that can in any way deny me the pleasure and the privilege of living today as though everything were complete and perfect. "For behold, I create new heavens and a new earth: and the former shall not be remembered, nor come into mind." My whole confidence and expectancy is of much and more, of good and of better. The future is bright with hope and fulfillment. The present is perfect, and there is no past.

May 19

I Surrender All Fear, Doubt or Uncertainty and Accept the Gift of Life Today

Fear not, little flock; for it is your Father's good pleasure to give you the kingdom.
Luke 12:32

WE should always keep in mind that we are beneficiaries of life. We do not put the chicken in the egg, nor the oak tree in the acorn. Rather, we take them out. We did not create the divine presence nor the law of good; we commune with this presence and use the law. Therefore, Jesus said that it is your Father's good pleasure to give you the kingdom. It is our business to receive it. And in doing this we follow the same method that any scientist would, for the scientist knows that he did not create the laws that he uses or the principles which he employs.

IT is my Father's good pleasure to give me the kingdom. Today I accept this kingdom, which it is the pleasure of the heavenly Father to give to me, and I accept it in its fullness. Today shall contain joy and happiness; today shall be filled with peace, and through it all will be running the silent power of spiritual forces, which will harmoniously and happily govern my thoughts, decisions and acceptances so that everything I do will be done without effort.

I lay all weariness aside and accept the life-giving, invigorating, dynamic power of the Spirit, knowing that It vitalizes every organ of my body: It flows with power and strength and purpose through everything I do, even as It leads me gently down the pathway of life. Today is the day that God has made, and I am glad in it. And when evening comes, the cool shadows of peace shall fall across my pathway and the quiet of the night shall enter into my soul, while the beatitude of the Spirit flows through me as a river of life.

May 20

Today I Proclaim My Divine Inheritance

Neglect not the gift that is in thee...
I Timothy 4:14

IF two persons were exactly alike, one would be unnecessary in the scheme of things. Emerson said that imitation is suicide. The divine spirit never made any two things alike—no two rose bushes, no two snowflakes, no two grains of sand, and no two persons. We are all just a little unique so that each may wear a different face, behind which is the same, the one and the only presence, which is God. It is right and necessary that we should be individuals. Unity does not mean uniformity. Unity means that everything draws its strength, its power and its ability to live from one source. One life flows through everything.

This life is never monotonous; it is forever doing new things in you and in me.

REALIZING that the divine has made me just a little different, I affirm that I am one with this original Spirit and that It is doing something new through me today. Therefore, everything I do shall be original; it shall be like a new creation. There will be a new enthusiasm, a new zest for life. Even the old songs I sing shall be a little different because of a renewed influx coming from "the maker of all music" and "the master of all singing."

Realizing that the divine Spirit is flowing through me in an individual way, I accept the genius of my own being. I know that the original artist is doing something new through me today. Therefore I do not imitate others, for each is a king in his own right, each is a divine being on the pathway of an eternal unfoldment. Gladly do I recognize and unify with the genius in others, but always keeping the uniqueness of my own personality. All the presence there is, is flowing through me in a little different way. All the creative genius there is, is thinking in me in an original manner. I invite the inspiration, the illumination and the guidance of God, and gladly cooperate with it.

May 21

The Spirit Within Me Communes With Everyone and Everything

...thou shalt love the Lord thy God with all thy heart, and with all thy soul, and with all thy mind...and...thy neighbor as thyself.
Mark 12:30, 31

WHEN we let the love that is within us go out to the God who is in all people and the divine presence that is in all things, then we are loving God with all our heart and with all our soul and mind because we are recognizing that the Spirit within us is the same Spirit that we meet in others. This is loving our neighbors as ourselves.

THE love that is within me goes out to the God who is within all people. I recognize the divine presence everywhere. I love and adore this presence. I know that it responds to me. I know that there is a law of good, a law of love, forever giving of itself to me. This divine and perfect law is circulating through me now. Its rhythm is in my heartbeat; its perfection is in every organ, action and function of my physical body. Love and perfect life circulate through everything. This love and this life I accept as the truth about myself, now and forever.

This same love, this same presence, this same law of good, I recognize in others. It is a divine presence, a holy presence, and a perfect presence. It is a law that heals and makes whole, that prospers and makes happy. This is the law of my life. This is the good that I meet everywhere. I know that the only power there is and the only presence there is, is love, the living Spirit Almighty. There is no condemnation, no judgment and no fear in me. I feel that I belong to the world in which I live. I love people and am loved of them. I have a deep sense of confidence and trust. I feel that I am secure in life and that I need not be anxious about anything.

May 22

I Free Myself From Every Sense of Condemnation Either Against Myself or Others

He that saith he is in the light, and hateth his brother, is in darkness...
He that loveth his brother abideth in the light...
I John 2:9,10

WHEN John said that it is impossible for us to remain in the light while we hate someone else, he was pointing to the same truth that Jesus had in mind when he said, Forgive, and you will be forgiven. We could not expect the law of good to operate for us alone, shutting all others out. It is only what we share with others that really is ours. We are so constituted that when we think evil of others or condemn them it is impossible to escape this condemnation for ourselves. This is why Jesus said, "Judge not that ye be not judged, for with what judgment ye judge ye shall be judged." Everything that goes out comes back again. Our thoughts and acts move in circles.

I BLESS myself for the good I would do and I bless everyone for the good they would do. I recognize the presence of God at the center of my own being, and I know that the divine Spirit within me responds to the same Spirit in others, comforting, unifying and making whole. There is no criticism, no false judgment, no unkindness in me. My whole thought and feeling is one of praise, of thanksgiving and blessing.

Today I am living as though this moment were eternity. I am recognizing that the kingdom of good is at hand. Seeing the divine in everything, I know that the divine in all things responds to me. Receiving the silent blessing of the Spirit, I permit this blessing to enrich the life of everyone I meet, to bring comfort, faith and good cheer to everyone I contact. Therefore, I walk in that light in which there is no darkness, in that love in which there is no fear, in that life in which there is no death.

May 23

I Do Everything With Reliance on the Law of Good

All power is given unto me in heaven and in earth.
Matthew 28:18

WHILE Jesus said that all power was given to him in heaven and earth, at another time he said that he of himself could do nothing. This sounds like a contradiction until we understand the subtlety of its meaning. Jesus realized that there is but one power and one presence and he knew that we all live in this presence and by this power. He also knew that when he surrendered himself to the presence, that is, when he thought the thoughts of God after Him, then the power would automatically respond to him. Therefore, in surrendering himself to the presence of good he commanded the law of good. This is fundamental to our whole concept of what we believe and the way we use it. For we use the law of good, which of itself is entirely independent of us, like all other laws of nature. Responding to the presence of love, we use the law of good. This is what meditation, affirmation and prayer mean.

I AM now depending on the power that is greater than I am and the law of good that is available right here and now. I identify my life with the presence and the power and the love of God. I recognize the divine presence within and around me, and in all people.

If there is anything in me that denies this presence or this power, I loose it and let it go. I am surrendering myself in faith and with complete conviction to the acceptance that everything necessary for my well-being, my physical, mental and spiritual self-expression, is now operating in, through and around me. I know that everything I do shall prosper. I know that the one life, which is God, is my life now. Therefore I accept this gift of life and love, for myself and for all people.

May 24

Today I Loose All Condemnation; I Judge Not and I Am Judged Only By the Law of God

...forgive us our debts, as we forgive our debtors.
Matthew 6:12

WHEN Jesus said that we should not judge lest we be judged, he was stating the action of the law of cause and effect. If we wish a complete clearance from any sense of condemnation about ourselves, we must first be certain that we have released all condemnation of others from our own minds. When we do this we meet others in a new light and reaching back of all judgment and criticism, establish a relationship between the Spirit that is within them and the same Spirit that is within us, for God is one in all people.

REALIZING that love is the great motivating power of life, and knowing that God must be at the center of everything, today I am meeting this God in everyone and seeing the manifestation of His life in everything. If there is any condemnation or animosity in me, I gladly loose it. I loose it and let it go as I turn to that silent presence within me which gives all and withholds nothing.

Giving and receiving, loving and being loved, I rejoice with all creation and find in field and flower and running brook, in the sunshine and in the stillness of the night, that one presence which fills everything. I enter into the harmony of eternal peace, into the joy of knowing that I am now in the kingdom of God, from which no person is excluded. My yesterdays are gone forever, my tomorrows stretch forth into an endless future of pure delight. And from out of the invisible there come to me these words: Today thou art with me in paradise.

May 25

Every Negative Thought or Condition Is Erased From My Experience and I Walk in the Joy of Ever Increasing Good

He shall call upon me, and I will answer him: I will be with him in trouble; I will deliver him and honor him. With long life will I satisfy him, and shew him my salvation.
Psalm 91:15, 16

THIS passage contains a great promise. Not one of something that is to transpire in the future, but rather, a good that should be transpiring in the present moment in which we live—right now and right here. Therefore we should accept this promise and its fulfillment.

I NOW accept this promise in its fullness. I do believe that every good thing necessary to my success already belongs to the kingdom of God, which I know is at hand. I am expecting good to happen. I anticipate success. I believe that divine intelligence guides me into happiness and wholeness, because I know that God is happy and whole; therefore, I know that I am living right now in the spirit of wholeness and happiness. I am looking through the eyes of happiness at the presence of wholeness, and accepting it.

I accept that God is love, and knowing that God is in all people, I meet this love which is everywhere. Therefore, I love and I am loved. Knowing that God is the great giver, I accept His gift and do myself become a giver to life. All I have I give, and all that God has I receive. The kingdom of God is at hand today. I enter into it with joy. This kingdom contains all that belongs to the life of good. It contains all people and all things. Forever the life of this kingdom flows through me in happiness, in peace and in love.

May 26

I Lift Up My Cup of Acceptance Knowing the Divine Outpouring Fills It to the Brim

God is able to make all grace abound toward you; that ye, having all sufficiency in all things, may abound to every good work.
II Corinthians 9:8

WE lift up our cup of acceptance to the divine bounty when we think affirmatively and with gratitude to the giver of all life. Daily we should practice affirming that our cup is filled and running over, always remembering that what we affirm for ourselves we must affirm for others. Living and letting live, giving and receiving, loving and being loved, our cup of acceptance will be filled from the horn of God's abundance.

I AM living in the continual expectancy that every good thing in my experience shall be multiplied. There is neither doubt nor uncertainty in my mind. Every denial is transformed into an affirmation, every negation into an acceptance, every "no" into a "yes." I know that the Spirit of God has made me, and the breath of the Almighty has given me life. I have complete confidence in this Spirit. I know that I am loved of It and needed by It. I feel at home with It.

Today is filled with blessing for myself and others. The past is gone and I gladly loose it and let it go. The present is filled with peace and joy, and the future with hope. Gratefully I accept the presence of love and divine givingness, and gladly I extend this love and givingness to everyone I meet. I am made whole with the wholeness of the Spirit. Gently but with complete certainty, I am guided into right action and successful accomplishment of all good desires. This I accept. This I experience.

May 27

Every Part of My Body Is in Harmony With the Living Spirit Within Me

...I am the Lord that healeth thee.
Exodus 15:26

SPIRITUAL mind healing has long since passed the experimental stage. We now know that we cannot tell where the body begins and the mind leaves off, and many of us believe that the actions, organs and functions of the physical body really are activities of the divine intelligence within us. To come to realize, then, that there is one body, which is the body of God, and which at the same time is our own body, is to indraw a greater spirit of life. We should daily affirm that:

THERE is one life, that life is God, that life is my life now. Every organ, action and function of my physical body is in harmony with the divine life. There is perfect circulation, perfect assimilation and perfect elimination. If there is anything in me that does not belong, it is removed. If there is anything that my physical being needs that it does not appear to have, it will be supplied. My body is daily renewed after the image of perfection with which it must be held in the Mind of God. "Be ye therefore perfect, even as your Father which art in heaven is perfect."

I affirm that my body is the body of God; it is a body of right ideas all working in harmony with each other. The life of the Spirit does circulate through it, the law of the Spirit does govern it, the love of the Spirit does sustain it. Therefore I sleep in peace and wake in joy and live in the continual acceptance that life is good. My whole experience is God. My whole life is God in action. For I am one with all life and all power.

May 28

I Use Divine Power in Practical Ways and Right Action Prevails in My Affairs

...What things soever ye desire when ye pray,
believe that ye receive them, and ye shall have them.
Mark 11:24

THERE could be no more explicit technique for effective prayer than this laid down by the Master himself. We actually are to believe that we already possess the object of our desire when we ask for it. We are to accept it even as we believe in the harvest which follows the spring planting. Therefore, every spring should be one of hope and every harvest one of fulfillment. We must learn to accept the good we desire and affirm its presence in our experience, here and now.

REALIZING that there is a law of good that governs my affairs, I loose every thought of doubt, fear or uncertainty and accept the good that I desire, here and now. Realizing that this law of good not only knows how to create, but must contain within itself all the details of its own creation, I let go of every thought of outlining and accept the perfect answer today. Feeling a deep sense of gratitude and joy because of this, I live enthusiastically and with calm and happy anticipation of more yet to come.

Because there is no sense of strain in this, I relax in quiet contentment while at the same time realizing that what the law of good does for me it must do through me. I declare that I not only know what to do but I am impelled to act, to move objectively. For this is not a dream I am entering into, or an escape from any present condition which is unhappy or unwhole. This is really the act of fulfillment, the moving into a greater sphere of action and life with certainty, calm confidence and limitless trust. Today everything in my experience shall be reanimated, reborn and increased. Gladly I accept my good and place no limit on the divine givingness.

May 29

Today I Feel the Active Power of God in Everything

...One God and Father of all, who is above all, and through all, and in you all.
Ephesians 4:6

THE key thought for our meditation today is the idea that there is an active presence of the creative Spirit in all our affairs—not something passive, but something that is moving in and through everything we do. We should affirm that this divine presence is everywhere, that it is always active in, around and through us.

BELIEVING that the divine Spirit is at the center of everything and at the very center of my own physical being, I recognize this presence harmoniously acting in every cell, every organ and every function of my physical body. I praise It and bless It and recognize that It is doing Its work well and in harmony with divine love and divine life. Recognizing this same presence in everyone I meet, I salute the God in people and I know that as surely as I do this, the God in them will respond to the same divine presence that is within me. Therefore I love others and act in unison with them.

Recognizing the one Mind that governs everything, consciously I affirm that this same intelligence is governing my affairs. It is within me and around me at all times, directing, guiding, governing, controlling and leading me happily to the fulfillment of all good purposes. Recognizing all nature as the handiwork of God, I see beauty in everything. I am one with the wind and the wave, with sunshine and cloud, with everything that God has created.

May 30

Nothing Can Go Forth From Me But Goodness, Truth, Love and Kindness; Therefore Nothing Less Than Goodness Can Come Back to Me

...If we love one another, God dwelleth in us, and his love is perfected in us.
I John 4:12

EVERY heart responds to the warmth of love. Every mind yearns for its embrace and no life is complete without it, love really is the fulfillment of the law of good. Love alone can heal the world and cause people to live together in unity and in peace. Believing that love is the great lodestone of life and that love alone fulfills the law of good, quietly I say to myself:

I BELIEVE that God is love. I believe that love is at the center of everything. Therefore I accept love as the healing power of life. I permit love to reach out from me to every person I meet. I believe that love is returned to me from every person I meet. I trust the guidance of love because I believe it is the power of good in the universe. I feel that love is flowing through me to heal every situation I meet, to help every person I contact. Love opens the way before me and makes it perfect, straight and glad.

    Love forgives everything unlike itself; It purifies everything. Love converts everything that seems commonplace into that which is wonderful. Love converts weakness into strength, fear into faith. Love is the all-conquering power of Spirit. As a child walks in confidence with its parents, so I walk in confidence with life. As a child, through love, trusts its parents, so I put my whole trust in that love which I feel to be everywhere present, within, around and through me—within, around and through all people.

May 31

Today I Enter Into My Kingdom of Joy, Into My Inheritance of Happiness

Thou wilt show me the path of life: in thy presence is fullness of joy: at thy right hand there are pleasures forevermore.
Psalm 16:11

JAMES Whitcomb Riley said: "As it's give me to perceive, I most certainly believe, when a man's glad plumb through, God's pleased with him, same as you." Jesus said that he came that we might have more life, not less. There is nothing in the thought of God that should produce sadness or depression; rather, it should be quite the reverse, because faith, conviction and love should give us such confidence and such a sense of security and faith in the good that our lives should run over with joy and we should indeed be able to sing: "Joy to the world, the Lord has come."

REALIZING that the Lord who is to come is not far off but an inward, intimate presence, closer to me than my very breath, I affirm that there is nothing in me that can doubt this presence or limit the power of good. There is nothing in me that can separate myself from the love of God, the joy of living, and the law of good.

I affirm that this divine presence is leading me on the pathway of peace. It is directing my thoughts, my words and my actions into constructive channels of self-expression. It is uniting me with others in love, in kindness and in consideration. Therefore, today I accept the joy of life. In gladness I recognize the kingdom of God that is within me. I know that today the law of good is bringing into my experience everything necessary to my happiness. And knowing there can be no good to myself alone, for God is in all people, I affirm for others that which I accept for myself.

June 1

I Am True to My Highest Principles

"Thou shalt not profess that which thou dost not believe. Thou shalt not heed the voice of man when it agrees not with the voice of God in thine own soul."
Emerson

TO profess is easy, to practice is not easy. All people proclaim their belief in God, but they rely on material help in every problem and pray as a last resort. I now take my stand with myself. I have no one other with whom to deal. I am in my own world, and I now place God at the center and know that good appears at the circumference. I refuse to declare my faith in God and still continue in my old material patterns of behavior. Today, the Lord becomes my physician, my lawyer, my counselor and my coworker. I lean not on my own understanding; I depend on Him who projected me as His own. I shout from the housetops my own divinity. I cry out to all, my dependence on the indwelling Spirit.

I am not a metaphysician in name only, I practice what I believe. I pray my way out of every problem, and prove God in every experience. The confines of my thinking extend to include the good of all. I truly practice the brotherhood of man. I see each soul as God sees him, and declare that his place in my life is one of blessing. I am not under the material influence of nations, economic levels, nor world conditions. I am an independent creation of a perfect Mind living in the atmosphere of my own consciousness. What I decree in Mind is my experience in the world. I know but one standard and one principle—the truth. To these I dedicate my thought, my motives and my responses.

Within me is the true Mind of the Spirit. It invites me to partake of Its ideas, and to prosper in all my ways. It whispers thoughts that are contrary to human opinions and worldly wisdom. But, I listen to the inner wisdom and act in accordance with it. No man can dissuade me, no group can alarm me. I know the right, and I do the right. I am true to my highest knowledge of and to my greatest vision of God and to my greatest vision of spiritual man. I am undaunted by others; I am true to my belief.

June 2

I Am God's Mind Made Visible

"The life of the soul in conscious union with the Infinite shall be for thee the only real existence."
Emerson

I LIVE in God, the one Mind, the one principle and the one truth. Body, world and material conditions are secondary to my consciousness, which is forever active in God's Mind. I am a mental being in a universe of mind-action, and the law of Mind is mine to use in ways of righteousness and in ways of peace. One with the infinite I walk the pavements of time untouched by error and upheld by the Spirit. From me proceeds the good, and to me comes the divine. All of life is now offering itself to me, and I drink deeply of its healing waters. My thirst for truth is quenched, as I realize the truth of myself as God made visible.

The material world is not my prison, and my work is not my supply. I am the conscious director of my life, and destiny depends upon me for its fulfillment. I am the creator of circumstances, not their victim. I sow the good and reap the plenty. I give out that which is of God and take in that which is of good report. One with His perfect Mind I rejoice in thinking the ever-expanding ideas of truth. Time and space are my tools, and thought is my only creative power. Unbound and free, I live with ease in my knowledge of God and of His eternal presence in my fellowman. Duality erased is unity made manifest. My one good is God, and my one action is good.

I walk as a person of power. I act as a person of love. I speak as the voice of truth. I live as an example of what God can do in man. Within me there is a peace and around me there is right action. The Almighty is my strength and I never fail my highest ideal. True to all that God expects me to be, I live in right relationships with all whom I meet. I am a blessed experience to friends, coworkers and family. God is visible in all that I do, say or think. Today is my opportunity to reveal my real self.

June 3

Today Is Unconditioned by the Past

"Teach men that each generation begins the world afresh, in perfect freedom; that the present is not the prisoner of the past, but that today holds captive all the yesterdays, to judge, to accept, to reject their teachings, as they are shown by its own morning sun."
Emerson

THE infinite Mind being eternal is not concerned with past, present nor future. It knows me as a timeless being. It offers to me all that It is, and never frowns at my lack of acceptance. In a timeless God I allow my human thinking to become aged by experience, and then my complaints are many, and my excuses are profuse. I use the past to explain the limitations of the present, and I fail to realize that only my acceptance of the past gives it power. I now free my thinking from all past patterns and step forth this day as a new creature in Christ. Too long have my alibis ensnared me. They are as nothing when I declare the truth.

I am of God's generation. My habitation is eternity, and my continuity is beyond question. Time is my own measurement, and God knows only the now. I accept myself as free from the past, creative in the present and rejoicing in the future. I inherit the ideas of God, and I dispense them with order and efficiency. Fresh impulses come to me, and new experiences unfold before me. God's man is never of the past, for God knows no past. God's man is the man of the hour, the moment, the split second. I am that man now. Unconditioned by mistakes, I can make none. Unconditioned by disease, I am health. The world does not determine my prosperity, I alone determine it. God is all that I am.

The sun of truth shines in my world and reveals the good that is at hand. Gone are all false leanings on family, heritage, and background. I am today what I am because of my consciousness. Background is merely a record, it is never a fact. Born of the Spirit, I am the Spirit and no man can convince me otherwise. I rejoice in the now and live in the present, finding God in every moment.

June 4

I Rise Out of the Old to Walk With God in the New

"Religion in the mind is not credulity, and in practice is not form. It is a life. It is the order and soundness of a man. It is not something else to be got, to be added, but is a new life of those faculties you have. It is to do right."
Emerson

THE world would have me tarry in the old, the traditional and the past. But, the infinite urges me forward, bidding me to keep pace with the fresh ideas emerging from the divine Mind. The truth is ever new to me. Today's inspiration is God's action urging me to do a creative work. Within me now is the order and soundness of God's man. I need add nothing more to my wisdom, for His Mind is mine, and I now produce good works. I practice my knowledge of God. I give factual evidence of my faith. Whoever sees me this day sees the Spirit at work through me. I do the right and loving thing.

The years ahead are bright with promise. They will be to me what I cause them to be. I can repeat the past, or I can create new and better experiences. God wants me to do the latter, and I now resolve to do it. If God is forever making all things new, then He is forever making me a new person. This constant improvement is now the basis of my thinking. I think and act today in accordance with my plan for the future. My present faith in good brings that good upon my pathway. Today is better than yesterday, and tomorrow will be heaven on earth. No longer chained by the past, I freely create a new heaven and a new earth.

My religion is of today, for my God is present today. I acknowledge Him in all my ways, and allow His Mind to direct my paths. Right now I am a spiritual being, and I never shall be less. New ideas are the foundation of my life today, and I am their living representative. God walks as man through the affairs of my world, and I am that man of God. All power is mine to use. All blessings are mine to share. I am victorious over the past, and I am radiant with the possibilities of the now. I open my whole being to the next great good that is even now appearing in my experience.

June 5

What I Decree Today Happens

"A man contains all that is needful to his government within himself. He is made a law unto himself. All real good or evil that can befall him must be from himself."
Emerson

I STAND in a universe which responds to me. My world being a subconscious intelligence must respond to my conscious thought, act upon it, and produce what I decree. It has no power to resist me, and no way of not doing what I direct. I act upon the one Mind and the world of form reacts to me in direct response. My word is power. My thought is a direction to the universal power and presence. My active treatment is a command to the subconscious to produce what I want. Knowing what I really want, I now speak with authority to my own mind, and the sum-total powers of the universe automatically produce my command in form. This is my power and my authority as a son of God.

Jesus bid the waves be still, and they calmed at his word. I now look out upon the troubles of my own experience, and declare "Peace, be still." Jesus demonstrated to all that God's power is the only power. I am a center of this power, and it seeks my recognition and direction. My thought directs it and my emotions motivate it. I am the only authority in my world. I may give this authority to others, to situations or to conditions, but it is my free choice to do so. God's action through me is only conditioned by me, and I now give it freedom to act for my good, by directing it to do so.

Nothing can happen to me, unless I am the channel through which it acts. I now refuse all evil, all inharmony and all disease. My mind is centered in the good, the true and the wise. Projecting good, I experience good. Wise ways of the Spirit, I know what to do and speak my word to accomplish it. In me there is wisdom born of God. In me there is love born of the infinite love. I now decree their release into my experience. I decree my own good, and this makes it a good to others. I accept the responsibility of life. I declare the truth and my world must mirror only truth.

June 6

I Know My Own Divinity and Appreciate It

"The purpose of life seems to be to acquaint a man with himself. He is not to live in the future as described to him, but to live in the real future by living to the real present. The highest revelation is that God is in every man."
                                                                                                                                        Emerson

ALL Mind operates at a center within me. All love seeks an outlet through me. God's action in me is my own real self, and to it I now devote my attention. I know myself as God knows me, and all disbelief is erased from my consciousness. Contemplating myself as a spiritual being, I realize the vast possibilities before me. I am unconditioned by the world, for I am Mind in action. I now become the person I have always hoped to be. Finding the Spirit within me, I change all my opinions of myself. No more self-limitation, no more self-condemnation. Today, I am God's creation and as such I move forward in life.

Watching my momentary thinking, I realize the reason I have not accomplished my heart's desires. All stumbling blocks have been unconsciously created by myself. I am determined to cease my own self-imposed restrictions. God has placed no limitations upon me, and I accept my freedom to prosper. Acknowledging myself as God's beloved expression, I think straight and make right decisions. I now act from the God-Mind indwelling me, and my actions are worthy of truth. God speaks, acts and loves by means of me. Around me is an inviting presence, and within me is all the Mind of truths. Knowing myself as God knows me, I move ahead to great accomplishments.

I appreciate the God action indwelling me. I appreciate the life that animates me. I praise and give thanks for my own divinity. I see this same divinity in my fellowman. All men have goodness in their hearts and greatness in their souls. I am one with the good in all. I am one with the universe and its spiritual source. I am one with God and act as His representative. Today, all men shall call me blessed, and the world will be a better place because of my actions. I am Divine and release goodness.

June 7

I Rely on God Alone to Meet Every Situation

"Instead of that reliance which the soul suggests, on the eternity of truth and duty, men are misled into a reliance on institutions, which the moment they cease to be the instantaneous creations of the devout sentiment, are worthless."
Emerson

I FACE my world with a courage born of my knowledge of God. I am never alone, never deserted and never without aid. My reliance is on Him who brought me forth to express His life divine. Indwelling me, there is a center of Mind and love, where power awaits my recognition. From this inner Christ I draw greatly on God. The inexhaustible action of divine Mind is the power of my thinking, and I have the courage to do all things. Directed from within, I see the falsity of external authority. God in the midst of me is my power and my deliverance from all that would beset me.

Steadfastly knowing my inner strength, I am no longer appalled at what I need to meet. Challenges change to opportunities; problems to possibilities. Urged forward by divine truth, I proceed into correct action and bring forth right solutions. I am no longer the victim of verdicts, whether they be medical, economic, age, social or financial. I have but one divine verdict upon me—God declares forevermore that I am His eternal son. That alone is true of me, and knowing this I have no fear. His whole Mind and love are mine to use for right activities, and I use them with ease.

As there is no power opposed to omnipotent Mind, there is no power opposed to me as Its beloved outlet. I now erase all opposition within my own thought, and am a free and open channel for omnipotence. I face all things with faith, cheer and the expectancy of good. I am a spiritual optimist, for I know that with God's help everything works together for good. My life is now a victorious one, and problems dissolve as I think the truth. Today is filled with victory.

June 8

My God Indwells Me as Mind and Love

*"The nameless Thought, the nameless Power; the super-personal Heart—
he shall repose alone on that. He needs only his own verdict.
No good fame can help him, no bad fame can hurt him."*
                                                            Emerson

THERE is but one infinite Mind, and It indwells me this day as the source of all life, all knowledge and all possible good. This Mind is also love. It is a complete unity of all that ever has been, ever will be. I know myself as Its vehicle of operation, and It acts without hindrance through me. Not to the outer world do I look for help, but to the inner source I turn for the full supply of every need. In this inner consciousness of security I am no longer impressed by material fears. All manner of evil may appear to assail me in my hectic world, but the peace within bids me to believe it not.

Divine love maintains the calm of my being. It disciplines and balances my emotions. Anger and hysterics are impossible to experience, for within me there is nothing to cause them nor react to them. I face my world poised and at peace. I face the arguments of my fellowman with the clear understanding that they will not twist my judgment nor lead me to wrong conclusions. God's Mind is the only basis of my decisions, and thus all my affairs must prosper. With love and intelligence as the foundation of my thinking, I do all things with ease and with efficiency. God's action in me is wonderful.

I am independent of fame and slander. I am a spiritual being in a spiritual universe and only my estimate of myself is true. Others may proclaim my faults, outline my mistakes, and declare my weaknesses. Not one word of these is true. God in the midst of me cannot see evil, hear evil or speak evil about me nor anyone else. Only that which is true of the Spirit is true of me. I know my spiritual worth. I affirm my thought as the divine thought, and my heart as being of Him whose heart is the heart of all. I am untouched by human opinions, and I offer none. God indwells me today as Mind and love.

June 9

I Accept Myself as a Center of Divine Release

"Yourself, a newborn bard of the Holy Ghost, cast behind you all conformity, and acquaint men at first hand with Deity."
Emerson

I ACCEPT myself as the outlet of the infinite. I believe in my divine origin, my persistent inspiration, and my destiny of good. I know that God gives freely of Himself to all, and my share is great. In me the Divine is seeking to create new trains of causation, which will enrich me and increase the good of all who know me. The power which spoke through Moses, Isaiah and Jesus is the power which acts through me. I have within me all the creative powers of spiritual genius, and I accept them and use them this day. What others have done in the past, I can do now, and even greater works can I do.

I acquaint men at first hand with deity. My actions as well as my words give evidence of my spiritual understanding and development. My reactions to unpleasantness reveal my inner poise, security and peace. In all situations I bear witness to his Mind which directs me and prospers me. Freely I give of myself to all, and richly the Father gives to me of His inexhaustible self. I behold the Christ in every man, and I refuse all human speculations of evil. I refuse to accept, contemplate or seek anything less than the perfect, the true and the fine. No man can convince me of error, for I know from my own experience that God is the final reality, and untruth fades before the light of my own understanding.

I am God in action, for there is nothing else for me to be. Creative ideas indwell me, and my environment welcomes their complete expression. I am unopposed, for the one power and the one presence is the cause, continuity and conclusion of my life. I am a center of divine release and from me there flows this day the glory of God to all the other sons of Heaven.

June 10

I Let Life Move Me Forward into Greater Good

> *"People wish to be settled; only as far as they are unsettled is there any hope for them."*
> Emerson

THERE are no anchors in my world to fasten me to any one situation forever. I accept the ever-changing, ever-unfolding action of God in my experience. I have faith that life impels me into greater good for myself and for all who comprise my world. I appreciate the past, but it cannot bind me to any person, place nor thing. It is now a neutralized memory of good, and its knowledge is available to me, but its negative power is gone. No more weeping for what might have been. Today is the day of glory, and tomorrow is alive with the possibilities of creative self-expression.

There are no impediments to the divine impulse within me. My consciousness is cleansed and awaits all new ideas with expectancy. These ideas will take me out of the present mediocrities into the heaven of fresh conditions. As I let life move me forward I find joy on every hand and love in every heart. New friendships, new opportunities, new environment and new experience appear to be enjoyed and to be praised. I do not miss the patterns from which I have emerged, for greater good is mine today than I have ever known before. I bless the old, but I welcome with open arms the new.

I let changes take place in my life. I know they must, and I know they will, whether I say yes or no. All changes accepted as a spiritual adventure are for the good and I now begin the discovery of God in every new condition. Buried in all men is the treasure of the kingdom of God. I seek it, and I find its coffers overflowing with kindness. I have no enemies, for God's friendship comes to me through every relative, coworker and contact. I break all chains which bind me and walk free into God's great experience of life. New forms of good come to me, emanate from me, and appear around me today.

June 11

I Dare to Put New Ideas Into Practice

"Let me admonish you, first of all, to go alone; to refuse the good models, even those which are sacred in the imagination of men, and dare to love God without mediator or veil."
Emerson

I LOVE God, and I appreciate the inspiration which His Mind is pouring into mine. Without this inner source of refreshment, I would soon experience stagnation and despair. Not for me are the hard roadways of discouragement and failure. With my keen knowledge of the Spirit I face only pathways of pleasant success and certain abundance. Many may call me irreligious, but I do not care. Dearer than all else is the knowledge that I am the son of the Father and unto me He gives all of Himself in full measure. Of this I am certain now and forevermore.

I have courage to put new ideas into practice. I dare to act as a spiritual being would act, for I am one who knows his divine origin. The world may not understand me, and may even condemn me, but I stand unmoved in my determination to prove that God is the only power there is. My thinking is forward and my actions are creative. Nothing stands between me and my desired accomplishments, for I am an open channel for the inflow and the outflow of God. The Lord God omnipotent operates through me. My Spirit and I together walk as one united activity of life.

In a world that is weary of the commonplace, I originate new conditions of good. I inaugurate God's ideas in a material world, and its seeming materiality, melts away and reveals my heaven here and now. My faith is great and I am determined to break new paths through the wilderness of human opinions. There is a light that leads me on, when all would turn me back. I am an inspired and creative expression of infinite Mind. I need not to be understood by men, for I am understood by the indwelling Spirit which motivates me. Pioneering in the ways of truth, I prove for all to see that the greatness of God does dwell in the hearts of men.

June 12

I Enthusiastically Spread the Truth

"Nothing great was ever achieved without enthusiasm. The way of life is wonderful; it is by abandonment."
Emerson

THE concept of my omnipresent God is too wonderful to keep to myself alone. I spread my larger understanding of God abroad to all who will listen. I am enthusiastic about life as God in action. Having given myself to the infinite presence, the infinite Mind and the infinite love, I can shout from the housetops the value of this new way of life. Gone are all the fears, the terrors and the blasted hopes. To me there has come the joyous abandonment to Him who knows what to do and how to do it. I have never been so free, and never been as happy.

All men should know the truth and be freed from their own misconceptions. I accept the challenge to so live that all who contact me shall find their freedom, their health and their prosperity. My light shall so shine that all men seeing my good works shall glorify my Father in heaven. My enthusiasm for God is catching. Others see the light in my face and seek the same enlarged consciousness of good. As they seek, they find, and in their finding pass on the same light to others. I am starting a chain of truth-minded people which shall encircle the globe and heal the nations.

The mantle of the Christ is upon my shoulders. The sword of truth is in my hands. The breastplate of righteousness protects me from all evil. I show forth the glory of my inner Christ, and whoever thinks of me receives a benediction of illumination. The whole Spirit of God is in full action through me, and I have courage to do the right and loving thing at all times and under all circumstances. His Mind is mine, His love beats in my heart. The contagion of true holiness is tremendous. I share my God with my world.

June 13

I No Longer Interfere With the Higher Mind

"We are wiser than we know. If we will not interfere with our thought but will act entirely, or see how the thing stands in God, we know the particular thing, and every thing, and every man."
Emerson

I HAVE faith that the Mind of God not only created this universe and man, but also forever maintains Its creation within Its own bosom, nurturing and furthering the perfect plan and the divine concept. The Divine forever knows what to do and is forever doing it. Being all in all, It is never conditioned, never inhibited and never limited. I am the outlet of all that Mind is, and I am always in the presence and always using the power of God. I cannot escape my divinity, try as I may. I cannot be a failure, for God will always win out in the long run. God uses me as His channel for good.

My best planned ideas will fail me if they are founded upon selfish principles. Each time I work for my personal gain and disregard others, I am interfering with divine action, and I merely punish myself. The divine order and law will always prevail, despite my human will. I cannot change God, but I can change myself. I now cease all interference with the divine plan of my life. I stop deciding long-range plans for the future. I accept the fact that I am wiser than I know. I am wise enough to let life unfold in Its own way and for its own purposes.

I respect my world, for in it I see the action of God take place. I respect my fellowman for he was not made by himself, but God created him for a purpose. I respect myself and my own abilities, recognizing the Divine within that seeks to make me greater than I am at the moment. My consciousness turns with confidence to God, and His ideas appear in me in perfect order and on time. Letting the infinite Mind have Its full sway in my thinking makes life easy and right. I can never falter nor fail, for I am governed by Mind and by Mind alone. Divine ideas impel me forward today, and I rejoice in my many demonstrations.

June 14

All Life Impels Me to Right Action

"For the Maker of all things and all persons stands behind us and casts his dread omniscience through us over all things."
Emerson

IT is time that I definitely improve my life. I have lingered too long with half-truths and alibis. I am willing to face myself squarely and honestly. Without true inspiration, I have made many mistakes, and I am weary of the hard work that my material thinking has caused me. The wisdom of the infinite is available to me, is actually within me, and I now let it guide me into perfect ways. I start an improvement program based on spiritual inspiration. The universe is planned for everyone's success, and I now expect mine. God is backing me up, and there is no power to prevent my demonstration.

The one Mind acting in me is my source of ideas. Divine thinking impels me to right action and right decision. He who created me abides in me and directs me. From this inner point of true control and true direction, I look out at my problems and see their immediate solution. I refuse to believe that I am blocked, delayed or frustrated. God is all power, all wisdom and all action. All of God is with me, and all of God is for me. Knowing this, I cannot fail. I rejoice in this newfound freedom of letting God do the work. I rest in the divine action of the law of good.

Improvement appears on every hand, and I see a new day dawning. The night of fear has passed, and the light of God defines my pathway. I anticipate this day to be a good one, and tomorrow to be even better. I glory in my newly discovered abilities. I appreciate every good impulse that the divine Mind delivers to me. I hold my consciousness open to guidance. In complete confidence I face each task and all impatience deserts me. I find love and cooperation in all people, and I offer them only harmony and affection. Heaven is where I am, and I enjoy its perfect peace. I accomplish all that I need to do with ease, for God indwells me as Mind.

June 15

Divine Ideas Come to Me at Every Moment

"The soul's communication of truth is the highest event in nature, since it then does not give somewhat from itself but it gives itself and becomes that man whom it enlightens."
Emerson

I ACCEPT the responsibility of being alive in God's great universe. Truth seeks to give itself to me, and I open my mind to it. I let down all the bars, I unlock all the gates of human wrong thinking. I expect to have my consciousness flooded with inspiration as the infinite Mind uses me as Its channel for expression. I allow the Divine to enter and absorb me, I become the Divine incarnate. This is what Jesus knew, and now I know it. He sensed his responsibility to so think, act and be that God would find no closed doors in his mind. I shall do likewise.

I am the living expression of all that God is. I am not a body using a mind—I am Spirit in complete authority over my world. I am a receiver of divine inspiration, and a communicator of divine love. The potential of a perfect life is given me to use, and I develop it in fullness. I am not hindered by myself, for no longer do I claim material infallibility. I know that my senses may deceive me, my world may wrongly influence me, and only my own thinking determines my experience. I give myself to the truth, and the truth sets me free from all previous wrong conclusions.

The one Mind is the source of my life. Ideas are the beginning and end of demonstration. I see myself as a mental being in a universe of mind-action. I declare the truth and the truth becomes my experience. I receive and affirm God's ideas and they bless and prosper me. My health is perfect because His Mind is perfect. My affairs are in order, because order is the way God works. Prosperity cannot pass me by, for his ideas in action through me guarantee my abundance. Every instant of this day is potent with God, and his unfailing inspiration is mine, and I accept it.

June 16

Importance Is the Order of the Day

"Every moment when the individual feels himself invaded by it (Truth) is memorable. By the necessity of our constitution a certain enthusiasm attends the individual's consciousness of that divine presence."
Emerson

EACH day is the new order offering itself to man. In the divine plan, all yesterdays are canceled and all tomorrows are speculation. This is the day the Lord hath made, and I accept its importance. None of my affairs are under the verdict of yesterday. Health, peace and abundance are dependent only on this day. Mind negates the past and affirms the present. God's ideas vitalize and create new vistas of demonstration. I realize the value of this day, and refuse to allow it to be dominated by the past or by the future. My God is of the present, and his ideas rule me at this moment.

I am invaded by truth, and I welcome its rules in my thinking. No false reports can register their misconceptions in my mind, for God alone thinks in me and God has righteous judgment. The invasion of truth is welcomed by me, for then I can let go of my own false sense of responsibility. I turn over the affairs of today to a Mind which knows exactly what to do. All my questions are answered by my inner intelligence. All my fears are dissolved by my inner love. I lift my thought to the one Mind in the calm assurance that no mistake can ever be made. God governs me now.

All things are important, for all things bear witness of the idea which created them. I look at the details of my experience and find the Divine facing me. God looks at me through every situation, every person, and every feeling. Omnipresent love infolds me and omniscience is mine. I value the inspiration that infiltrates my consciousness, for it is God bidding me to do the right and loving thing. I prosper as I let the larger Mind and the greater intelligence dominate me. God is always a welcome guest in the home of my thinking. I bid His ideas come and live with me. Today is the most important day. I have ever lived, and I prosper in it.

June 17

I Find the One in All

"We live in succession, in division, in parts, in particles. Meantime within man is the soul of the whole; the wise silence; the universal beauty to which every part and particle is equally related; the eternal One."
Emerson

I HAVE faith in one God, one action of love, and one life that is in all and through all. God must be one—for my life bears witness of a unity of creative action, that I, alone, can upset. This eternal one Mind acting through one law is never confused by the stupidity of man. It remains forever poised in its own self-knowing, and this is the Rock of Ages to which I can always turn when my own thinking has led me astray. I am never alone, never forsaken by the truth. Its patience is forever, and as I return to its premise It welcomes me and gives me all that It is.

Details can no longer exhaust me, and my variety of duties shall no more disturb me. In all that I have to do there is a single power and a single Mind operating, and It directs my ways and makes light my burdens. I arise out of the many and find rest in the one. I now accomplish all that needs to be done, with inner peace and poise. No longer distracted, I work with ease. Life is a pattern of wholeness, and all details fall into their right place and are completed with ease. I am overshadowed by wisdom and embraced by love. It is good to know this and to feel the one divine presence.

I now am able to find the beauty of the Spirit in all things. The commonplace becomes the threshold of God, and every minute action glows with the harmony of the Spirit. Nothing I do is too menial, for God greets me in every action, and peace enfolds me as I work. All false pride is swallowed up in the victorious attitude of God's work in me, through me, and by means of me. I am the vehicle of the truth, and I am worthy of the divine trust. I dedicate this day to the allness of God. I perceive His face in every face I see. I do His work in every job. I glorify my Father by living as His son.

June 18

Let Heaven Happen to Me Today

"From within or behind, a light shines through us upon things and makes us aware that we are nothing, but the light is all."
Emerson

WITHIN me now is the light of life, and I let it reveal its perfect nature in all that I do. I am willing to step aside from all petty thinking and place God first and foremost in my experience today. I know that more good is seeking to express through me than I can ever know. All that the Father-Mind has is within me offering Itself to me. Peace is in my environment, prosperity is in my finances and health rules my body, as I let God dominate my consciousness. It is a great relief to know that I need not work, but merely know truth and let it happen to me.

The allness of Spirit includes me and all my world of affairs. Heaven is my natural setting, and I appreciate its generosity of beauty, harmony and order. I give God the freedom to be in me what His Mind has chosen to be. Out of the infinite comes all the good I want and need, and it appears now at this time in my life. Through me shines the glory of God and from me flows the beauty of the Spirit. As I grant full authority to divine Mind, I can rest from all labor and watch my affairs operate with ease. I have peace in my soul, rest in my body, and joy in my world.

It is a great relief to know that people, things and situations are not dependent upon me but upon God: I withdraw all claims of personal achievement and give all honor and all glory to Christ in me who doeth all the true work. The universe is divinely operated, and all my personal affairs are a part of this divine action. Therefore, they are now governed by intelligence, motivated by love and they prosper. Heaven is mine today. Joyously I greet all men as brothers, for we are all one in the kingdom. One God, one fellowship of man, one universal order, and one heaven in the present. Greater good than this I cannot know, for I am one with my Father.

June 19

I No Longer Indulge in Negatives

"We lie open on one side to the deeps of spiritual nature, to the attributes of God. Justice we see and know Love, Freedom, Power."
Emerson

THE spirit of the Lord is within me, and I am resolved to live positively. The Bible states that man is the image of a perfect God. Therefore, I must have the potential of perfection, and this perfection must be positive. I now align myself with the positive side of life. It is divinely natural to be positive, optimistic and expectant of good. These are the bases of all healing, for they are the way God works through me. If God is my life, then I should express health. If God is my supply, then I should express abundance and freedom in finance. I have faith that these ideas are true, and that they now act for me.

No one causes me to worry, nothing causes me to fear. All evil is wrong self-indulgence. As an individualized center of divine operation, I can no longer afford the luxury of fear and worry. I refuse to pay their price, for God's free faith is mine to use without cost. It offers Itself to me without stint, and I accept it with joy. I know that my right thinking controls my destiny. I know that the key to all experience is in my own consciousness. I set my thinking on the truth and I do not waver for a single moment. I am steadfast in my loyalty to Him who made me of Himself.

God loves the positive person, for then all of Mind has a free outlet for Its Ideas. Knowing this, I become the person God loves, and all right action uses me as a center of distribution. To me comes the holy purpose, and from me flows the healing power. I heal myself and others. I think health, act as health, and speak health at all times. I am no longer sick, tired or worn out. God in me is positive life, health and vitality. I radiate the positive. I rejoice in the power of right thinking. My whole experience is now changed into greater good, and my thinking expands it forevermore. I dedicate my mind to His, and I rejoice in positive results.

June 20

I Am a Growing Mind in an Unlimited God

"The life of man is a self-evolving circle, which, from a ring imperceptibly small, rushes on all sides outward to new and larger circles, and without end."
Emerson

I DECIDE to grow in wisdom and in understanding. I decide to give up the half-truth and base my whole life upon the one truth which forever imparts itself to me. No more good and evil, no more right and wrong. God alone is good and truth alone is right. I refuse to stagnate at any intellectual level of knowledge, for all true wisdom comes from growth with understanding. What I now know is merely the doorstep to what I shall know. Greater ideas of God come to me each moment, and these cause me to walk forward with consistent enlargement of consciousness. I thank God that I can grow in His ways.

The seed falls into the ground and dies in order that the plant may appear. I let every area of my subconscious become the soil of a larger life. I declare that every idea I now have shall die that greater ideas shall appear and thereby make me a greater expression of life. I refuse to stay as I am, and I refuse to live by past thinking. The doorway of the future opens to me only in so far as I let new thoughts govern me today. Tomorrow will be what I am thinking and feeling today. Knowing this, I now receive from the indwelling Spirit those ideas which will improve me.

I am receptive to growth. I desire more good than I have, and I know that Spirit through me will provide it. I acknowledge but one source for my present and future good—the Mind of God. I am an evolving, growing expression of a limitless principle and an ever unfolding love. I grow out of all ignorance into all truth. I evolve out of all pettiness into all tolerance. I emerge from disease into permanent health. Whatever needs to be done to make me a greater instrument of divine life and love is now being done in me. I let all changes necessary to growth take place. I love to see the old patterns dissolve and the new ones appear. I thoroughly enjoy growing in grace and in truth.

June 21

I Know That Sickness Is Unnecessary to God's Creation

"We cannot describe the natural history of the soul, but we know it is divine. But this I know, that these wonderful qualities did not now begin to exist, cannot be sick with my sickness, nor buried in any grave; but that they circulate through the Universe: before the world was, they were."
Emerson

I ACCEPT myself as a healthy, whole person endowed with divine life and the wisdom to maintain it in freedom of action. I am unconvinced by all the reports of disease and their many classifications. I condemn no one who believes them or experiences them, but I am certain that God is unaware of illness. I have faith that the intelligence which created my body will maintain it in perfect action, if I will cooperate. In me the Spirit of wholeness abides and remains untouched by the errors of body. The Christ in me is never ill, and never depleted. God in me is the same yesterday, today and forever.

My life and its health is dependent upon my knowledge of God and my practice of spiritual truth. I now increase my understanding of the divine idea of life, and let this idea be in me a power. Perfect God around me, perfect life within me. I am maintained in wholeness of body and health of mind. I am not subject to any ill, I am owned and operated by Him who made me to be His own. There is nothing in my subconscious mind to cause, maintain or erase disease. I have denied the power of evil, sickness and death. I have affirmed my health, strength and vitality as God's offspring, and this alone shall I experience.

God's action through me is perfect and complete. My whole being is receptive to life and joy. I love health, for God is health. I rejoice in health, for life is joyous, creative activity. Nothing disturbs me, for the calm peace of faith is mine today. My thinking is based on truth, my emotions are balanced in love. I gladly cooperate with every idea of health, and these ideas come to me from all directions. All people speak health to me. I radiate health to them. I am healed and whole because my mind is centered in the Lord who is health to His people. I give thanks that never again shall I know other than health.

My Religion Is of Today's God

"As soon as every man is apprised of the Divine Presence within his own mind—is apprised that the perfect law of duty corresponds with the laws of chemistry, vegetation, astronomy, as face to face in a glass; then we have a religion that exalts, that commands all the social and all the private action."
Emerson

THE world of today is my world, the cause of it I consider in today's language. I see my world as the operation of an intelligence which must be Mind, a power which must be the law of that Mind, and a unity which must bear witness of divine love. While I respect the beliefs of the past, yet I must seek my God today. I can accept a perfect Mind, an unalterable law and an interpenetration of love. This is understandable to me, and workable by me. I believe myself to be of divine importance. I believe that He who brought me forth indwells me and acts through me. God in me is my reason for being.

Indwelling me is a center of divine action. Omnipresence personalizes itself in me, and I am its distributing center. I live under a law of Mind action, and into that law I place the cause of the things I desire. God wants me to have what I want to have, and the law produces my good for me, as and when I want it. Being a law, it cannot oppose me, but must obey my will. This is the hope of my being, this is my cause for rejoicing. I live in a universe that fulfills my every positive desire, when I definitely state this desire into the law of Mind. Greater good could no generation have.

My God gives me my freedom for all experience. Good can be mine, and evil can be mine. I, alone, decide the picture and I, alone, experience the result. I live in a perfect Mind which knows me as Its perfect image and likeness. I now choose to have a heavenly experience, and the law now creates it for me. I love to live the life of freedom in a God which ordains good for me. Health, peace and prosperity belong to me, and they now function in me and around me, because I have accepted the divine gift. I respect the God of all men, but I know one Mind, one presence and one power as the truth today.

June 23

I Simplify My Understanding of God

"Whenever a mind is simple and receives a divine wisdom, old things pass away—means, teachers, texts, temples fall; it lives now, and absorbs past and future into the present hours."
Emerson

JESUS was not interested in the logics of theology, he was primarily concerned with the Spirit of man. I now turn to the Spirit within me, and find It in all Its greatness and all Its peace. There is an interior Christ-Mind that baffles all reasoning, and is beyond all human explanation. In me at this moment, God abides in fullness, in richness, in omniscience. My life today is the life of God. My thinking this day is accomplished because the God-Mind thinks through me. My capacity to be a great and loving person is because greatness born of the Spirit indwells me.

From whence I may have come is of little importance to me. Where I shall go upon leaving my present body, I am willing to leave to the wisdom of the Father of us all. Today I am alive as a creative soul, and I will so live that today the action of truth shines forth through the works of my thinking, and the words of my mouth. The Divine is a perfect simplicity. Life flows through me, love seeks an outlet from me, and power is mine to use as I select. My use of the Spirit is not dependent upon my education, background or environment. God in me acts through me as I recognize It.

I am not dependent upon theological beliefs. God and I are one process, one life and one joyous Spirit. I am in the Father and His Mind indwells me, and inspires me at every moment. I have an invisible church in my consciousness, and in it I silently acknowledge the beauty of my present life in God. The inner altar of truth feeds me with its living bread of ideas and its vital wine of creative action. I no longer seek an outside God and an exterior temple, for I know that I am the temple of the living God and that all of His creativeness is mine to use and to enjoy. I have a simplified concept of God.

June 24

I Recognize But One Mind, The Mind of God

"There is one mind common to all individual men. Every man is an inlet to the same and to all of the same. He that is once admitted to the right of reason is made a freeman of the whole estate."
Emerson

IF there is but one mind, then God must be that Mind, and therefore God must be my mind now. The unity of creation is evidence of one creative cause, and the process of creation is indicative that this cause is pure intelligence in action. The world in which I live is the Mind of God made visible. The body I wear is intelligence clothing me with a vehicle of accomplishment. The works of my consciousness, my hands and my efforts are the outlets through which I release the one Mind into form. I now accept the responsibility of knowing myself as the Mind of God in action.

Knowing all men as the means by which the one Mind acts, I know true equality. I am no greater than anyone else, and no other soul is greater than I am. All races and all creeds express the one God, the one life and the one truth. Differences, variations and discrepancies are of no importance. God in me is the only reality, and all men are my brothers living with me in the kingdom of good. All life in all forms is God in action. There is nothing too simple to express beauty, and nothing too great to express pure wisdom. God appears to me in all things and through all people.

My thinking is now determined by the one Mind. God's thoughts being premised upon good sustain my every creative action. Evil disappears from my experience, for there is nothing but the good to contemplate. The holy Spirit of pure truth abides in me and uses me as Its distributing center. I am now free to demonstrate what I want, for the one Mind delivers to me the full results of my own concepts. I affirm the good, the true and the perfect. I affirm one cause, one source and one Mind. Absolute peace indwells me, and love creates through me the desires of my heart.

June 25

I Accept Myself As the Health of God

"Mind is the only reality, of which men and all other natures are better or worse reflectors."
Emerson

THE natural state of all life is health. Life is so organized that under normal circumstances it must be health. Left to its own devices the action of God in man maintains him in health. Therefore, I let the Divine be in me what it planned to be, and my health is automatic. I remove every mental and emotional obstruction to the already perfect intelligence governing my body. I am a spiritual being, operating through consciousness and experiencing body. My body cannot make me ill, for Mind alone is cause. I rejoice in my victory over disease.

I refuse to believe that I am the victim of any situation. The Divine in me is always in full charge of my experience, and the power of God is greater than the power of disease. His Mind in me knows only perfect action and perfect results. I join with God in the knowledge of perfect man, perfect life and perfect health. I erase from my own subconscious any pattern, ideal or belief that is contrary to God. I know that deep within me is the cleansing action of Spirit, and my soul is delivered of all evil; I am healed by the perfect thought of the divine Mind.

My consciousness is alerted to truth. My body responds to health. Today, I shall have all the energy, vitality and strength I shall need to accomplish without strain. I shall have power at every moment. I shall have wisdom in every decision. God can never desert me, and His indwelling action shall maintain me in ease of body and clarity of thought. His Mind is my mind now. I am strong, fearless and creative. I have nothing to fear, and no evil to anticipate. The radiant eternal health of God is in every cell of my body and the one Mind maintains this health in me today.

June 26

This Is the Best Day of My Life

"The genius of man is a continuation of the power that made him and that has not done making him."
— Emerson

I HAVE faith in an unlimited God, my own unlimited possibility, and an unlimited world in which I function. I see all restriction as temporary negative experience which can be healed by my highest thought of God. Today, I am determined to live as a free agent of an unlimited Mind that knows only my possibility and is not interested in my own wrong beliefs. God wants me to express Him today. God has not finished creating, and His plan for me unfolds with certainty and with precision. I let Mind be in me what It has planned to be, and my success is sure.

This twenty-four hours is my opportunity to prove the reality of truth. At every moment the Mind of God leads me into my good. I am never forsaken, and never left alone. No human opinions can govern me, and no wrong decisions can be made. By my recognition of God as my own real self, the one presence actually controls my environment, and divine Mind dominates my thinking. This negates all evil, and I am free to express perfect life. I behold myself as a successful outlet of divine ideas and a joyous creator of lasting benefits. I think rightly of God, of myself and of my fellowman.

Today I am born afresh of the Spirit. No past beliefs hold me in bondage, for God in this day knows only the good of this day. His Mind in me holds no carryovers from yesterday. My past mistakes are nullified, and I shall never again believe in two powers and their resultant disunity. I have one God, and that one is the power in me to produce for me what I select. I have good cheer, for I see nothing but good before me. Today is the day of victorious results bringing to pass greater demonstrations than I have ever known before. Prosperity of all kinds is mine because I let divine Mind produce it for me.

June 27

My Selection Determines My Experience

"There is One Mind, and all the powers and privileges which lie in any, lie in all; and I, as a man, may claim and appropriate whatever of true or fair or good or strong has anywhere been exhibited."
Emerson

THE universe is a spiritual system, and it gives to all men alike. God in His creation knows no great nor small. It knows me only as an outlet of Its ideas and Its love. To me is given all power in mind and in control of matter. My authority is from on high, and the material thought of man cannot negate it. I stand in control of my experience. As my thinking determines my control of situations, I now assume my divine prerogative and think only of the things I desire. No evil can withstand my determined spiritual mentation. The gates of hell may open, but the windows of heaven shall still outpour me a blessing and triumph will always be mine.

In the one Mind I am an unlimited action of intelligence, power and love. This is my birthright. This is the divine legitimacy of my being. To this end was I created, and for this cause have I come into the world. I bear witness to perfect life, complete wisdom and ever unfolding possibilities of greatness. I remain forever unconditioned and free. My selection of truth now determines my demonstration of health, peace and prosperity. Knowing only God and His permanent goodness, I can select only that which will unfold my capacities and enlarge my usefulness. Today, I definitely do this.

I refuse to believe in evil, to experience it, or to speculate upon its possibility. All the sense testimony which can be arrayed in favor of evil is a useless argument. I have set my eyes on the good. I have established heaven in my consciousness, and there is no power in darkness and ignorance. The light of life is mine and in me it illumines my mind and maintains my faith. God alone is my beginning, continuity and conclusion. Love alone is my outer experience, and prosperity pours into my experience in profusion. I have selected that which will endure, and God giveth the increase.

June 28

The Problem of Evil No Longer Intrigues Me

"These facts have always suggested to man the sublime creed that the world is not the product of manifold power; but of one will, of one mind; and that one mind is everywhere active, in each ray of the star, in each wavelet of the pool; and whatever opposes that will is everywhere balked and baffled, because things are made so, and not otherwise."
Emerson

GOD dominates my whole experience. There is so much of God everywhere in my life, that I cannot see any opposite. My health cannot know disease and my prosperity cannot know decrease. I am completely convinced that God is the only power, Mind is the only reality and love is the only atmosphere. Evil is a word without meaning. I perceive the truth and the truth has set me free from all false speculations. Within me, around me and through me there is nothing but pure Mind. I bask in Its eternal embrace; I think in Its eternal consciousness of good.

The problem of evil no longer fascinates me, for I see it as nothing. Negatives are merely my misunderstanding of positives. My attention being diverted from the unworthy causes it to disappear from my observation. I can see only that which is of good report. My eyes are now too pure to behold any viciousness in creation. God appears to me in all things, in all people and in my own uplifted thinking. All resistance to problems is erased, because the problems are merely my opportunities to prove God as the only cause. I accomplish with ease, where others struggle to make ends meet.

God's Spirit in me appreciates my recognition of Itself, and outpours upon me all of Its qualities, ideas and aspects. All life moves to grant me the ability and the power to do what I know is right and fine and true. The inner upsurging of divine intelligence and creativeness impels me to right decisions and right actions. There is nothing to fight, there are no battles to be won. The victorious truth of my being expresses as me, and dominion over all the good is mine to use. All positives are mine. All virtues belong to me. All of God is revealed to me, and I demonstrate my happiness.

June 29

I Refuse to Experience Sickness, Poverty and Unhappiness

*"Good is positive. Evil is merely privative, not absolute;
it is like cold which is the privation of heat.
All evil is so much death or nonentity. Benevolence is absolute and real."*
Emerson

I HAVE free will as a part of my divine birthright. This great power of mind is mine to use, and the law of Mind must fulfill my direction. I now declare my freedom from all evil. I refuse to be dominated by illness, fear, lack and frustration. God never made them, and I will have nothing to do with them. God in me knows only my perfect self, and this alone I recognize, affirm and accept. Having the power to reject the undesirable, I now declare my freedom from evil. Never again will negatives rule my thinking. I am the perfect creation of a perfect God, and I know it.

My body is divinely created, and divinely operated. It is not subject to the ills of the flesh, for my flesh is spiritual substance and cannot be defiled. No sickness can come upon me, and no medical belief can enthrall me. I am the health of the Spirit. I am the life of God made manifest. I control my thinking and discipline my emotions. My vitality is sufficient for every demand made upon it. I am never unhappy, for God in me is the joy of living. Outer pleasure I enjoy, but my inner joy is not dependent upon it. My real happiness is from my knowledge of God as the joy of my being.

I refuse to experience poverty, lack or financial limitation. I live in a universe of divine design and it knows no lack of abundance. Everywhere prosperity is rampant. Money seeks me through every person, thing and situation. His richness is mine, and I accept it. I enjoy the money I have, and I use it with wisdom. There is no virtue in lack, and I now dismiss it from my world. I am the child of a rich and abundant God. The eternal providing principle supports and maintains me in freedom. I have manna to eat which no man can see, I have a living water of life to drink, and I am free of all evil.

June 30

I Give My World Love, Justice and Temperance

"For all things proceed out of this same spirit, which is differently named love, justice, temperance, in its different applications, just as the ocean receives different names on the several shores which it washes."
Emerson

GOD must act by means of me, for otherwise I have no purpose in life. I am; therefore that which caused me to be, must have a reason for my being. I have confidence that the infinite Mind knew what it was doing as It released me into the world. I have a divine purpose and a spiritual reason for being. I am not an accident of fate, nor a victim of inheritance. I am a living soul equipped to display the attributes of God in my world. I have within me the potentials of greatness, yes, the glory of God as He acts through man. To me is given the Mind, life and love of God, and I accept my role in the divine plan.

I live, because God is life. I love, for within me is a love greater than I have ever known. I am kind to others, because God in me knows their love, their integrity and their hopes. I have at the center of my being all the Mind of truth. His ideas are mine, and His ways are my paths of peace. I know the real meaning of spiritual justice. I judge no man by his outer actions. I judge only righteous judgment. God is man in his own real self, and though his outer actions may camouflage this, it still remains true. I behold the truth in every person. I see God in every face.

To live in the presence is to live always in balance. I have true temperance, for I am guided by a wisdom that always guides me rightly. I indulge in the good, and fast from all evil. I find my every hunger and thirst satisfied by an inner manna of the Spirit. I live with wisdom, and allow my fellowman to do the same. I have the spiritual intelligence to perceive the difference between temperance and intolerance. I live and let live. I love and let love happen. I have faith in my concept of truth, and respect my fellowman's concept as well. I live in God, and I express His love, justice and temperance.

July 1

I Am One With All Men

Have we not all one Father? Hath not one God created us?
Malachi 2:10

ARTHUR Compton, in *The Freedom of Man*, tells us that science has discovered nothing which contradicts the idea of a universal Mind or Spirit to which men are as Its, or His, children. It would be impossible to converse with each other unless there were a common medium, or, as Emerson said, "one mind common to all individual men." It is impossible to depart from this divine presence, to be separated from this heavenly Father, which is the parent Mind. Since God is everywhere, wherever we are God is.

TODAY I know that there is one Spirit in everyone I meet. Realizing that there is one heavenly Father, I know that there is a brotherhood of humanity. There are no aliens, no strangers. The divine image in me cannot be separated from the divine image in others. I see God in everyone I meet. The Spirit that is within me responds to the Spirit within them, for we have one Father.

I neither condemn nor make excuses for another's seeming shortcomings. I endeavor to help him to know that God at the center of his being reveals to him his perfect being. In the kingdom of God within him no false beliefs exist. No self-frustration nor inner conflict can exist in heaven within him. When I can really see God in the person who is in great need, I prove my consciousness of oneness. I am one with the Spirit in all people.

July 2

I Express Divinity

We all, with open face beholding as in a glass the glory of the Lord, are changed into the same image from glory to glory...by the Spirit of the Lord.
II Corinthians 3:18

BEHOLDING the image of perfection in everything, dominion is added to glory. This refers to the continual progression of the soul. Since God is infinite, our expansion is progressive and eternal. No matter how much good we experience today, the infinite has more in store for us tomorrow. We should look forward to this expansion with enthusiastic anticipation. The march of life is not a funeral dirge, but a song of triumph.

GRATEFUL for each success and each new advancement, I advance to new and greater revelations of truth. Knowing that the Spirit within me is free, I am no longer bound by the patterns of yesterday. Freedom is made manifest through my thoughts, in my words and actions.

The good that I experienced yesterday is going to be multiplied today. I cast this good upon every wind of heaven, knowing that it goes out to bless. I condition my mind to accept greater good for myself and others. I wait calmly, but with joy, for new experiences to come to me, for new opportunities for service. I expect my mind to be flooded with new ideas. I know that the Spirit of the Lord is with me and that the glory of the Lord is around me.

July 3

I Am Peace

*Peace be both to thee, and peace be to thine house,
and peace be unto all that thou hast.*
Samuel 25:6

PHILLIPS Brooks said that "peace is the entire harmony between the nature of anything and its circumference." "House" is a symbol of the physical body and of "that house not made with hands eternal in the heavens." House is a symbol of any of the "vehicles, bodies or habitations of the soul" on any or all planes. The Bible speaks of the House of Bondage and the House of Freedom. Symbolically, it tells us that we must come "out of the land of Egypt, out of the house of bondage;" that we must be led by the divine Spirit into that true home which is heaven. Jesus said that "in My Father's house there are many mansions."

TODAY I permit my mental house to be at peace. I know that my true home is heaven and that the kingdom of Heaven is at hand. Today I enter into this permanent home. I consciously move in and make my dwelling place in this house of peace and gladness.

The perfect life of God now expresses through me. As the sun dissolves the mist, so my knowledge of truth dissolves all pain and discord. There is nothing for me to fear. God is my life, my strength, I claim my true sonship. I claim my divine inheritance of perfect life. Today I am made perfect through conscious union with the source of all life. I have peace in the household of the Lord.

July 4

I Am Love

There is no fear in love; but perfect love casteth out fear...for God is Love.
I John 4:18,16

THERE is no fear in love and there is no liberation from fear without love. Fear is based on the supposition that we are unprotected, rejected, friendless. If the fearful Mind would entertain love and the harmony and peace that go with it, it must turn from everything that denies this love, and trusting in divine guidance, open its being to the influx of love, not just love of God but love of everything, for love is all-inclusive.

"I WILL fear no evil for thou art with me." Today divine love and infinite tenderness sustain me. In order that I shall not separate myself from this love, I endeavor to see it reflected in everyone and everything. I shall permit only that which is loving, kind and true to find entrance or exit through my consciousness. Thus I shall be assured that I am bathed in the warm glow of that love which casteth out all fear.

Becoming conscious of myself as I really exist in the mind of God, I shall find that I am walking in pathways of peace; that something within me like a magnet attracts that which belongs to itself. This something is love, the supreme impulsion of the universe. I know that I have no existence apart from this love. As I grow in the knowledge that I am one with the Spirit, I know that I shall grow in the ability to use the love within me.

July 5

I Receive My Good

Whatever things soever ye desire, when ye pray,
believe that ye receive them, and ye shall have them.
Mark 11:24

HOW simply Jesus tells us that whatever we need we shall receive if we believe that we have it! Is it so hard, then, for us to believe that the divine gift is forever made? Prayer is a sincere desire to enter into conscious union with the divine presence and to receive from it every good thing that makes life worth while.

THE truth leads me into a more abundant spiritual life. It also leads me into the possession of everything necessary to my well-being here on earth. When I discover the inner kingdom, with its spiritual gifts, the material gifts which shadow forth this inner kingdom will also make their appearance. I now learn to forget the wrong that may have appeared in my outer world, and, turning with gratitude to that inner light, I think upon those things which are good. In doing this I become emancipated from my previous bondage.

My prayer today is one of affirmation. It incorporates a complete acceptance of the divine beneficence and the eternal givingness of the Spirit. Today I lift high my cup of acceptance, knowing that the universal horn of plenty fills it to overflowing. This shall include everything I need, whether it be health, happiness or wisdom. Today my mind is open and my consciousness receives the kingdom into itself.

July 6

I Have Protection

He that dwelleth in the Secret place of the most High
shall abide under the shadow of the Almighty.
Psalm 91:1

THIS is a song of hope, a psalm of praise, the acknowledgment of an overshadowing presence, the most high good, to which Jesus gave the name, "Our Father which art in heaven." We have a right to know that in so far as we live in accord with the Divine we are protected by Its omnipotent law. "His truth shall be thy shield and buckler." The knowledge of truth will ward off the darts of evil, for evil is as night before the onrushing day; it is as darkness dissipated by the rising sun; it is as a fire extinguished by the waters of Spirit.

"Fear thou not for I am with thee…I will strengthen thee…I will uphold thee." "For I, the, Lord thy God, will hold thy right hand." It is when we turn from all belief in separateness that we find the indwelling Spirit. When we have dismissed all fear, then we know that God is love. When we have turned away from every sense of weakness we know that God is strength. Jesus said we cannot serve both God and mammon, and the Gita tells us that we must do away with the pairs of opposites before we can enter into peace.

TODAY I put on the whole armor of faith. I place before me the shield of divine wisdom. I surround myself with the conscious knowledge of the overshadowing presence. Therefore, I fear no evil, for Thou art with me.

July 7

I Am the Truth

Ye shall know the truth and the truth shall make you free.
John 8:32

JESUS implies that there is a truth which known automatically will demonstrate itself in our experience. What could this truth be other than a consciousness of our union with life? It is wonderful to contemplate this spiritual and exalted idea of truth, that truth which frees us from the tyranny of fear and the thralldom of fate. It is not in our stars, nor in our environment, that we should look to discover this pattern of truth. The truth which Jesus proclaimed would make us free, lies only in the conscious communion of the soul with its source, the conscious union of man with God, the conscious union of the heart's desire with the source of its being.

"Be yourself today regardless of what happened yesterday." We are in bondage only to a false sense of the self. We are in bondage because we judge the possibility of the future by the limitations of the past. We are in bondage because we do not realize that "He maketh all things new."

TODAY I commune with the spiritual truth in everything. Today I know that the truth makes me free from fear, doubt or uncertainty. Today there is a song in my heart as I gladly proclaim that truth which is the revelation of divinity through humanity.

July 8

My Spiritual Body

Know ye not that your body is the temple of the Holy Ghost which is in you?
I Corinthians 6:19

EMERSON said that "God builds His temple in the heart," and Seneca that "He [God] is to be consecrated in the breast of each." St. Augustine said that "the pure mind is a holy temple for God." To realize that God is in us, with us and for us, is the first step toward understanding that we are the temple of the Holy Ghost. Bishop Wilberforce tells us that "the conscious mind is the temple of the Christ Mind." We must so control the conscious mind that the Christ Mind may function through it. We must permit the Spirit to control the intellect.

"THIS is none other but the house of God..." "Know ye not that your body is the temple of the living God?" Then this body of mine is none other but the house of God. Therefore, infinite power, let me know only thy perfect life flowing into and through me.

Today I realize that my body is the temple of God; that there is the divine pattern of perfection at the center of my being. I shall not think of my physical body as being separated from this spiritual presence. The presence is the cause, the body is the effect, and the two are one. Therefore, I too shall exclaim: "In my flesh shall I see God."

July 9

I Am Mind

Let this mind be in you which was also in Christ Jesus.
Philippians 2:5

THIS means that we should recognize the divine incarnation, universal in essence but individualized in personal experience. The spiritual genius of Jesus enabled him to see that each is a unique representation, an individualized expression of one mind. The mind of God in us is the mind of Christ. At the center of every man's being the eternal Christ waits, knocking at the door of his intellect for admission. This is not a faraway presence, nor a future advent. The recognition of Christ can come to anyone at any time and under any circumstance. The consciousness that walked over the troubled waters of human experience, the inner calm that stilled the tempest, is accessible to everyone.

THE indwelling Christ tells me that the words which I speak are Spirit and life. There is a divine authority at the center of my being which announces itself in every act. I have implicit confidence in that invisible part of me which is my share in the God nature, my partnership with the infinite, my oneness with all that is. Therefore, I shall not doubt nor fear, for my salvation is from on high and the time of its appearing is today.

I know that the Christ in me is always triumphant. I know that Christ in me is one with God; there is no separation, no isolation, no oneness. There is a divine companion who walks with me and in whose light I see the light.

July 10

I Am Spirit

Now there are diversities of things, but the same Spirit…
It is the Spirit that quickeneth.
I Corinthians 12:4 and John 6:63

OUT of unity comes variety. All things are made from one formless substance. The invisible essence of everything is pure Spirit. It is a realization of this Spirit at the center of everything that enables us to see God in everyone. "It is the Spirit that quickeneth." When we recognize the Spirit in anything or anyone, there is an equal reaction from the Spirit back to us, and we are made more alive through the divine influx which follows our recognition.

I BELIEVE there is but one power and presence in the universe, which is God, the living Spirit Almighty. Therefore, disregarding any appearance which seems to contradict this divine fact, I press forward with the certain knowledge that I am forever one with the invisible presence which is able, ready and willing to direct all my ways. I know that "her ways are ways of pleasantness and all her paths are peace." Today I walk in these ways of pleasantness and "no wind can blow my bark astray."

Today I am resolved to see the Spirit in everything; therefore, today I know that my own spirit is quickened. I know that there is an inner presence in everything I shall contact which will respond to me. I know that everything is alive, awake and aware with this presence; that in all the changing scenes of my experience I shall be contacting this one presence. Therefore, I go forth to meet the Divine, to enjoy His bounty and consciously to live in His house forevermore.

July 11

God Is My Identity

Be ye therefore perfect even as your Father which is in heaven is perfect.
Matthew 5:48

THERE is a pattern of perfection at the center of everything. This the saints and sages of the ages have told us. There is, as the Platonists taught, a prototype of perfection at the center of every form. It is this spiritual prototype with which the mind should identify itself, for this is the Father in heaven within us. Nothing has ever violated the integrity of this inner kingdom. It exists forever in the bosom of God and we are in Him even as He is in us.

THE most high is enthroned in my soul; the divine Spirit exists at the center of my being. Knowing that divine power can accomplish anything and realizing that faith in this divine power draws it forth into my experience, today I exercise complete confidence in the invisible. I permit that Mind to be in me which was also in Christ Jesus.

Today I consciously identify myself with the supreme presence which inhabits eternity, and finds a dwelling place at the center of my own soul. By some deep inner spiritualization, I penetrate the mask of separation and discover the unity of all life. I identify myself with this unity, finding Christ within and knowing that "Christ is God's." I recognize my union with all the power, all the presence and all the life that there is.

July 12

I Am Success

They that seek the Lord shall not want any good thing.
Psalm 34:10

SUCCESS does not mean the accumulation of wealth, the maintenance of position, nor a supremacy of power. Success means a life free from the burden of anxiety and liberated from the thralldom of fear. There is no successful life without peace or without that inner spiritual certainty which knows that the soul is on the pathway of good, forever expanding into the conscious union of God with man.

TODAY I expect every good thing to come to me. Everything that is worthy of the soul, I anticipate. Everything that belongs to the Spirit, I accept. Everything that partakes of the nature of the divine reality, I claim as my own. Today I identify myself with abundance and success. I know that my destiny is divine, that my destination is certain, that the kingdom of heaven is at hand. I know that this kingdom contains everything necessary to my well-being. In gratitude and with joy, I receive this kingdom into myself.

I live in the consciousness of success. I awaken its greater possibility within my imagination. I feel it at the center of my being. My whole consciousness expands, and my enthusiasm glows with the heat of divine fire. There can be no obstruction to my success. Every path is open before me, and "I shall dwell in the house of the Lord forever."

July 13

I Have Divine Guidance

Be strong and have good courage…for the Lord thy God, He it is that doth go with thee; he will not fail thee, nor forsake thee.
Deuteronomy 51:6

WE all wish to know that the divine presence goes before us and we all have a right to feel this assurance. Every man is a unique presentation of the divine Mind, a separate, without being a separated, entity in the universal Spirit. Every man is, as Emerson said, "dear to the heart of God." We should all develop an increasing consciousness that we are protected and guided in everything we do, say or think.

I KNOW that new and wonderful ideas will come into my consciousness today and that I shall be compelled to act upon them intelligently. I am assured of divine guidance, I feel that it will be impossible for me to make any mistake; that even though I should start to move falsely, my movement will be corrected. I feel as though I am being constantly watched over and protected.

Today I know that the Spirit goes before me, making plain my way. I feel that everything I do shall be prospered and I fully accept that I am in partnership with the infinite. It is my desire that only good shall go from me, therefore I have a right to expect that only good shall return to me. I live under the government of good and am guided by the spirit of God. This I affirm; this I accept.

July 14

I Have Faith

The life which I now live in the flesh I live by the faith of the Son of God.
Galatians 2:20

FAITH is more than an objective statement. We do not have perfect faith while any subjective contradictions deny the affirmation of our lips. This is what the Bible means when it says we must know in our heart. Heart symbolizes the innermost center of the being. When the intellect is no longer contradicted by our emotional reactions, by unconscious doubts and fears, then the word of our mouth will immediately bear fruit.

TODAY I have faith that my word shall not return unto me void. Today I surrender myself completely to this faith, for I know that there is a creative Spirit which gives substance to this faith and which will provide the evidence of this substance in actual fact. I expect, then, to meet my good, and I rejoice in the anticipation of this good. I know that my faith operates through an immutable law and that there is no possibility whatsoever of its failing.

My faith leads me into complete self-expression. It awakens inner spiritual forces that have the power to do anything. My faith transcends the limitations of fear, of physical pain, of mental depression. My faith leads me into the pathway of righteousness. My faith unites every experience I have with the eternal. My faith in God reflects itself unto everyone I meet, thereby making practical my faith in man.

July 15

My Own Communion

My delight is in the law of the Lord and in his law doth he meditate day and night.
Psalm 1:2

THERE is always a silent communion going on between the individual soul and the invisible presence. This communion should become a conscious union of the self with the over-self, of the mind with the Spirit, of the personal with the universal. As the artist communes with the essence of beauty and gives birth to form, so our minds should commune with the divine presence.

TODAY I commune with the Spirit. In nature I see the Spirit manifest. In everyone I meet I shall commune with the living Christ, the divine presence in him, sensing its perfection, realizing its beauty, and being consciously aware of its love. Today I hold silent communion with that invisible presence which peoples the world with the manifestations of its life, its light and its love.

I declare the presence of Spirit; I worship the God within me. Knowing that the Lord is in His holy temple, and that everything on earth is subject to His will, I bless the place where I now stand. This attitude of blessing sheds a new light on my environment and I see beauties hitherto hidden. Even the commonplace takes on a new glow, and I hear "a voice out of heaven, saying, behold, the tabernacles of God is with men, and he will dwell with them, and they shall be his people."

July 16

I Have Sympathy

My little children, let us not love in word, neither in tongue; but in deed and in truth.
I John 3:18

HUMANITY and divinity will be identical when we recognize divinity in humanity. We must learn to see through the apparent, to judge not according to appearances, to realize that at the center of every man's soul God is enthroned. Sympathy and compassion are the ties that bind us together in mutual understanding and in the unified attempt to uncover the divinity in each other. Sympathy is the most gentle of all human virtues, for it is the outpouring of the divine givingness through man.

TODAY I extend the hand of sympathy to everyone I meet. I permit my inward vision to penetrate every apparent obstruction, every obstinate attempt to cover up the Divine, every ignorant misuse of the law of good. I withdraw the veil that hides my real self and in so doing, unveil the reality in others. Today I love as never before. I draw close to the Spirit in everything and everyone.

I know that God's action is right action and that all things work together for good in my experience. My word shall objectify itself as cooperation, sympathy and love. I am not afraid to make demands upon myself. I recognize the harmonious self which I am, and I know that this self will find its perfect expression. I am receptive to new and greater ideas of good for myself and others.

July 17

Christ in Me

Till we all come in the unity of the faith, and of the knowledge of the Son of God, unto a perfect man, unto the measure of the stature of the fullness of Christ.
Ephesians 4:13

THE Bible tells us the real man is Christ. This Christ is the perfect, invisible presence back of, in and through every living soul. Just as there is but one God or first cause, so there is but one man, the manifestation of the divine Spirit in and through all people. Throughout the ages this Christ has come with some degree of clarity to those who have meditated long and earnestly upon the nature of the divinity that is in everything.

I ACKNOWLEDGE this true self, knowing that it will instantly supply me with whatsoever things I need. I consciously re-enter the kingdom of heaven within me. I sit at a table of the Lord and partake of the divine banquet, the wine of Spirit and the bread of life. I know that the master at the table is my own indwelling Christ, that part of me which is perfect in God, that immortal self which is birthless, deathless and changeless. I know that my host is God, the living Spirit Almighty. I live, move and have my being in this divine presence.

Today I permit Christ to be born in my consciousness. Today I realize that Christ is the universal son appearing through every deed of goodness, truth or love. As I unveil the Christ in my own nature, I know that the countenance of the same Christ will be revealed to me through others. I enter into my divine inheritance through the recognition of my union with the supreme Spirit.

July 18

I Use Divine Law

Commit thy way unto the Lord; trust also in him, and he shall bring it to pass.
Psalm 37:5

IT is written that the law of the Lord is perfect; therefore, when we commit our ways unto the Lord, we automatically are using this perfect law even in the most trivial things of life. To this law there is neither great nor small. It is always responding to us by corresponding with our mental attitude toward it. Our mental attitudes can be consciously controlled; therefore, we can always make conscious use of the law of good.

The law of Mind brings all ideas into expression according to man's thought; therefore, we know that our positive vision brings right action in all of our affairs. We do not try to influence people nor attempt to bend them to our will. But we do know that what we sustain in our consciousness will be established in our experience. When we know that God action is right, and depend on God action and not on personalities, whatever is necessary to the fulfillment of our vision will be included in our experience.

TODAY I have faith in the law of God. Today I guard my thinking, consciously endeavoring to think affirmatively and with faith. I believe that the law of the Lord will bring every good and perfect thing to me and will bless everyone whom I hold in consciousness. Knowing that the law of good operates through my word, I speak this word with implicit confidence, with complete acceptance, and with absolute abandonment to good.

July 19

I Have True Understanding

Wisdom is the principal thing; therefore get wisdom: and with all thy getting get understanding.
Proverbs 4:7

AS all Scriptures tell us, true spiritual understanding comes from perception of the divine unity back of all things. Knowledge is of the intellect; wisdom and understanding are of the heart. Those who have had true spiritual understanding have always taught us of the unity of good; that we are one in essence with the Spirit. They have told us that the unreal never has been; that the real never has ceased to be.

"I will not leave thee nor forsake thee." Our divine nature never deserts us. Like the prodigal son, we may wander into far countries of despair, but the divinity within us ever gently urges us back to the center of our true being; it ever reminds us of its presence.

TODAY I permit my spiritual understanding to penetrate everything which seems opposed to good. Back of all variety, I perceive the one cause, the one presence, the one purpose. Today I align myself with this divine presence that runs through everything. I open the gates of my consciousness with enthusiasm and through recognition and acknowledgment, permit the Spirit of wholeness, the Spirit of oneness to flow through me. I know there is one God, one spiritual man, one perfect law, and one eternal life.

July 20

I Forgive

I have blotted out, as a thick cloud, thy transgressions...
For, behold, I create new heavens and a new earth;
and the former shall not be remembered, nor come into mind.
Isaiah 44:22, 65:17

WHATEVER the mistakes of yesterday may have been, today is a new creation. Turning from the errors of the past and no longer carrying with us the sorrows and mistakes of yesterday, today we may enter into a new experience. But it is only when we forgive everyone that we may feel certain that the weight of condemnation is lifted from our own consciousness. We should refuse to carry the negations of yesterday into the positive atmosphere of today, for today the world is made new in our experience.

When we criticize another person we are apt to become involved in his psychological reactions. This does not help the person we censure but draws us into the confusion which we are observing. We must recognize that each person is a law unto himself within the cosmic law. Each person has the right to his own ideas and beliefs. We cannot understand a person's actions until we know the beliefs which are motivating him. Only from the inner self can motives be explained.

TODAY I loose all condemnation. I judge not and I am judged only by the law of good. There is no animosity, no criticism, no hatred. I shall behold the face of love, of beauty and of peace in everyone I meet. I know that every right motive has the blessing of the Spirit and that there is nothing that opposes this blessing or denies divine givingness.

July 21

I Give Freely

Give, and it shall be given unto you; good measure, pressed down, and shaken together; and running over.
Luke 6:38

WE all wish to receive, but how many of us desire to give? If, as Jesus intimated, receiving is the other end of giving, then the more we give, the more we shall receive. "Who loses his life shall find it." We should give the best we have to each other and to the world. This gift of life is made without effort. It is complete abandonment of the self to life, a conscious letting go of all the tight strings of our being, a loosening of the divine gifts within us. Only when we have learned to give all shall we be in a position to receive all.

GOD "preparest a table before me in the presence of mine enemies…my cup runneth over." Realizing that the table of the Lord is ever spread with the bounty of the eternal givingness, and knowing that my inner shepherd attends my every need, I realize that my cup of joys runs over with the gifts of life. Unhesitatingly, I give to others. I share my kingdom with all.

Today I give myself unstintingly to life. I unloose the wellsprings of my being and make a complete deliverance of the self to life. This I do with joy, withholding nothing. I shall not do this with any hope of reward, but in the glad joy for the opportunity to increase my own livingness. Everything that I have belongs to the world. Giving, I shall receive the world back into my own consciousness.

July 22

I Have Illumination

Lift up your heads, O ye gates; and be ye lifted up, everlasting doors; and the king of glory shall come in.
Psalm 4:27

THE gates represent the place in our consciousness where the divine flows into the human. The light which artists painted around the saints represents the light of heaven. Illumination or cosmic consciousness is a reality. This is what Jesus referred to when he said, "Let your light so shine before men, that they may see your good works, and glorify your Father which is in heaven."

AS the dawn of illumination breaks and the shadows of evil flee, the hills of God are touched with the glow of divine rays. I wake to the thought that I am one with all life. I lift mine eyes to the sky and sing with the joy of one who beholds the eternal presence in everything.

Today I lift up my consciousness to the light and I know the king of glory will come in. Today I keep this inner light, this candle of the Lord, trimmed and burning, for I know that the bridegroom, which is Christ, my true self, will enter my consciousness. I know that there is a divine radiance emanating from everything. I know that in this light which emanates from the very center of everything there is no darkness at all. In this light, I see the light.

July 23

I Am One With All

Hear O Israel: The Lord our God is one Lord…I and the Father are one…
Who hath seen me hath seen the Father.
Deuteronomy 6:4; John 10:30

PERHAPS the most difficult thing for us to realize is that one life runs through everything, one presence manifests in everything, and one person individualizes through everyone. But unity does not mean uniformity. We do not all have to be alike, think alike, or act alike, but the world is learning that we must all act in union. The infinite one manifests in infinite variations, each rooted in the one but each divinely unique in its own right. Good, bad; high, low; across, above and beneath, are all one to the infinite Mind.

TODAY I find my union with life. Today my imagination reaches back through all differences to the universal sameness. Today I know that I am in Him, He is in me, we are one. Today, I sense this divine union of the soul with its source and of all people with the infinite.

I know that I am not isolated from the all-good, but as one with it. Therefore, I am not afraid, even when the billows roll and the wind sweeps by, for there is a divine hand guiding my ship; there is an invisible presence at the wheel. I lift the sails of faith and let the winds of love fill them with the mighty power of the divine presence. My boat rides upon a sea of pure Spirit and finds safe anchorage in a haven of delight. I am one with God.

July 24

I Have Companionship

I am a companion of them that fear thee, and of them that keep thy precepts.
Psalm 119:63

WE all long for intimate relationships; we wish to feel that we are one with people. This yearning, which every normal person has, emanates from an unconscious but spiritual perception that we all are one in life itself. Where there is no sense of rejection there will be no loneliness.

I NO longer reject myself. Knowing that I am one with all people in the Spirit, I receive everyone as a friend. I establish a close and intimate relationship with everyone I meet—something goes out from me and becomes unified with them. I include all and exclude none. Higher than all differences is that union of the soul with its source; beyond all differentiation, the infinite person is enshrined in the sanctuary of my own consciousness. One with all people, I enjoy this divine companionship. I embrace the infinite in everyone and in turn am embraced by it.

I know that my presence upholds and blesses everyone whom I contact, and that a healing power goes forth from me. I know that today I shall be able to help everyone whom I meet. There is a song at the center of my being which everyone hears, a joy which everyone feels, a strength which is imparted to all. I place upon everyone I meet the seamless robe of Christ, the garment of truth which is the unity of God and man. All men are my friends.

July 25

I Have Power

So God created man in his own image…And God blessed them and God said unto them…replenish the earth, and subdue it; and have dominion over the fish of the sea, and over the fowl of the air; and over every living thing that moveth upon the earth.
Genesis 1:27-28

IT is because the Spirit of God is incarnated in us that we have dominion over the world of effects. This dominion is exercised in such degree as we sense its true meaning. It is written that we have dominion over evil, not that we have dominion in or through evil. Spiritual dominion is exercised only as we rise above that which denies the divine goodness.

TODAY I exercise my spiritual dominion through the recognition that good alone is real, that God is the only presence and love and the only power. Today I rise above the sense of separation into a consciousness of my union with good. Today I understand the power of God flows through me to everything I contact.

I declare that my God-given dominion is exercised over everything I do, say or think. I am guided by divine intelligence which goes before me and makes perfect my way. I exercise dominion over my environment, over every circumstance and condition that I contact. I know that the divine Mind, operating through me, will arrange all my affairs in harmony and in prosperity. Divine power flows into my thought and work. Peace and harmony attend everything I do. Love and protection are ever present. I am guided, guarded and sustained by an everlasting strength, power and wisdom.

July 26

I Am Intuitive

Before they call I will answer; and while they are yet speaking I will hear.
Isaiah 65:24

INTUITION is not a product of the intellect nor is it something which developed in the process of our evolution. It is a thing in itself. That which is instinct in the animal, blindly, unerringly leading it to food, water and shelter, becomes intuition in man, consciously perceived. Instinct is intuition acting unconsciously; intuition is instinct elevated to the point of self-awareness. They are identical. Intuition is omniscience acting omnipresently; therefore, whether or not we believe it, it is ever present with us.

TODAY I know that the presence of divine Mind in me will guide me aright. It will set me on the path of right action. It will direct my footsteps. It will counsel my mind. Today I am aware that there is a light which dispels ignorance, fear, superstition and doubt, and sets me, safe and sane, on the pathway of truth.

I feel that my being is so close to the Divine that there is no separation whatsoever. "If ye abide in me, and my words abide in you, ye shall ask what ye will, and it shall be done unto you." Knowing that I abide in the Spirit of truth and that the Spirit of truth abides in me, today I open my whole consciousness to divine guidance. I realize that my entire being is in the hands of a higher power, that my thought is molded by the divine will, that my mind responds completely to the indwelling presence which is God.

July 27

I Receive My God

Ask, and it shall be given you; seek and ye shall find; knock, and it shall be opened unto you.
Matthew 7:7

HOW can we receive what the mind refuses to entertain? Should we not, then, consciously develop the ability to receive more? We make life little and mean and limit our own possibilities when we refuse to accept the whole gift of God. We should open our consciousness to a receptivity of the Divine. There will never be any point of saturation because God is infinite. We cannot contract the infinite, but we can expand the finite.

"THE word is very nigh unto thee, in thy mouth, and in thy heart." Realizing that God has placed the power of life in my own mind, today I am resolved to use this power in accord with the nature of the divine Mind. I shall no longer look for God in some distant place, but shall find Him directly at the center of my own being.

Today I ask and know that I shall receive. Today I seek and know that I shall find. Today I knock and know that it shall be opened unto me. But what is it that I ask for? What is it that I really seek? It is to discover God in everything, to see the Divine manifest in everyone, to come into close and conscious communion with life. Today, then, I receive the gift of God in its fullness, unstinted, complete.

July 28

I Give Thanks

*O Lord, thou art my God; I will exalt thee,
I will praise thy name; thy kingdom is an everlasting kingdom.*
Isaiah 25:1

PRAISE and thanksgiving are salutary. They not only lighten the consciousness, lifting it out of sadness and depression; they elevate consciousness to a point of acceptance. Praise and thanksgiving are really attitudes of recognition. They are affirmations of the divine presence, the divine abundance and the divine givingness. It is only when we live affirmatively that we are happy. It is only when we recognize that the universe is built on affirmation that we can become happy.

I GIVE thanks for my happiness. It cannot be taken away from me; rather, it increases daily in my experience. It is always more and never less. I experience the joy in which Jesus proclaimed when he said, "I am come that they might have life, and have it more abundantly." I bless everything I contact. I praise God in all things.

Today, through praise and thanksgiving, I recognize the divine presence in everything. In the midst of darkness I shall sing a song to the dawn, for I know that the eternal light dissipates all darkness. Today I shall recognize the beautiful and the perfect in everything. I shall call it forth with praise and thanksgiving, blessing the spiritual reality back of all things.

July 29

I Have Health

The Lord will take away from thee all sickness... I am the Lord that healeth thee.
Deuteronomy 7:15; Exodus 15:26

HEALTH is a state of wholeness in mind and in body. The body is the servant of the mind, and the mind is the offspring of pure Spirit. Thus the Bible tells us that we are spirit, soul (or mind) and body. These three really are one, and supposed to work in perfect unison with each other. They do this when the mind lifts its countenance to the Spirit, permitting Its flow of harmony, unity and beauty a clear passageway. The body will always reflect this inner poise.

REALIZING that the source of all being is within and at the center of my own being, I consciously unite myself with this center and with this source. I expect to be made whole. I expect to radiate health and vitality wherever I go. It is my will, my desire and my acceptance that I be made whole.

Today I know that my health, my physical well-being, as well as my mental poise and peace, are drawn from an infinite source of perfection. Today I know that the Lord, the law of good, is the healing presence of life forever restoring my mind and my physical being. I pray to, or commune with, this Spirit within me. Thus I am made whole.

July 30

I Have Joy

Sorrow is turned into joy before Him… Thou hast put gladness in my heart…
Thou hast turned for me my mourning into dancing;
Thou hast put off my sack cloth, and girded me with gladness.
Job 41:22; Psalms 4:7, 30:11

WE cannot conceive of the Spirit as sad or depressed. There is ever a song at the center of everything. This song is reflected in all nature, turning "mourning into dancing." To put off sackcloth means turning to a complete reliance on the Divine. To be girded with gladness means to cover ourselves with the threefold nature of good. This is a symbol of divine protection. Turning the mind to God and recognizing the omnipresence of love, causes us to rejoice, as we recognize that in Him (pure Spirit) we live, move and have our being.

I KNOW that happiness is God's will for me and for everyone. I also know that I cannot gain happiness without giving it, therefore I do not expect to be happy unless I make others glad. I radiate happiness to everyone. There is a sense of joy at the center of my being which everyone will feel. There is no insecurity in this happiness, no sense of impoverishment or fear, no feeling of doubt.

Today I turn from everything that depresses, and sing a song of praise, of gratitude and of joy. I am going forth to meet joy, singing the song of the triumph of Spirit over all apparent negation.

July 31

Today I Wait Upon the Lord Within Me

The eyes of all wait upon thee; and thou givest them their meat in due season.
Psalm 145:15

KNOWING that the divine spirit is everywhere, and realizing that everyone who asks receives, today I ask of my spiritual self that it shall come forth afresh; that it shall direct every decision with intelligence and that it shall make perfect my way before me.

REALIZING that the Lord of life is my true inner self, the incarnation of God in me, I learn to lean upon this divine shepherd; to accept every desired good as though it were already an accomplished fact; to let nothing enter my thought that would contradict the allness and the goodness of the Spirit. The divine shepherd is ever with me, guiding, counseling and leading me into pathways of peace and security.

Jesus lifted up his eyes and said, "Father, I thank thee that thou hast heard me. And I knew that thou hearest me always." This assures me that divine power can do anything and that divine love will not refuse any good gift. Since the divine gift and the divine giver are one, and since God is both peace and joy, I know that everything which transpires in my experience today will bring peace and joy. I know that everything will bring happiness and success. I rest in calm expectation, in enthusiastic anticipation of every event that is to transpire, because I wait upon the Lord within me.

August 1

I Am Cause, Not Effect

Behold now, I have ordered my cause; I know that I shall be justified.
Job 13:18

GOD made man in His own image and likeness, and I am that person now. God is the Creator of heaven and earth, so I am the creator of my own heaven and my own earth. I stand in the midst of my own consciousness and assume control. No longer am I acted upon by my world. I now am *cause* to my world. I act in mind, and my world reacts in matter in direct response to my demand. I am cause, not effect. I am Spirit releasing Itself into form under freedom. With my new sense of spiritual responsibility, I create in my experience blessings for myself and good for my fellowman.

Having taken my stand as the cause of my own experience, I now create the unique, the unusual and the different in my world. God's ideas are always new ideas. They never repeat. With my consciousness acting in its true place in the divine Mind, all things are made new and fresh in my world. Old patterns of routine and monotony are demolished, and a new mental structure of flexibility and ease is mine. I let go of the past with joy. I accept the responsibility of right thinking in the present, and I expect only new forms of good in the future.

I act upon the plastic substance of the universe with intelligence and authority. My world cannot make me sick, poor or unhappy. My world has no power or authority over me. I tell it what to do, and it does it. As I think the ideas of God, heaven appears as my world. Health, happiness and peace are mine today, because in my freedom to use God's law of mind, I create them and rejoice in them.

August 2

I Am Healed of Worry

*Behold, his soul which is lifted up is not upright in him:
but the just shall live by his faith.*
Habakkuk 2:4

FAITH in God, the good, is natural to man. Instinctively man knows that the Mind which created him works through him. I now declare my faith in God, and I prove this faith through my actions. My full attention is now devoted to seeing good everywhere and in all people. I know that within me God upholds my search for truth and guides me all the way. I know that the divine plan for me is in action; and I have complete trust in God. Only good surrounds me, and only good comes to me. I am assured of perfect peace and complete prosperity, for I fear not.

I refuse to worry this day. Despite all the negatives that may claim my attention, I shall not deviate from my affirmation of faith. One power alone is active within me and my affairs. One mind alone rules and governs my life. Nothing but God is true, and nothing but good will happen. The Lord is with me and upholds me in every situation. Everything that needs to be done, shall be done, on time and with ease. Every need will be met by the Spirit, which works through me. God in me is equal to every demand made upon Him. I am certain of this.

I trust the great law of Mind to bring my demonstrations to pass without any worry on my part. I declare the truth, and the law produces the truth in my world. Never again will I question my own ability to make my demonstrations. God honors my thought, and the law produces it. Calmly I face today, and declare it to be the best day I have ever known. My good is where I am, and it is now revealing itself to me. Freed of worry and filled with faith, I have a heavenly experience today.

August 3

I Refuse to Be Disturbed

Try constantly to keep the mind steady, remain in solitude, with mind and body free from desires and possessions.
The Bhagavad-Gita

THE universe is always orderly, and my life in it should be one of order, harmony and peace. This I now accept as truth. Henceforth, no situation shall confuse me, for I will not accept confusion. My mind, and only my mind, determines the appearance, the continuity and the end of confusion. I know that I can think in terms of order, and that all ideas do unfold with order and ease. I am determined to live in peace this day.

My consciousness is at peace, for it is now rooted and grounded in God. All my thinking is premised on God's ideas. Only good appears in my world, and all my reactions are now dedicated to good. There is nothing in me to cause confusion, or to accept confusion from others. I know that my thought determines my experience, and I now think rightly and lovingly about myself, my world and my fellowman.

My faith is great. My peace is complete. I see a divine order and a divine pattern in all situations. I behold myself living with ease and in harmony with God and with man. People react to me in orderly ways. Every situation is a blessing to me and increases my good. I move forward into larger experiences of prosperity, because my mind is clear and my goal is in sight. No longer can the world tell me what to do. I am poised and established in the one Mind, and nothing can disturb the calm peace of my soul. I declare peace, and peace is mine, for God responds to me as I think His way. I assume that my world, in all its ways, is filled with right action. I live in faith, and I demonstrate order with ease.

August 4

Today I Make My Demonstration

*For there is nothing hid, which shall not be manifested;
neither was anything kept secret, but that it should come abroad.*
Mark 4:22

THERE is just as much of God in this day as in any other. There is no reason why I cannot make my demonstration now, if I am willing to discipline my thought and feeling. All that God is, is present in my world now. All the ideas I need are in my consciousness now. My thought, being the action of infinite Mind, is all powerful. I now accept my spiritual responsibility to make a definite demonstration. No more vague thinking, and no more hoping that it will happen. Today it will happen, for God is the only presence and the only power in my life.

Every hour is alive with God's perfect action. Infinite Mind is instantly and permanently available to me, for I am its beloved outlet. I claim my good, and subconsciously accept my good. That good is now appearing, and I train my eyes to see it, and my thought to expect it. There is no delay to this action, for it is God's action through me. There is nothing to prevent my demonstration, for all doubt is removed from my thought. I am immersed in the perfect action of Mind which is already moving to complete my desire.

At this instant my good appears in orderly ways. The law of Mind accepts this demonstration as completed. It has already accomplished every act necessary to its production. I relax and let God do the work. I hold my thought firmly to the completed idea. I discipline my emotions to the accomplished mood. I am absolutely certain that my idea is appearing in form. I have full confidence in the law. My faith is complete, and my soul rejoices and gives thanks, now, that it is done. Father-Mother God, I thank thee for this full demonstration *now*.

August 5

I Am Divinely Optimistic

But the eyes of the wicked shall fail, and they shall not escape, and their hope shall be as the giving up of the ghost.
Job 11:20

GOOD is even more possible than evil, for it is God, while evil is only a temporary, false appearance. The hopeful have always managed to lift the world a bit and to bless their fellowman. With their eyes upon good, they have walked forward on a pathway of blessings. I now join with all who have placed God at the center of their lives and who know that truth alone is real. I clasp hands with the men and women who have proven the power and the presence of God.

Before me lies an eternal possibility which awaits my exploration. It bids me come to its gates and enter in to partake of its immeasurable good. Even though my world tells me that much is impossible, I still declare my possibility in God. I know that nothing can be withheld from me, if my consciousness is clear and positive. The good I seek is seeking me. The pathway I walk is always forward. If any man cannot walk forward with me, then I release him with a blessing, but I press on to my good. My footsteps are not deterred by people, places or situations. God walks by means of me, and to His forward action there is no impediment.

My future is dependent upon my conscious awareness of infinite Mind. The fears of the world and of the people who have not yet awakened to truth have no power over me. I alone determine what next year shall bring. As I am established in good, each year shall improve my consciousness, and bring greater joy to me. Nothing can prevent my progress, for God is with me, and the power of God acts through me with wisdom. I am divinely optimistic.

August 6

All Power Is Mine to Use Today

And I took the two tables, and cast them out of my two hands, and brake them before your eyes.
Deuteronomy 9:17

POWER is the capacity to imitate and demonstrate an idea. What God has done on the scale of the universal, I can do in my own world. When the God Mind initiates an idea, a new good appears for man. When I initiate a holy idea and carry it through to its logical conclusion, I am fulfilling my divine destiny. Around me is the power of infinite Mind forever revealing new greatness of mind, ease and possibility. I now attune myself to the true source of ideas, and I execute them in my experience. I have all the power I need, for Mind alone is power, and Mind thinks by means of me.

As I use power rightly I become a blessing to the world and a success to myself. I select ideas as carefully as I would select a precious gem. I want only those ideas which are worthy of my highest spiritual development. The ideas I have selected include health, prosperity and creative self-expression. These ideas now move through my thinking, backed by my affirmations of truth. They must accomplish their full demonstration in my life, for the law of Mind does the work.

There is no power outside of the Spirit within me. I formerly believed that situations, people and problems had power, but now I see rightly. Today, I stand at the center of my world as a distributor of power. I deliberately choose to have God's power in my life act as my perfect health. I open my whole body to its inflow and operation. I select the idea of joy, knowing that as power flows through me the process is a joyous one. The only power I have is God, but that is sufficient to revolutionize my being.

August 7

I Am Determined to Know Truth

And now the Lord shew kindness and truth unto you: and I also will requite you this kindness, because ye have done this thing.
II Samuel 2:6

THE truth is that which is really so, and God alone is truth. Too long have I accepted half-truth and false speculations of evil as being true, when only the real is permanent. With my mind established in truth, I look at all my fears and see them as nothing. I know that they have hampered me for too long a time, but now I am free, for I see them as they really are. Never again will the old race ideas of age, lack and disease intrigue my mind and confuse my soul. I am the free creation of Spirit, and I know the truth of freedom.

The truth of my life is that God's action is my activity. This is always healthy, strong and moving forward through finer expressions of body. God acts through me as vitality and power. I am not under the laws of a human body, for my true body is God's idea of man. This is my real body now, and in it I am living with joyous freedom of movement.

The truth of my world is that it is heaven right here and right now. Despite my limited viewpoints and human mind opinions, my real world is heaven. In this heaven of the presence of God I do that which is pleasing to the Christ within me. I live with ease, and I accomplish great things. The ever expanding activity of God frees me from the past, blesses me in the present and makes great the future before me.

I am determined to know truth this day. In all people, I behold God's perfect man. In all situations I behold the glory of God unfolding. I expect miracles to happen, for nothing can inhibit the action of God, which is the truth of my life.

August 8

My Faith in God Is Great

Even from everlasting to everlasting, thou art God.
Psalm 90:2

THE Mind which conceived me is with me. The power which has brought me this far attends me all the way. Heaven is where I am and love fills my environment. All power is in action through me and I accomplish my good works with ease. I am as certain of these truths as I am of life itself. There is no doubt or question in my mind. I know a perfect God, a complete Mind and a definite law. I do not go to It, for I am already in It. I do not seek It, for I already have all that God is and can ever be.

Having accepted this full understanding of truth, I now live in such a way that I prove my faith. I dedicate my thought to true and positive ideas. I dedicate my feelings to divine love and divine understanding. I let my human ego become as nothing, for I desire that only the Christ ideas govern my life. I rise steadfastly out of all pettiness in human relationships. I live as a spiritual being, and I acknowledge all with whom I live, play and work as sons of God. I face the future with joy, for I see idea after idea unfolding in perfect order. The future will be good, and I now have health, peace of mind, and security.

My universe is alive with good, and I have dismissed evil forevermore. I know that I am upheld and maintained by God, and by God alone. I know that my thought demonstrates instantly the desires of my heart. I have faith in all that is good and true. I have faith in a protecting presence and an indwelling power. Today, I rejoice and am glad.

August 9

I Control My Thought

Thou art of purer eyes than to behold evil, and canst not look on iniquity.
Habakkuk 1:13

FREE will does not mean that wrong thinking is justifiable. Infinite Mind created man a free soul in order that man might experiment with varying combinations of right ideas. I am free to think in all possible ways about the good, the true and the perfect. There are endless possibilities of right thinking and of right action. I now assume dominion of my mind and emotions, and dedicate them to positive goals. I enjoy the infinite variety of divine ideas, and I contemplate their possibilities of making me a new creature expressing spiritual discernment.

My faith in God is so great that I have no faith in evil. I cannot conceive of evil's power, for I know that God alone is power and is presence. Life to me is an affirmative action of thought. I think affirmatively this day, knowing that good is created, maintained and extended by so doing. I drink of the living water of spiritual truth, and am never thirsty for error again. I eat of the heavenly manna of God's ideas, and never again hunger for old experiences. I look forward with my mind and create good ahead of me. I do this deliberately, for my future will be the result of my thinking today.

God's thoughts are now my thoughts, and good appears instantly wherever I look. Thinking rightly of God and of man is a joyous and easy accomplishment. My mind is centered in heaven, and good is established in my earth. Ideas of good appear in my consciousness continuously, and I give them free action through me. I am in full control of my own destiny, and I now create good alone. Recognizing only the one true source of my thinking, I experience only the one possible effect in my experience—the effect of good. Controlled, poised and sure, I see God everywhere as I think His thoughts with Him.

August 10

I Am Victorious

Ye shall know them by their fruits.
Matthew 7:16

I HAVE faith that God, the good, is all there really is. Always, I am supported by the action of good, the action of God. Problems are merely the acknowledgment of the power of evil. I now refuse to believe that any situation can confuse me, make me sick, or limit me. Either I live in God, or I live in nothing but material belief. I now choose to live in God, and immediately I renounce every thought of negation. I assume victory over my world, my body and my finances. God in the midst of me is victorious over the doubts of my mind. Joyous accomplishment saturates my life, and victory is mine now.

I let divine ideas work in me, for I know they are powerful and quick to accomplish their ends. They arrive in my consciousness equipped to demonstrate themselves, and I give them my loving attention. God's ideas functioning within me are my only source of power, health and peace. These alone make my life victorious and undaunted. I meet every hour of this day with a deep inner conviction that I am spiritually able to handle every situation with poise. Order prevails; love is in control; and peace is the result.

I face all problems with inspiration and an expectancy of handling them with ease. I know that from a center within me, I control the events around me. I am calm and victorious at the center, and therefore my world is calm and victorious at the circumference. Christ in me is my hope of glorious achievement, and around me all things work together for good. Inspired by divine Mind, I act with wisdom in all matters. Enfolded in divine love, I handle all personalities with love and understanding. Undaunted by things and people, I am always in control of my life, and victory is forever mine. Today is the day of spiritual victory.

August 11

God's Presence in Me Is Life, Love and Wisdom

> *When the mind is cleansed by the grace of wisdom,*
> *he is seen by contemplation—the One without parts.*
> Mundaka Upanishad

GOD is Mind, and I exist in a universe of mind-action. My thought and my feeling are now governed and controlled by the Spirit within me. Gone are all my doubts and fears. Gone are all my false conclusions about life. I know, and know that I know, that life, love and wisdom are within me.

The life that I live is perfect in purpose and perfect in plan. I align my thinking with life's purpose, and I live in accordance with its plan. My expectancy is great, for I know the law of mind, and I know that right results are now appearing. I rejoice in health. I rejoice in strength. I rejoice in vitality. Only increased creative activity is before me, and I am equal to every situation that life offers me.

The love that is mine to give is from God, and I give it into my world with ease. I love to love with the love of God. I love to free my fellowman in love. I love to feel that all people everywhere are one with me, and are a blessing to me. This deep inner love gives me peace of mind. It gives me a feeling of being worthwhile. It makes me know that I am loved by others. All love is mine to give this day.

The wisdom of God is the true inner motive of my consciousness. I make right decisions. I think clearly and I act wisely. I have order in my mind and in my affairs. All things work together for good, because the wisdom of the infinite Mind is my wisdom now. I live with ease, for my thinking is right, and my world responds to my decisions. I claim good judgment. I claim the integrity of God as mine today.

August 12

I Fear No Evil

*The net of Heaven is cast wide. Though the mesh is not fine,
yet nothing ever slips through.*
The Tao Te Ching 73

THE omnipotence of God forever surrounds and maintains man. All power is instantly available, at every point in space and in every instant of time. As man knows this, all fear is erased from his consciousness. I join with all who know God as the only power and presence in their lives. I have absolute faith in the goodness of life and the indestructibility of Spirit. God in me is my resource, and nothing can harm me. I know that I am the cause of my experience, and I erase fear from my mind, and evil cannot appear in my world. Love attends me wherever I go. Peace envelops me at every moment, and God will never leave me comfortless.

I rejoice that my knowledge of good has destroyed my belief in evil. The more I know of God, the less I can create or experience difficulties. I steadfastly watch my thought, and eliminate every suspicion of fear and negation. Through the doors of my mind only good ideas pass, and only righteous judgments issue. Good is my experience, now and forevermore. I have complete security because I keep my consciousness free from false conclusions about evil. I know that no evil can happen to me unless it happens through me, and that I will not allow. I consecrate my consciousness to truth, and thereby think the truth and experience the truth. Evil is not the truth, and has no place in me or my affairs.

The endless possibilities of life are before me, and nothing can prevent spiritual development. I know that I am growing in spiritual wisdom and in factual demonstration. Every victory over evil increases my realization of its lack of power and authority in my life. I am the victorious creation of triumph in all my ways.

August 13

There Is Peace in My Soul

My mercy embraces all things.
The Koran

THE universe remains forever in perfect balance. No thought or creation of man can confuse the eternal heavens. The perfect action of intelligence maintains its creation in peace, order and harmony. This is the true state of the world in which I live. Around me in normal activity, and within me is a peace born of God. As I know this, and accept this, I relax and let the infinite Mind do its perfect work through me. Peaceful thoughts flow through my mind, and rest flows through my body.

Nothing can disturb me, for I am anchored in peace. I am led beside the still waters, and my soul is refreshed. Never again will the confused opinions of men have power over me. False speculations of the human mind no longer intrigue me or lead me into chaos. Now, I am firm in the truth and the power of its word. I do not accept appearances as truth. I have spiritual shrewdness to see good where others see evil. Peace is mine today, and no person or situation can confound me. I know that the harmony of heaven is where I am, and in all that I do. Poise is my attitude and order is my vision.

Recognizing peace as my normal environment, I give peace to others. My presence in any group is calming. My speech reflects my inner peace. I speak of those things which are true of God and true of God's spirit in man. By my silent thought I still the troubled waters of other minds. I know that peace is natural to all people, so I seek its center in all whom I know. The healing peace of God radiates from me, and I am a blessing to my world. This day I am peaceful, loving and wise.

August 14

I Choose to Live Wisely

Thou wilt keep him in perfect peace whose mind is stayed on thee: because he trusteth in thee.
Isaiah 26:3

ALL that is good is available to man. God never limits Himself, and God never limits man. Man is consciousness in the one Mind, and all ideas are given unto him. I now choose to live with wisdom today, by selecting only true ideas to function in my mind. No one governs my thinking but myself. No one forces me to worry, or forces me to have faith. Either of these is mine as I select. I choose faith, for I know that I am maintained by the power of the universe. I have full confidence that my life is rich in goodness, and prospered by love. My faith in God keeps my mind positive.

I choose health today. Right thinking is spiritual medicine. My thoughts are worthy of God, and a blessing to man. My whole consciousness is positive and constructive. I know that health is God's free gift to me. I know that my body responds to my thought, and wholeness is mine. Fatigue is impossible, for strength never fails me. Disease is no more, for there is nothing in me to cause it. Joyous, healthy ideas saturate my consciousness, and God's life saturates my body. God's presence in the weather blesses me. Heat and cold do not affect me, for my life is warm with love.

I choose to be a blessing today. Every act I perform brings good to someone. Every thought I think brings healing to my fellowman. I know that God uses me as a mighty channel of good, and I love to do the works of Him who sent me. I let my light shine so that all men, seeing my good works will glorify God. Love fills my heart, and power fills my mind. Richly I give to my world, and richly my world gives to me. Wisdom, born of the Spirit is mine. I have chosen Him who will never fail me. I love to live the life of God.

August 15

I Am Receptive to God's Ideas

For the word of God is quick and powerful...
Hebrews 4:12

ALL of God is available to every person. Nothing is ever withheld from a sincere seeker of truth. The infinite Mind releases all of Its ideas to every receptive consciousness. I now receive ideas direct from God, and I assimilate them and express them. These ideas are perfect and complete, revealing to me all that I need to know for this day. My way is now easy, for I know what to do at every instant, and order does prevail. I am inspired by God to do right and to live abundantly. No more doubt, no more questioning, I know exactly the way to go, the thought to think, and the love to express.

God's ideas fill my mind, and there is no room for any wrong thoughts. I claim my health, my prosperity and my full self-expression. As I make these claims, the infinite supplies everything I need to fulfill them. All power is given unto me to demonstrate the desires of my heart. All life surges through me as health. All prosperous ideas quicken my consciousness, and money comes to me from all directions. I deny any and all negative thoughts which seem to contradict this truth. I know that God backs me up in every situation with right ideas. These ideas move me forward into ever-increasing joys of life. I shall never hesitate again in moving forward with wisdom.

What every great spiritual teacher did, I can now do. The same ideas which inspired them, inspire me. God gives of Himself with lavish abundance, and I rejoice to receive His ideas now. All of good is before me, as I accept this inspiration from on high. I give thanks for my freedom from all problems, and my ability to meet all situations. The Lord is with me, now and forevermore, and I am sustained by His truth.

August 16

I Accomplish With Ease

God is faithful, and he will not let you be tempted beyond your strength, but with the temptation will also provide the way of escape, that you may be able to endure it.
I Corinthians 10:13

INFINITE Mind is forever in action, producing good. This action is the activity of man. I now realize that I am an outlet for the perfect action of a perfect God. Therefore, my yoke is easy and my burden is light, for God does the work. I am a center in the divine Mind, and I direct the action of that Mind through me. My work is to let God's action flow through me into creative and valuable results. This takes the burden of hard work off my shoulders, and I accomplish all things with ease.

My work is easy, for I let the Spirit within me do it. I know that there is no need to struggle for a living, for God acting through me makes easy my job. I now relax and know that within me right action is taking place, and that I am inspired to right results. My life is the life of the Spirit, and my work is to release this Spirit, and I now do it. As I let this action take control of my work, everything I need appears at the instant I need it. All the strength I need is within me, and never fails me. All the wisdom I need is within me and guides me constantly.

I do not believe that I have to work hard to be successful. I only know that success is mine to the extent that I let spiritual ideas work in my mind, and love work in my heart. I approach whatever needs to be done with confidence that I am equal to the situation. I lean upon the indwelling Spirit, and it never refuses to respond to my call. Letting God do the work assures me of perfect results. My mind is receptive to God, and I am divinely sustained by his action through me. Success is no longer before me; it is now where I am, appearing in all that I do.

August 17

Believing in God, I Expect Immediate Results

Lo! We have shown man the way, whether he be grateful or disbelieving.
                                                            The Koran

GOD is unconditioned by time, space or belief. As the perfect expression of this infinite Mind, I am not under the laws of time, space and belief. The instantaneous action of Mind produces immediate demonstrations in my experience. No longer do I wait for my good. No longer do I hope, trust and expect. I am now established in instant results.

The Lord is with me. The Lord is where I am. The action of God is taking place now in my affairs. What needs to be done is already done, for Mind sees the end from the beginning. Cause and effect are one action. Prayer and demonstration are one unit. There is no longer a beginning and an end, a treatment and a healing. In my consciousness there is only the complete understanding that at this moment all is accomplished, and I already have what I formerly thought I needed to have.

Having erased the concept of time and space from my thought, I now claim my perfection of mind, body and affairs. I claim it as an actual fact now; not tomorrow but today; not in an hour but at this instant. The world cannot limit me; man cannot inhibit me; and God is for me. No more alibis; no more delaying mind-action. God, and God alone, is in action through me, and I have all that I can use of his intelligence and love. Within me perfection is; around me perfection has appeared. Duality has been dissipated, and unity has been established. I thank God for this, and act upon this premise. All that is good is mine, and all that is true is mine now. My world blesses me. My body is a joy to me. My friends and loved ones are perfect spiritual beings now. It is all here, and it is all mine.

August 18

Not Tomorrow But Today, I Have What I Want

Now we have received, not the spirit of the world, but the spirit which is of God; that we might know the things that are freely given to us of God.
I Corinthians 2:12

THE future is bright with promise, but only in this day can the infinite Spirit reveal Itself to man. God at this moment is the reality of this moment. I have faith in the future, but I must act wisely in the present. My right and loving action in this day is my spiritual insurance for tomorrow. God is forever the same; so all of God is where I am and is now available to me. I start bringing to pass my hopes of the future by acting upon them today. God's idea of me includes my success right now. If God does not procrastinate, then I shall no longer do so. My demonstrations of truth are now taking place, and I rejoice in their appearance.

Today the unlimited health of God is mine. Today the unlimited abundance of God is mine. Today the unlimited love and peace of God are mine. These I affirm as present facts, and I expect immediate results. I dismiss all belief that it takes time to accomplish what I want to do. I know that Mind acts through my consciousness as I determine It shall act. I have decided that God's action is mine now, and my demonstration is not only in process—it is now completed. I accept with thanksgiving the full demonstration of my heart's desires.

Jesus healed instantly those who came to him. He fed thousands in a few minutes. The Mind that acted through him acts through me, with the same abilities. Knowing this, desired experiences follow. Affirming this, results appear on every hand. Each moment is filled with expectancy, for my faith is complete; and all impediments in my thought are now removed. Heaven is where I am, and evil does not exist. I have what I want, and I am that person God wants me to be.

August 19

I Am God's Unlimited Creation

The great, unborn Self is undecaying, immortal, undying, fearless, infinite.
Brihadaranyaka Upanishad

GOD is never limited by His creation. Omnipresence, omnipotence and omniaction are the eternal processes of Spirit. An unlimited God could only create an unlimited man, and I am that man now. My only foes are those of my own mentality. The universe is for me, and it wants me to succeed. I now assume my rightful place in God's universe and move forward to my own success in life. There are no limits placed upon me by the divine Mind, and I now free myself of my own limited thinking. I refuse to accept boundaries of success, for all of God is before me, and all His intelligence acts through me.

I am never the victim of circumstances. I create circumstances and adjust them as I please. God's creative power is my creative power. God's action in the acorn is not limited by the shell. God's action in me is not hampered by body, affairs or situations. Out from the center of my being comes the full action of life itself. Under the direction of my thought it produces for me my decisions. I select that which is progressive, creative and loving. The new creations in my world are flexible and bless me. As there are no fixed ideas in my mind, so there are no fixed situations in my experience.

Today, unlimited good is my experience, because the unlimited ideas of infinite Mind fill my consciousness. Every barrier is destroyed and every door opens. The divine plan of my life unfolds with ease, for there is nothing to prevent it. Increased good appears on every hand, and I use it with wisdom. I am the free expression of an unlimited Creator.

August 20

I See My World Clearly and Rightly

Blind is this world. Few are those who clearly see.
Dhammapada

GOD looks out upon His universe and declares it to be good. The eyes of the Lord are never dimmed. Perfect sight is my inheritance, and I see all things clearly, easily and normally. Through my eyes the light of the world enters my consciousness bringing me beauty and glory. I have spiritual vision in my consciousness, and perfect sight in my eyes. There is nothing to distort God's eternal beauty, for I look at it and see it as it really is. All creation is harmonious and in right proportion. My eyes see the harmony and balance of heaven in every scene. Looking for good in my world is easy, for God is everywhere, and His intelligence reveals itself on my pathway.

With my eyes focused on good, my day is blessed with demonstrations. There is no strain in seeing the hand of the Lord make glorious His creation. I look upon the riches of glory in all nature. I look upon the "image and likeness of God" in every person. Around me perfection awaits my recognition, and within me is the vision of true holiness. Beauty beckons to me in all things, and love calls out to me from all people. I dedicate my eyes to seeing God in all and through all this day.

The light of the world is the light of my eyes. I behold the truth in every situation, and the Christ in every man. Darkness cannot limit me, for the true light is from within. There is nothing to becloud my sight, for all life cooperates with me in seeing clearly. My eyes are blessed with clarity, and the kingdom of heaven is in view. God looks out upon His heaven by means of my eyes, and I let this perfect action take place. I need no help in doing this, for God's eyes are my eyes now.

August 21

The Light of Truth Is Mine

God is light and in him is no darkness at all.
I John 1:5

THE word light, as used in the Bible, is the symbol of spiritual illumination. It is the inner capacity in man to perceive a divine idea and to assimilate it into his consciousness. Any idea assimilated into consciousness must then express in man's experience. I now claim that the light of truth is mine. I am aglow with divine possibilities. My mind is open to the influx of spiritual ideas, and I rejoice as they enter my mind and are assimilated into my consciousness. I know that my world is filled with light, for there is only light within me to shine forth in it.

There can be no darkness, no fear and no depression in me, or in my experience, for God is the light of my life. All evil is dispelled, and all truth is revealed. The Spirit within me is my sure guide to right action. I live in light, for my mind is filled with light. Ideas appear on time and in order, telling me what to do and when to do it. With an illumined mind, I live with ease today. All good appears within me and is projected from me.

This light within me is shared with my friends. I give them good counsel, great inspiration and helpful thoughts. The Christ in me shines forth to quicken the Christ in them. My only contribution to them is one of good. No criticism, no pessimism, just the steadfast knowing that God takes care of them, and His light is within them as their true guide. Wherever I go I am a blessing to man and a joy to God. The light that lighteth every man is within me, and I share it with others. I am spiritually illumined, and I know truth and give truth today.

August 22

God Takes Care of Me

Thou compassest my path and my lying down, and art acquainted with all my ways.
Psalm 139:3

OMNIPRESENCE surrounds me, and omniscience is mine. Never for an instant does God separate Himself from His creation. Always there is an abiding presence and a beneficent power. I am forever established in my good, for wherever I am, there is the law to produce it. I am never forsaken and never alone. As I turn in thought to God all love appears in my heart, and all peace acts in my mind. People unconsciously respond to the Christ within me and share their good with me. I have divine protection all through the day and night.

There is nothing to fear, for divine intelligence is my inner security, and I am led in paths of blessings. A loving presence enfolds me and a security not born of man is mine. Never again will I fear the future, regret the past, or be anxious in the present. I have absolute faith in the power of God where I am, and wherever I may go. "The Lord is my shepherd, I shall not want." Heaven is where I am, and God is my only reality. The truth has set me free of fear, and I walk undaunted the pathways of God. Immersed in my good and aware of it, I laugh at fear and declare my faith.

The Spirit is within me as definite guidance and complete success. I am protected from all evil, for divine intelligence inspires me to right action. God knows I am successful, healthy and peaceful. I now join with God in this. All other human speculations are as nothing, for God alone is true and success alone is possible. I let God act in my world, and I know that divine love upholds me in righteousness and peace. Always the Lord is at hand, yea, even within me. I am blessed and sustained by the Christ within my soul.

August 23

I Am Spirit

I have breathed into many of My spirit.
The Koran

THE image and likeness of God must be a perfect expression of Spirit, and I am that expression now. Therefore, I use my body with wisdom, but I am not limited by it. It is effect and not cause. God's true knowledge of me is that I am a spiritual being using body as vehicle. The Spirit within me is now in full control of my body. It renews it, repairs it, and glorifies it. My body responds to these spiritual ministrations, and is radiant with health and vitality.

The Spirit within me inspires my mind with perfect ideas and true wisdom. Its action in my subconscious is one of cleansing and healing. It breathes through my consciousness the breath of life, and all fixed opinions are dissolved and dissipated. My old ideas and patterns cannot control or limit Spirit. God in the midst of me is the only real power, presence and reality. I let the indwelling perfect pattern of me be the truth of my mind today. Without using introspection or self-analysis I merely know that God's spiritual concept of me is the activating center of my mind. All my mental and emotional processes now accept the orders and decisions of the spirit, and I have perfect mental health.

I am a perfect spiritual being, living in a perfect spiritual body, and operating in a perfect spiritual universe. This is not merely an ideal; it is the truth. I am free from all false conditioning of matter or of mind. I am Spirit, and God alone is cause in my experience. I accept this perfect concept of myself, and my whole being gives evidence of it.

August 24

The Action of God Fills My Life

The spirit of man is the candle of the Lord, searching all the inward parts of the belly.
Proverbs 20:27

THERE is a purpose and a plan in all creation. The divine intelligence has always known what it was doing. It now knows why it created me, and it is urging me to fulfill my destiny. All of the action of God is where I am, and is in action through me at every instant. What I need is seeking me. What I want, I now have, for all of God is mine. Infinite Mind acts in fullness through Its creation, and I am impelled to right action.

This perfect action of Mind within me governs and directs me in pathways of blessedness. All health is flowing through me. God's health is complete, and I am incapable of experiencing disease. Vitality quickens my body, and my strength is unlimited. Fatigue cannot operate in me today. I am strong in the truth, and am vitalized by it. I accept the perfect action of God as health, and I radiate this to others. My strength is sufficient for every demand of life.

Prosperity is the full action of God in my world of affairs. Business is good, for business is the circulatory action of ideas. I accept money as an activity of the Spirit, and I use it with wisdom. I accept the freedom which money gives to me. I rejoice in an inflow and an outflow of money. God's ideas circulate in my consciousness, and God's money circulates through my affairs. Divine inspiration gives me an alertness to new ideas, and a keenness of discernment. My business activities are established in wisdom, expansion and abundance.

The full action of God in my life is perfect peace. The thoughts of God in my consciousness maintain me in poise and harmony. Order greets me wherever I go. I am balanced by truth, and the words that I speak give evidence of my conviction that God acts through me.

August 25

I Have Perfect Life

But thou art the same, and thy years have no end.
Psalm 102:27

THE life of God is the life of man; for there is only one life. This life must be perfect, for it is the action of a perfect intelligence and a beneficent power. The Mind which acts as life, being a unity, could not conceive disease, for such would destroy its unity. Therefore, life is perfect, spiritual and eternal. I am the expression of life, so there can be nothing in me but perfect health at every instant. Disease cannot operate in me, for I refuse to let it. I recognize illness as unnecessary and a failure on my part to know my life as the life of God.

I believe in one God, so all life must be one life. There cannot be a sick life and a well life. There is only one life, acting in one way, as health, vitality and freedom of action. This is my life now, and I rejoice in it. My body is eternally made new by it, and my consciousness is eternally refreshed by it. Every cell that is not perfectly expressing God's life is now cleansed, renewed and restored by my right thought about life.

Life cannot know age; it does not measure time. Life can only act in my body in one way, as health. Life, being greater than I and wiser than I, cannot be defeated by my wrong thinking. It always is itself, and upon my recognition, it becomes its perfect health in me. This is now true, and my health is permanent and complete. My thought is dedicated to health, and my emotions respond to health. Regardless of all so-called material causation of disease, I stand firmly in mind on the platform of health. I refuse to believe that any situation or condition can make me ill. God is my health, now and forevermore.

August 26

God Gives of Himself Through Me

To be in accord with the eternal means to be enlightened.
The Tao Te Ching

ALL that God is, man can reveal in his individual world. All the ideas of good are within man's consciousness seeking outlets through him. Knowing this, I now behold myself as a distributing center of divine activity. I know that truth comes to me in order that I shall release it in my world and be a blessing to my fellowman. I accept this joyous responsibility, and the words of my mouth are henceforth acceptable to God and to man. Each sentence I utter is potent with love, wisdom and goodness. I speak the Christ word with poise, assurance and power.

Through the meditations of my heart I give truth to my loved ones, friends and fellow employees. I think of the ideas of God, and with a refreshed mind I release these thoughts in scientific prayer to all whom I know. I contemplate health, abundance and peace, and know these belong to every man. I definitely direct my thoughts to bless and heal my companions along the way. I let myself be a channel of healing, an instrument of the Almighty. Divine love in the midst of me is released by me in vision. From the divine center within me love flows out through my world, and the glory of God is made manifest in all whom I know.

The holy Spirit of right action is my gift to every man this day. Each person who meets me is seen rightly by me. I see the good, the true and the perfect in him. God's Christ at the center of each soul calls to me for recognition and praise. I give my silent acknowledgment of good to all, and they respond with joy. Through me God gives of Himself, and nothing within me impedes this action. I let God bless His world through me today.

August 27

I Enjoy Life Today

The Infinite is the source of joy. There is no joy in the finite. Only in the Infinite is there joy. Ask to know the Infinite.
Chandogya Upanishad

OMNIPRESENCE surrounds me; omniscience inspires me; and omnipotence is mine to direct. All things bless me, and all people benefit me. I look out upon my universe and love it, for He who made it indwells it. He that made me, acts through me with ease, for I let God be in me all that He desires for me. God's vision of me as a perfect expression of life is my vision of myself. There is nothing to cause me to feel regret or sorrow, for I recognize but one Mind-God. I know beyond the shadow of a doubt that good is my only experience today.

It is as easy to be joyous, as it is to be sad. It is as easy to think of God, as it is to think of trouble. I devote my consciousness to joyous ideas, and I experience happiness in my world. When others point out to me their troubles, I immediately correct my thought and proclaim order and right action. I never hesitate to declare the truth. He who hesitates to speak truth is lost in untruth. I speak positively, yet lovingly. I stand firmly for what I know is truth, and I am not afraid to say so. Never again will I indulge in false sympathy, or a belief that evil has power. God alone rules my life with His joyous activity of ideas.

I am divinely enthusiastic about the possibilities of the present. All of God is for me, and things are turning my way. Life offers me all that I can take. Beauty seeks my eyes, and love seeks my heart. I give all glory and all honor to God, and there is nothing but gladness in my soul. My feet are planted on holy ground, and the whole universe invites me to enjoy the game of life. Right thinking is my greatest asset. Right living is my true vocation. I love to live the life which is God.

August 28

My Universe Is Flexible

Jesus Christ the same yesterday, and today and forever.
Hebrews 13:8

CHANGE is the law of human experience, for only God is permanent. The infinite Mind is forever conceiving new ideas, and the infinite law is forever producing new forms. In the midst of this flexibility I live, move and have my being. Life is consciousness flowing through forms, but never restricted by forms. Therefore, the situations in my world cannot restrict me for long. The instant I think a new thought, a new form begins to appear. Every static condition in my life must be the result of my failure to think new thoughts. I now dedicate myself to spiritual flexibility.

Freely and joyously I let life flow through my experience, bringing new events to pass. Situations and people come into my life to bless me, and in their own season go forth from my life blessed by me. I am a growing consciousness in God, and better conditions are constantly appearing for me to appreciate. As I let go of the old, the new appears. As I seek a larger group of friends, I grow in the expression of love. As I visit new places and purchase new things, I expand my consciousness.

I let go of prejudices and fixed opinions. I am willing to see God's action in every man. I pass no judgments, and I refuse all finalities. I open my whole being to changes for the better. I also allow my friends to change and enjoy the new experiences in their lives. I am flexible and pliant to all forms of good. God is continuously bringing new ideas into my mind, and new events to my world. This is the joy of living. I am free to change into a greater person, and I now let God's greatness manifest in me.

August 29

All of God Is My Inheritance

*Wisdom is good with an inheritance:
and by it there is profit to them that see the sun.*
Ecclesiastes 7:11

HE who created me, acts through me. He has never loosed me from His eternal embrace. Infinite Mind is my father, and infinite love is my mother. Unto me, their beloved creation, they have given fully of themselves. All power in heaven and on earth is mine, for my inheritance is incorruptible. I may not believe this at times, but it is the truth. Though I let my human mind deceive me, still the heavenly presence enfolds me, knowing that I shall awaken to truth. Too long have I dreamed that the world could hurt me and people disturb me. I now realize that I am a son of God, and free to live with wisdom and plenty.

Health is my inheritance. Divine Mind is incapable of knowing other than strength and wholeness. The health that created me acts through me. Pure life flows through my body, as pure thinking flows through my mind. I inherit every tendency to perfect living.

Prosperity is my inheritance. Around me is all of God; within me are the unlimited resources of Mind. The bounty and fullness of Spirit are mine this day and forevermore. I accept this abundance and use it with wisdom.

Ideas are my inheritance. Infinite Mind sustains Its creations in all their ways. I have unlimited ideas of good to express. I always know what to do, when to do it, and how to do it. Never a hesitation on my part, for God has revealed right action for every moment. With this inheritance I am always well and prosperous. The riches of this universe invite me to partake of their goodness, and I accept them with joy.

August 30

Heaven Is My World Today

So heed God, you men of wits, so that you may prosper.
The Koran

THE unlimited action of God surrounds me on every hand, and I rejoice to see it. It merely seeks my recognition to become my experience today. Resolutely I turn to the good, the perfect and the true, and claim these as my world and my experience. They respond with ease, for they await my acceptance to be real to me. God's beauty is in every person; God's intelligence is in everything; and God's unalterable law is maintaining order. All this is mine, for It created me to rejoice in It and be glad.

Perfect good surrounds me, perfect life acts through me. I can make every dream come true and every demonstration come to pass. No restrictions, save my own inabilities to see God in all and through all. I lift my eyes and behold greatness in every man, and healing in every heart. The peace which has never been disturbed is now revealed to me. The divine plan is now obvious to me, and I am amazed at what I can be. I can move with ease, for all life is impelling me forward into new and greater experiences. Now, I see the nothingness of evil, the stupidity of blaming the past and accepting limitation in the future. This will never confuse me again, for the allness of God is mine today.

In this heaven of God's presence is revealed my own possibilities. I will become the person God intended me to be. There is nothing to prevent my spiritual evolution. I grow in grace each hour, and I find more and more of God in my present environment. Where yesterday I saw a problem, today I see a possibility. I am at ease. Life is more fully mine than ever before, and I never cease to thank God for all that His Mind has revealed to me.

August 31

Divine Love Loves Through Me

Grant that these forms may penetrate within our hearts.
Atharva Veda

THE mood of the infinite Mind is one of love. The action of intelligence takes place in loving ways. What God hath wrought has been by means of love. Knowing this, I realize that the love of God uses me as a center of distribution. If I let my mind be a center of God's intelligence, I must also let my heart be a center of His love. Living the life of truth is a warm and joyous experience. I let God's ideas rule my mind, and I let God's love act through my heart.

There is nothing within me to impede the love of the Spirit. I now release all personal opinions about others. I let go of all hurts and prejudices. I let the full action of divine love act through me and be the basis of all human relationships. I am unified with the good in every man, and all else becomes as nothing. I have no interest in other people's faults. I keep my attention on the divine possibility within everyone I know. God's love is at the center of all, and it forever moves in perfect action through all. I am blessed and prospered by divine love. It enriches my soul and it prospers my consciousness. It frees me from the errors of human judgment, and makes me to know that I am one with all good.

With love in my heart, I forgive and forget all untruth. The true spiritual man is all I know of each person with whom I live, work and play. All else is unimportant, for God's love in me is interested only in the good, the true and the perfect. I think rightly, and I love greatly. This love flowing out from me is felt and recognized by others. In turn they love me and judge me according to God's standards. I love to let love express through me.

September 1

I Accept the Fullness of Life

And God said, Behold, I have given you every herb bearing seed, which is upon the face of all the earth, and every tree, in the which is the fruit of a tree yielding seed; to you it shall be for meat.
Genesis 1:29

YOU know that life cannot withhold itself from you. All that life is and has is fully given to you to enjoy. The life of God is perfect and eternal. It is the essence of everything that is. Life is God's gift to you. It is always ready to manifest itself through you in its entire fullness.

You are a self-choosing mind in a divinity which permeates everything. You are always in the midst of life, a life that lives eternally and lives through you now. Therefore, you need not be disturbed by the passage of time, the movement around you, nor the variations of experience through which you go. There is something within you that remains unmovable, that always speaks directly to you, saying, "Be still and know that I am God." Say:

CONSCIOUSLY, I draw upon the life that is mine. I know that the fullness of life, which is divine in its origin, eternal in its presence, and forever available is mine. The life of the eternal Spirit is my life. The infinite riches of its being are mine to enjoy.

The vitality, the wisdom and the peace of God are mine. I accept them in fullness, in joy and in peace. My thought is a gateway to illumination; it is the secret place of the utmost high within me. I accept the fullness of life this moment. I accept life as a glorious experience, a spiritual adventure.

September 2

I Live Fully Today

Behold, the kingdom of God is within you.
Luke 17:21

THE wisest man who ever lived said there is a truth which can set you free from fear, want, unhappiness and finally death itself. He said that this truth is already within you. Suppose you accept this spiritual wisdom, since the one who gave it was able to prove his claims. Don't you think that this great and glorious person was telling you that the kingdom of your good is here today?

Now, this means that evil, no matter what face it wears, or what form it takes, or how many people believe it, is never a thing in itself. Jesus did not say that evil has no reality as an experience. He did say that you should not judge according to appearances. He said that you are to live as though the kingdom were already yours. No matter what the negations of yesterday may have been, your affirmations of today may rise triumphant over them. Cease weeping over the mistakes of yesterday and steadfastly beholding the face of the great and divine reality, walk in that light wherein there is no darkness. Say:

I KNOW that every negative condition of the past is swept aside. I refuse to see it or to think about it. Yesterday is no longer here; tomorrow has not yet arrived. Today is God's day. God's day is my day. Today, bright with hope and filled with promise, is mine. I am alive, awake and aware—today.

September 3

I Sing Life's Song of Joy

Do not be anxious about anything, but in everything, by prayer and supplication, with thanksgiving let your requests be made known unto God.
Philippians 4:6

YOU are part of the universal Mind, one with the universal substance. You live, move and have your being in pure Spirit. All the wealth, the power and the goodness of this Spirit exist at the center of your being. You experience this good in such degree as you accept, believe in and feel it. As you enter into life, feeling the divine presence in everything, more and more you will hear a song of joy singing at the center of your being. You have only to be still and listen to this song of life, for it is always there. Say:

KNOWING that the loving Presence is always closer to me than my very breath, I have nothing to fear. I feel Its loving protection around me. I know that a song of joy, of love and of peace is forever chanting its hymn of praise and beauty at the center of my being, therefore, I tune all unhappy and negative ideas out of my mind. I turn the dial of my thought into the sunshine of life, into brightness and laughter, into the joyous presence of radiant Spirit. I lay aside all anxiety, all striving, and let the law of divine love operate through me into my affairs.

Joyfully I anticipate greater abundance, more success and a deeper peace. Joy wells up within my mind and life sings its song of ecstasy in my heart.

September 4

His Law Is Written In My Heart

The energy of God is Power that naught can e'er surpass, a Power with which no one can make comparison of any human thing at all, or any thing divine."
Thrice-Greatest Hermes

SINCE the only life you can have is the life of the Spirit within you, you need but permit Its radiance to flow through your thought into self-expression. You are surrounded by a dynamic force, a great surge of living power. You are immersed in and saturated with the vital essence of life. Its presence permeates everything, binding all together in one complete whole. Say:

BECAUSE my whole being is the life of God in me, I have nothing to fear. Everyone I meet is part of the same wholeness in which I live. Every person I meet is a center of the great unity of life. It is this center of life that I meet in all persons. It is this unity in and through all that I respond to. I cannot wish anyone harm, nor does anyone desire to harm me. Through my consciousness of love, which is the very essence of goodness, I transform any apparent imperfection into the perfect idea of true being.

I am knowing people as God knows them. I am seeing everything as God must see it. His law is written in my mind and felt in my heart. I see God everywhere.

September 5

I Exercise My God-Given Dominion

*They feast on the abundance of your house;
you give them drink from your river of delights.*
Psalm 36:8

THERE is a God power at the center of every man's being, a presence that knows neither lack, limitation nor fear, sickness, disquiet nor imperfection. But because everyone is an individual, he can build a wall of negative thought between himself and this perfection. The wall which keeps you from the greater good is built of mental blocks, cemented together by fear and unbelief, mixed in the mortar of negative experience.

Now you are to tear down this wall, to completely destroy it. The view which this wall obstructed is now seen in all its grandeur. The sun never really stopped shining and the river of life forever flows. Every man's experience is an attempt to merge his own being with this eternal river, not to the loss of his identity, but to the discovery of that self which has never wholly left its heaven. Say:

I KNOW that there is a presence and a perfect law irresistibly drawing into my experience everything which makes life happy and worthwhile. The good that I receive is but the completion of a circle, the fulfillment of my desire for all. I have placed my reliance in the power, the presence and the perfection of God. Therefore, I have dominion over all apparent evil. I repudiate all its claims, cast out every fear of, or belief in, that which is not good and exercise the dominion which by divine right belongs to me.

September 6

I Live Eternally in the Household of God

> *The perfect man, along with other men,*
> *gets his food from the earth and derives his joy from his Heaven.*
> Kwang-Tze

YOU live in the house of God. The household of God is a household of perfection. It is "the secret place of the most high" within you and within all. The inmates of this household all are divine. They will become as divine to you as you permit. As you look at them they look at you, for this is the way of life. Everything responds to you at the level of your recognition of it.

In the household of God there is no jealousy, no littleness or meanness. It is a household of joy, a place of happiness and contentment. Here is warmth, color and beauty. Seen in this light, your earthly house symbolizes the kingdom of divine harmony in which no one is a stranger. Say:

NOTHING is alien to me. Nothing enters into my experience but joy, integrity and friendship. The good I would realize for myself I realize for all others. I cannot desire a good for myself other than the good I desire for everyone else. I know that in the household in which I live the host is God, the living Spirit Almighty; the guests are all His people; the invitation has been eternally written for all to enter and dwell therein as the guests of this eternal host forever.

September 7

The Law of Good Brings Me Satisfaction

*Devotion is God-gnosis; and he who knoweth God,
being filled with all good things, thinks godly thoughts.*
Thrice-Greatest Hermes

THERE is a power operating through, a presence inspiring, an intelligence guiding, and a law of good sustaining you. Upon this presence, this power and this law you may place complete reliance. Because you live in this divine presence and because it is in you, you may know that the creative law of good, which is infinite, and which has all power, can do for you or bring to you, anything necessary to your complete happiness. Its whole desire for you is one of freedom and joy. Say:

I KNOW that freedom and joy are mine today. This freedom and joy express themselves in my experience. There is nothing in me that can obstruct their passage. I permit them to flow through me in all their wonder and might.

I am conscious of an infinite wisdom directing me. Whatever I ought to know I shall know. Whatever I ought to do I shall do. Whatever belongs to me will come to me. My every thought and decision is molded by intelligence and expressed through law and order in my experience. I not only think upon and realize the meaning of this truth, I am impelled to act upon it intelligently, creatively, without confusion, doubt, or hesitation. With joy I enter into the fulfillment of life.

September 8

The Protecting Power of the Infinite Sustains Me

> *Now that you have purified yourselves by obeying the truth so that you have sincere love for your brothers, love one another deeply, from the heart.*
> I Peter 1:22

AS a child turns to its parents for comfort, so every man is relying on God, whether or not he realizes it. This concept is so universal that it has been present in every age, with all people, and at all times. Jesus dared to place his hand serenely in the hand of the invisible. His works justified his words; his faith was manifest through his acts.

Nothing has happened to reality since this glorified figure walked the highways of human experience. With equal confidence you should believe in the protecting presence of the ever-available Spirit. Today you are to hold your thought steadfast in the realization that God withholds nothing from you. Therefore, prepare yourself for a life of joy, love, happiness and well-being. Say:

I KNOW that the law of God surrounds me with love and friendship. I let it radiate in my environment, bless everything I touch, make whole that which is weak, turn fear into faith, and accomplish the miracle of healing through love. I believe in myself because I believe in God. I accept life fully, completely, without reservation, holding to the conviction that good is the eternal reality, that God is the everlasting presence, that Christ within me is the eternal guide, that my life is complete today.

September 9

I Experience Abiding Peace

Heaven, Earth, and I were produced together, and all things and I are one.
Kwang-Tze

PEACE must exist at the center of everything or the universe itself would be a chaos. You already know this and believe it, now you are going to act upon it. You are not only going to believe in it, you are going to act as though it were true, because it is true. There is peace at the center of your being—a peace that can be felt throughout the day and in the cool of the evening when you have turned from your labor and the first star shines in the soft light of the sky. It broods over the earth quietly, tenderly, as a mother watches over her child. Say:

IN this peace that holds me so gently I find strength and protection from all fear or anxiety. It is the peace of God in which I feel the love of a holy presence. I am so conscious of this love, this protection, that every sense of fear slips away from us as mist fades in the morning light. I see good in everything, God personified in all people, life manifest in every event. Spirit is not separate from persons or events; I see that It unites everything with Itself, vitalizing all with the energy of Its own being, creating everything through Its own divine imagination, surrounding everything with peace and quiet and calm. I am one with this deep, abiding peace. I know that all is well.

September 10

Divine Circulation Animates My Being

There is no end or beginning to the Tao.
Kwang-Tze

THE Chinese sage said that Tao (meaning Spirit) "produces everything, nourishes everything, and maintains everything." It flows through and is in all things, being all that is. There is nothing outside it. There is a spiritual presence pervading the universe, welling up in your consciousness, always proclaiming itself to be the source of your being. The enlightened ones of the ages have told you that your recognition of life is God within you recognizing Himself in everything you do. Say:

I KNOW there is one Mind, one Spirit, and one body—the Mind, the Spirit and the body of God—the universal wholeness, the ever-present good, the all–sustaining life. Every organ, every function, every action and reaction of my body is in harmony with the divine creative Spirit. I could not ask for more; greater could not be given. I now seek to realize the significance of this one Mind and this one body. I now become aware that the one Mind is acting through my body in accord with Its own divine perfection, peace and harmony. The Divine circulates through me automatically, freely. Every atom of my being is animated by Its action. At all times I have a silent, invisible partner walking with me, talking with me, operating through me. I keep my mind open to its guidance, to its inspiration and illumination.

September 11

I Bear The Eternal Stamp of Individuality

It is sown a natural body; it is raised a spiritual body.
There is a natural body, and there is a spiritual body.
I Corinthians 15:44, 45

LIFE has set the stamp of individuality on your soul. You are different from any other person who ever lived. You are an individualized center in the consciousness of God. You are an individualized activity in the action of God. You are you, and you are eternal. Therefore, do not wait for immortality. The resurrection of life is today. Begin to live today as though you are an immortal being and all thought of death, all fear of change will slip from you. You will step out of the tomb of uncertainty into the light of eternal day. Say:

I KNOW that every apparent death is a resurrection; therefore, I gladly die to everything that is unlike the good. Joyfully I am resurrected into that which is beautiful, enduring and true. Silently I pass from less to more, from isolation into inclusion, from separation into oneness. Today, realizing that there is nothing in my past which can rise against me, nothing in my future which can menace the unfoldment of my experience, I know that life shall be an eternal adventure. I revel in the contemplation of the immeasurable future, the path of eternal progress, the everlastingness of our own being, the on-going of my soul, the daily renewed energy and action of that divinity within me which has forever set the stamp of individualized being on my mind.

September 12

I Am Spirit

*He discovereth deep things out of darkness,
and bringeth out to light the shadow of death.*
Job 12:22

THERE is a spiritual body which cannot deteriorate. This spiritual body is already within you. As much of it appears as is recognized. Spiritual perfection always responds to man's consciousness but it can respond only in such degree as he becomes aware of it. It is because this inward perfection is so insistent that you maintain a physical body, but because you are an individual with volition, you can, as it were, hang a curtain between your physical life and its spiritual cause.

Spiritual realization helps to withdraw this curtain. Every statement you make about your body, or belief you hold about it, with deep feeling which causes the mind to accept Spirit as the substance of the body, tends to heal. Say:

I REALIZE that there is a divine presence at the center of my being. I let this recognition flow through my entire consciousness. I let it reach down into the very depths of my being. I rejoice in this realization. I am now made vigorous and whole. I possess the vitality of the infinite. I am strong and well.

Every breath I draw is a breath of perfection, vitalizing, and renewing every cell of my body. I am born of the Spirit. I am in the Spirit. I am the Spirit made manifest.

September 13

The Spirit Goes Before Me

But the path of the just is as the shining light,
that shineth more and more unto the perfect day.
Proverbs 4:18

GOOD is at the root of everything, regardless of its seeming absence. But this good must be recognized. Since there is but one Spirit and this Spirit is in you and in everything, then everywhere you go you will meet this Spirit. You meet this Spirit in people, in places and in things. This one Spirit, which manifests Itself in and through all, including yourself, automatically adjusts parts to the whole. Therefore, you may accept with positive certainty that the Spirit within you does go before you and prepares your way. Your faith is placed in something positive, certain as the laws of life, exact as the principle of mathematics, ever present like the ethers of space, ever operating like the laws of nature. Say:

I KNOW that the Spirit within me goes before me, making perfect, plain, straight, easy and happy the pathway of my experience. There is nothing in me that can obstruct the divine circuits of life, of love, of beauty and truth. My word dissolves every negative thought or impulse that would throw a shadow of unbelief across the threshold of my expectation. I lift my cup of acceptance, knowing that the divine outpouring will fill it to the brim. I identify myself with the living Spirit—with all the power, all the presence and all the life there is.

September 14

Divine Power Is Mine to Use

The Perfect man is spirit-like. Great lakes might be boiling about him, and he would not feel their heat; the Ho and the Han might be frozen up, and he would not feel the cold; the hurrying thunderbolts might split the mountains, and the wind shake the ocean, without being able to make him afraid.
Kwang-Tze

EVERYTHING in nature is an individualization of one coordinating life, one law of being and one presence. But our minds have become so filled with that which contradicts this that even the truth has to await our recognition. You must learn to become consciously aware of the divine presence and the divine power, the wholeness of truth, of love, of reason and of a sound mind. Instead of dwelling on negative thoughts, cause your mind to dwell on peace and joy. Know that the power of the invisible Spirit is working in and through you now, at this very moment. Lay hold of this realization with complete certainty. Say:

I KNOW that I am a perfect being now, living under perfect conditions today. Knowing that good alone is real, I know that there is one power which acts and reacts in my experience, in my body and in my thought. I know that good alone has power either to act or react. I know that this recognition establishes the law of harmony in my experience, the law of prosperity, a sense of happiness, peace, health and joy.

Today I hold a communion with this invisible presence which peoples the world with the manifestations of its life, its light and love. I withdraw the veil which hides my real self and draw close to Spirit in everything and in everyone. I accept everything that belongs to this Spirit. I claim everything that partakes of Its nature.

September 15

I Know That My Redeemer Liveth

Of this same Spirit, of which I have already spoken many times, all things have need, for that it raises up all things, each in its own degree, and makes them live, and gives them nourishment.
Thrice-Greatest Hermes

IT has been written that Christ is your redeemer, also, that Christ is in you. You have been told that your redemption is at hand. You have been told to awake that Christ may give you light—Christ in you, the hope of your glory. All people are sons of God but only a few have completely recognized this. You have decided to live as though this were true. A deep and abiding faith has come to you. Therefore, you are fortunate among men—not that God has favored you above others; rather, you have chosen this path and you are going to walk in it.

Realizing that you may, in your ignorance, have been using the power of your mind negatively, you are not going to condemn yourself or anyone else because of this. If the light has come, the thing to do is to use it, forgetting the darkness. How can darkness have power over light? Say:

TODAY I realize that my good is at hand. Today I know that my Redeemer liveth in me. He is within me, now, today, this very moment, in this breath I draw, in the eternal now and the everlasting here. The Spirit within me refreshes me. I am saturated with the essence of life. My body is a vehicle for its expression, my mind its instrument. Today I shall endeavor to feel this presence as a living reality in my life. I shall see Him everywhere.

September 16

I Am Inspired From on High

All is the effect of all, one universal Essence.
Brihad Aranyaka Upanishad

JESUS, in utmost simplicity, proclaimed in the ecstasy of his illumination, "I and the Father are one." What do you suppose would happen if you believed this, not as a mere intellectual concept, but with deep inward feeling and an expanding sense of its meaning? Would you not sell all that you possess for this single pearl of utmost worth, this drop of water taken from the ocean of being, this mountaintop of revelation? If the wisest man who ever lived proclaimed this truth, should you not accept it, simply, directly, sincerely?

Perhaps this seems too good to be true, and yet, all nature is a living example, a continuous reminder, that there is a Spirit animating everything, a presence diffused, a law governing, a unity sustaining, a coordinating will binding all together, a unifying principle holding everything in place. Say:

I CLEANSE the windows of my mind, that it may become a mirror reflecting inspiration from the most High. Today I walk in the pathway of inspiration. There is an inspiration within me which governs every act, every thought, with certainty, with conviction and in peace. The key that unlocks the treasures of the kingdom of good is in hand. I unlock the doorway of my consciousness and gently open it that the divine presence may flood my whole being with light, illumine me with its radiant glow and direct my footsteps into pathways of peace and joy.

September 17

My Body Is a Temple of Spirit

If you keep your body as it should be, and look only at the one thing, the Harmony of Heaven will come to you.
Kwang-Tze

YOUR body is a temple of the living Spirit. It is spiritual substance. Since the Spirit of God had entered into your being, your life is spiritual. The supreme being, ever present, exists at the very center for your thought. This presence within you has the power to make all things new. Say:

THE perfect life of God is in and through me, in every part of my being. As the sun dissolves the mist, so my acceptance of life dissolves all pain and discord. I am free because the Spirit of life in me is perfect. It remolds and recreates my body after the likeness of the divine pattern of body which exists in the Mind of God. Even now the living Spirit is flowing through me. I open wide the doorway of my consciousness to Its influx. I permit this physical body to receive the living Spirit in every action, function, cell and organ.

I know that my whole being manifests the life, love, peace, harmony, strength and joy of the Spirit which indwells me, which is incarnated in me, which is my entire being. I open my consciousness to the realization that all the power and presence there is clothes me in its eternal embrace; that the Spirit forever imparts Its life to me. I know that the Spirit within me is my strength and my power.

September 18

My Word Accomplishes

So likewise thou in all thy speech
Swerve never from the path of truth.
Buddhism in Translations

YOU are either attracting or repelling in accord with your mental attitudes. You are either identifying yourself with lack or with abundance, with love and friendship or with indifference. You cannot keep from attracting into your experience that which corresponds to the sum total of your states of consciousness. This law of attraction and repulsion works automatically. It is like the law of reflection—the reflection corresponds to the image held before a mirror. Your life is a mirror peopled with the forms of your own acceptance.

How careful, then, you should be to guard your thoughts, not only seeing to it that you keep them free from doubt and fear—accepting only the good—but, equally, you should consciously repel every thought which denies that good. Say:

I KNOW that my word penetrates any unbelief in my mind, casts out fear, removes doubt, clears away obstacles, permitting that which is enduring, perfect and true to be realized. I have complete faith and acceptance that all the statements I make will be carried out as I have believed. I do everything with a sense of reliance upon the law of good, therefore, I know that my word shall not return unto me void. I accept this word and rejoice in it. I expect complete and perfect results from it.

September 19

I Claim My Divine Inheritance

Seek for the great [mysteries] and the little shall be added unto you; seek for the heavenly and the earthly shall be added unto you.
Fragments of a Faith Forgotten

"BELOVED, now are we the sons of God." Your kingdom of God is at hand. The riches, power, glory and might of this kingdom are yours today. You do not rob others by entering into the fullness of your kingdom of joy, your kingdom of abundance. You recognize that all people belong to the same kingdom. You are merely claiming for yourself what you would that the law of good should do unto all.

There is no law of human heredity imposed upon you. Evil has no history. Limitation has no past. That which is opposed to good has no future. The eternal now is forever filled with the presence of perfect life. You always have been, and forever will remain, a complete and perfect expression of the eternal Mind, which is God, the living Spirit Almighty. Say:

TODAY I enter into the limitless variations of self-expression which the divine Spirit projects into my experience. Knowing that all experience is a play of life upon itself, the blossoming of love into self-expression, the coming forth of good into the joy of its own being, I enter into the game of living with joyful anticipation, with enthusiasm. Today I enter into my divine inheritance free from the belief that external conditions are imposed upon me. I declare the freedom of my divine sonship.

September 20

Guidance and Wisdom Belong to Me

Thou hast begotten the Man in Thy self-born Mind, and in Thy Reflection and conception. He is the man begotten of Mind, to whom Reflection gave form. Thou hast given all things to the Man.
Fragments of a Faith Forgotten

REALIZING that all action starts in, and is a result of, consciousness, prepare your mind to receive the best that life has to offer. Become increasingly aware of the one presence, the one life and the one Spirit, which is God. Try to drop all sense of lack or limitation from your thought. The Spirit works for you through your belief. All things are possible to this Spirit; therefore, everything is possible to you in such a degree as you can believe in and accept the operation of Spirit in your life. There is something within you which is completely aware of its oneness with power, of its unity with life. Loose all thoughts of discord and fear, and permit the true pattern to come to the surface. Say:

I ALLOW the divine wholeness to flow through me in ever-widening circles of activity. Every good I have experienced is now increased. Every joy that has come into my life is now multiplied. There is a new influx of inspiration into my thought. I see more clearly than ever before that my divine birthright is freedom, joy and eternal goodness. The divine presence interprets itself to me through love and friendship, through peace and harmony. Knowing that life gives according to my faith, I lift my mind, I elevate my faith, I listen deeply to the song of my being.

September 21

My Faith Makes Me Whole

Yea, thou shalt not find any variableness in the way of God.
The Koran

FAITH is a mental attitude. A certain man came to Jesus, and, from the inspiration of his hope and the enthusiasm of the occasion, standing in the light of one whose wick of life was ever kept trimmed and burning, feeling the warmth and color of its eternal glow, exclaimed, "I believe!" This was a simple, sincere and enthusiastic response to the consciousness of one who had faith. But no sooner had he exclaimed, "I believe!" out of the enthusiasm of his will to believe, than old thought patterns arose to block his faith and he said, "Help thou mine unbelief."

Faith then is more than an objective statement. Perfect faith cannot exist while there are subjective contradictions that deny the affirmation of the lips. It is only when the intellect is no longer obstructed by negative reactions arising from experiences of doubt and fear, that the words of the mouth can immediately bear fruit. Say:

I BELIEVE with a deep, inward calm that my word of faith is the execution of spiritual law in my life. I have absolute reliance upon the law of good. I believe that the law of good will bring everything desirable into my experience. Today I proclaim my divine inheritance. I am rich with the richness of God; I am strong with the power of God; I am guided by the wisdom of God. I am held in the goodness of God, today.

September 22

I Partake of the Divine Bounty

This is the goodness of God: He bestoweth it on whom He will:
God is of immense goodness!
The Koran

TODAY you are to identify yourself with the more abundant life, to think on those things which make for peace, to dwell on the unity which underlies everything. As you poise yourself in the realization that you live in pure Spirit, new power will be born within you. You will find yourself renewed by the divine life, led by divine intelligence and guarded by divine love. Focus your inward vision on this indwelling harmony, knowing that as you contemplate its perfection you will see it manifest in everything you do. Say:

REALIZING that the Spirit within me is God, the living Spirit Almighty, being fully conscious of this divine presence as the sustaining principle of my life, I open my thought to its influx; I open my consciousness to its outpouring. I know and understand that good alone is real. I know that I am drawing into my experience today, and every day, an ever-increasing measure of truth and beauty, of goodness and harmony. Everything I do, say and think is quickened into right action, into productive action, into increased action.

My invisible good already exists; my faith, drawing upon this invisible good, causes that which was unseen to become visible. All there is, is mine *now*; all there ever was or ever can be, is mine *now*.

September 23

I Sense the Divine Presence Within Me

Conceiving nothing is impossible unto thyself, think thyself deathless and able to know all—all arts, all sciences, the way of every life.
Thrice-Greatest Hermes

THE Spirit of God is an undivided and indivisible wholeness. It fills all time with Its presence and peoples space with the activity of Its thought. Your endeavor, then, is not so much to find God as it is to realize His presence and to understand that this presence is always with you. Nothing can be nearer to you than that which is the very essence of your being. Your outward search for God culminates in the greatest of all possible discoveries—the finding of Him at the center of your own being. Life flows up from within you. Say:

I KNOW that my search is over. I am aware of the presence of the Spirit. I have discovered the great reality. I am awake to the realization of this presence. There is but one life. Today I see it reflected in every form, back of every countenance, moving through every act.

Knowing that the divine presence is in everyone I meet, the Spirit is all people, I salute the good in everything. I recognize the God life responding to me from every person I meet, in every event that transpires, in every circumstance in my experience. I feel the warmth and color of this divine presence forevermore pressing against me, forevermore welling up from within me—the wellspring of eternal being present yesterday, today, tomorrow, and always.

September 24

The Essence of Love Expresses Through Me As Harmony

Fulfill ye my joy, that ye be like-minded, having the same love, being of one accord, of one mind.
Philippians 2:2

"THE law of the Lord is perfect," and the law of the Lord is love. You are made perfect in the law when you enter into conscious communion with the love. It is only through love that the law can fulfill itself in your experience, because love harmonizes everything, unifies everything. You can never make the most perfect use of the law of your life unless that use is motivated by love.

As the artist weds himself to beauty, imbibing the essence or spirit of beauty that it may be transmitted to the canvas or awaken the cold marble to living form, so you must wed yourself to love. You must imbibe its spirit. This love is more than a sentiment. It is a deep sense of the underlying unity and beauty of all life, the goodness running through everything, the givingness of life to everything. Say:

TODAY I bestow the essence of love upon everything. Everyone shall be lovely to me. My soul meets the soul of the universe in everyone. Everything is beautiful, everything is meaningful. This love is a healing power touching everything into wholeness, healing the wounds of experience with its divine balm. I know that this love essence is the very substance of life, the creative principle back of everything, flowing through my whole being, spiritual, emotional, mental and physical. It flows in transcendent loveliness into my world of thought and form, ever renewing, vitalizing, bringing joy, harmony and blessing to everything and everyone it touches.

September 25

I Have Complete Confidence in the Law of Good

When Heaven and Man exert their powers in concert,
all transformations have their commencements determined.
The Texts of Taoism

THE good in which you believe can triumph over every evil you have experienced. You have a silent partnership with the infinite. This partnership has never been dissolved, it never can be. You are to have implicit confidence in your own ability, knowing that it is the nature of thought to externalize itself in your affairs, knowing that you are the thinker. You are going to turn resolutely from every sense of lack, want and limitation, and declare that the perfect law of God is operating in, for and through you. Say:

I HAVE complete confidence in my knowledge and understanding of the law of good. I not only know what this law is, I know how to use it. I know that I shall obtain definite results through the use of it. Knowing this, having confidence in my ability to use the law, and using it daily for specific purposes, gradually I build up an unshakable faith, both in the law and the possibility of demonstrating it.

Therefore, today I declare that the law of the Lord is perfect in everything I do. Today I believe in divine guidance. Today I believe that "underneath are the everlasting arms." Today I rest in this divine assurance and this divine security. I know, not only that all is well with my soul, my spirit and my mind—all is well with my affairs.

September 26

Spirit Permeates My Consciousness and Environment

For all the law is fulfilled in one word, even in this:
Thou shalt love thy neighbor as thyself.
Galatians 5:14

IT is only as you live affirmatively that you can be happy. Knowing that there is but one Spirit in which everyone lives, moves and has his being, you are to feel this Spirit not only in your consciousness but in your affairs. You are united with all. You are one with the eternal light itself. The presence of Spirit within you blesses everyone you meet, tends to heal everything you touch, brings gladness into the life of everyone you contact. Therefore, you are a blessing to yourself, to mankind and to the day in which you live. Say:

TODAY I uncover the perfection within me. In its fullness I reveal the indwelling kingdom. I look out upon the world of my affairs, knowing that the Spirit within me makes my way both immediate and easy. I know there is nothing in me that could obstruct or withhold the divine circuit of life and love, which good is. My word dissolves every negative thought or impulse that could throw a shadow over my perfection.

Good flows through me to all. Good shines through my thoughts and actions. Good harmonizes my mind so that love sings joyously in my heart. I am in complete unity with good.

September 27

I Am Bountifully Supplied From Divine Substance

For the Lord taketh pleasure in his people: he will beautify the meek with salvation.
Psalm 149:4

LIFE fills all space and Spirit animates every form. But since you are an individual, even the Spirit cannot make the gift of life unless you accept it. Life may have given everything to you but only that which you accept is yours to use.

Turning from every objective fact to the Divine, which is within you, is turning from conditions to causes, to that realm of absolute being which, through self-knowingness, creates the forms which It projects and enters into the experience which It creates. Thus the Spirit comes to self-fulfillment in everything. Through the manifestation of the power that is within you, you can project any objective experience which you may legitimately desire. Be certain that you are accepting this, that you are living in joyous expectation of good, that you are accepting abundance. Say:

TODAY I recognize the abundance of life. I animate everything in my experience with this idea. I remember only the good. I accept only the good. I expect only the good. This is all I experience. I give thanks that this good is flowing in ever-increasing volume. I do not withhold this good from others but proclaim that spiritual substance is flowing to each and to all as daily supply.

September 28

I Receive Because I Ask in Faith

> *But the fruit of the Spirit is love, joy, peace,*
> *long-suffering, gentleness, goodness, faith…*
> Galatians 5:22

"ASK and ye shall receive." This is one of the most wonderful statements ever uttered. It implies that there is a power which can and will honor your request. But it is only as you let go of the lesser that you can take hold of the greater, only as you drop confusion that you can entertain peace, only as you transcend doubt and fear that you can be lifted up to the hilltops of the inner life. In asking, you must identify yourself with the greatness of the Spirit. Permit your consciousness, through faith, to rise to a greater and broader realization of that divine presence which is always delivering itself to you. Say:

THROUGH the quiet contemplation of the omniaction of Spirit, I learn to look quietly and calmly upon every false condition, seeing through it to the other side of the invisible reality which molds, conditions and re-creates all of my affairs after a more nearly divine pattern. I know that my word transmutes every energy into constructive action, producing health, harmony, happiness and success. I maintain my position as a divine being here and now.

I know that in this consciousness of reality is the supply for my every need—physical, mental or spiritual—and I accept that supply in deepest gratitude. As I am filled with the reality I permit it to flow into my world of thought and action, knowing that it brings peace, harmony and order all around me. I have limitless faith in the unconquerable presence, the perfect law, and divine action.

September 29

The Healing Christ Abides With Me

Be not deceived; God is not mocked:
for whatsoever a man soweth, that shall he also reap.
Galatians 6:7

YOU have heard about the healing Christ who can come to you with power. Do you realize that this Christ is already here? This Christ is the incarnation of God in every individual. Not a person lives who does not at some time in his life sense this inward presence, this vision of the Divine which presses against us. It is seeking entrance through our thoughts. We must open the door of our consciousness and permit It to enter. It is willingness, acceptance and recognition that give entrance to the divine presence. It is faith and acknowledgment that permit Its creative power to flow through our word. Say:

TODAY I am opening my consciousness to a realization of the living Christ, the eternal sonship of the everlasting Father. I know that He dwells in me; I know that there is an invisible guide, a living presence with me at all times. With complete simplicity and directness, I recognize my divine center. Consciously, I unify myself with this pure Spirit in which I live, move and have my being. I am strong with the strength of the all-vitalizing power of pure Spirit.

I am sustained by divine energy which flows through me as radiant health and vitality. Every atom of my being responds to this divine presence. I completely surrender myself to it.

September 30

I Overcome Hate by the Recognition of Love

And the light shineth in darkness; and the darkness comprehended it not.
John 1:5

THERE is but one presence in the universe. Since it is in and through everything, it must be in and through you. This presence manifests itself in and through all forms, all people, all conditions. This presence is life itself. Its nature is love and givingness.

Negation may be an experience and a fact; it can never be an ultimate truth. Life cannot operate against itself. Always the negative is overcome by the positive. Good cannot fail to overcome evil. The meek alone shall inherit the earth. Finally, the consciousness of good must overcome the negation of evil. Finally, it will obliterate everything unlike itself, even as the sun dissolves the mist. Say:

I REFUSE to contemplate evil as a power. I know that it will flee from me; it dissolves and disappears in the light of love. I know that hate cannot exist where love is recognized. I turn the searchlight of truth upon every apparent evil in my experience. This light dissolves every image of evil. The manifestation of good is complete. Love makes the way clear before me. I am guided in an ever-widening experience of living. My every thought and act is an expression of the goodness which flows from life.

October 1

I Am the Perfect Creation of a Perfect God

So God created man in His own image, in the image of God created He him.
Genesis 1:27

WE cannot conceive of the nature of God as other than a perfect being, whose intelligence is forever creating, re-creating and sustaining a perfect universe inhabited by a perfect man. All the arguments devised by those who are unable to perceive this truth become as nothing when we look at our world and see God in every flaming bush and every act of nature. Only a perfect Mind could conceive this universe as it is. Therefore, we must look at our individual world and at ourselves as we believe God knows us to be. The garments of limitation are cast off when we begin to transform our individual minds with the belief that we are divinely created and divinely sustained. Our God is with us and our God indwells us as a perfect potential awaiting our recognition and releasement. We know that we are born of the Spirit, that we live this day in a perfect presence, and that we are filled this day with an unlimited power for good.

I HAVE faith that I am a spiritual being, unlimited and free. I am not merely a material body with a human mind working in a material world. This is an untrue picture of what I really am. I now lift my thoughts to the Mind of God and know with Him that I am His beloved creation in whom His pleasure abides. I am divinely quickened into new creative activities. All the ideas of His Mind now awaken within me, and I walk in paths of righteousness and ways of peace. Today I am the perfect creation of a perfect God, living in a perfect universe of order, love and endless possibilities. All is good and all is well.

October 2

I Have Nothing to Fear, For God Is All There Is

*Fear thou not: for I am with thee: be not dismayed; for I am thy God...
yea, I will uphold thee with the right hand of my righteousness.*
Isaiah 41:10

IF we believe in the omnipresence of God, we can handle the age-old problem of fear. Fear is the belief that God is absent. It is the only devil there is, and if it governs our thinking we experience the only hell there is. If we are overcome by it, we are headed for trouble and disease. Both the Old and the New Testaments tell us that this enemy can be overcome. But they tell us it can only be overcome within us, not by rearranging our affairs around us. Fear begins and ends within the mind of the one thinking it. The nightmare of its binding and restricting thought is broken as we turn to a belief in the goodness of God, the presence of a creative Mind and the feeling of a love that never fails. As we do this a peace steals upon us, a faith rises up again within us. The presence that sustained Jesus is also sustaining each of us at every instant. All that it asks of us is that we believe it and accept it.

"THE Lord is my shepherd; I shall not want. He maketh me to lie down in green pastures: he leadeth me beside the still waters. He restoreth my soul: he leadeth me in the paths of righteousness for his name's sake. Yea, though I walk through the valley of the shadow of death, I will fear no evil: for thou art with me." This is my belief. This governs and controls my thinking today. Nothing can stop my good from coming to me, for my mind is stayed on truth and love. Peace fills my whole being. There is nothing to fear, for God is all there really is. I claim this presence as my own. I trust in the Mind of God and all is well and all is good. I give thanks for a good day.

October 3

I Do Not Labor: I Work for the Glory of God and the Good of My Fellowman

Come unto me all ye that labor and are heavy laden, and I will give you rest. For my yoke is easy, and my burden is light.
Matthew 11:28,30

TODAY, as metaphysicians we should be clear in our thought as to the difference between *labor* and *work*. The word "labor" implies drudgery, while the word "work" implies creative activity producing a just and fair profit for all concerned. We are coworkers with God, coworkers with a Mind that knows exactly what to do and how to do it. If we cooperate with the indwelling presence of this universal God-Mind, It makes our routine activities creative and joyous experiences. If we condemn our jobs, our employers and our fellow workers, the law of cause and effect can only make our tasks heavier. Jesus said to those who disliked their employment that there was a way of working that was easy and a burden that was light. He told them to come unto his way of thinking and assured them that through this new and creative approach, a healthy change would take place in their business world.

MY work in life is to express God and His ideas. I do this joyously and lovingly in my home, my business and all my other activities. I have faith that the life, love and intelligence of Spirit sustain me at every instant. Therefore, I cannot be tired, exhausted or fatigued for within me is the sustaining power of unlimited Mind. I work with ease, with accuracy and with order. I know that through me God is giving something unusual and valuable into the world. I now release His Mind into the activities of this day. I dedicate and consecrate my thoughts and feelings to the love of God, the life of God and the perfect action of infinite Mind.

October 4

My Mind Is Established in God and Only Good Is Drawn to Me

No man can come to me, except the Father which hath sent me draw him.
John 6:44

WE believe that life to each of us is in accordance with our states of consciousness. Jesus is the illustration to this age that man's inherent divinity can be quickened into new activities of consciousness, and thus new and better conditions can follow. He knew that his mind was the individualization of God's Mind. He knew that as he thought rightly and loved greatly he would draw into his life people and conditions that were good. As we dedicate our thinking and feeling to the Mind and love of God, we too shall draw only that which is good, lovely and true into our experience, because our consciousness has no evil in it with which to draw the opposite. No evil can long exist in the mind of anyone who loves good and thinks rightly. It automatically dissolves, and as it leaves it takes with it the unpleasant aspects of life.

THE Father within me, my own eternal self, is now in full action through me, and I am cleansed of all that is unworthy of God. My consciousness is God's Mind, individualized as myself, and Its ideas are perfect. I am open and receptive to these spiritual ideas, born of my Father-Mother God. They are now established deeply within me, and they now direct my thinking and color my feeling. Thus, shall no evil come nigh me, for there is nothing in me to attract it. I give love, joy and creative activity in my world, and receive from it all that is good, and fine and true. I accept this, and it is the truth of this day. I rejoice, give thanks and am glad.

October 5

I Am Important to God and Necessary to Man

*A man indeed ought not to cover his head,
forasmuch as he is the image and glory of God.*
I Corinthians 11:7

IT is easy to discredit ourselves, indulge in self-criticism, and walk through life thinking we are unimportant. But, we forget one thing—God never makes a mistake. Infinite Mind can only create people with a value to themselves, and to the world. *Not one of us is unimportant.* The smallest and least-heard instrument of a symphonic orchestra is vitally important at the time it is used. Its music gives meaning and import to the entire ensemble. The universe suffers a sense of incompleteness whenever we indulge in self-condemnation. God made us to be important channels through which His Mind thinks and His love acts. Each of us has a definite and vital part to play in the whole life and love of this world. A unique and valuable contribution to the good of all seeks to express through us, and as we know this, we become valuable expressions of life.

I AM important to God, for His intelligence created me and works through me, and God never makes a mistake. Otherwise I wouldn't be here. My present work, environment and contacts are my opportunity to prove my spiritual worth. I rise in the dignity of my divine heritage and walk this world as a son of God. Today, I give love and creative thought to all I meet, and to all with whom I associate. I am a center through which God gives of Himself to His universe, and I know this and appreciate this. I have faith in myself and in my fellowman. I express in unique ways the gift of life, the power of thought and the holiness of love. I am important to God and necessary to man.

October 6

My Environment Is Saturated With the Presence of Good

Thou wilt show me the path of life: in thy presence is fullness of joy; at thy right hand there are pleasures forever more.
Psalm 16:11

IF we cannot demonstrate the presence of good where we are, we shall never be able to do it at what seems a better place. The human mind likes to think that distant pastures are greener, but we know they are not. *Good is the result of right thinking based on right motives.* It is not a location; it is an atmosphere which has to be revealed by us wherever we are. There is no more of the presence of God in a great cathedral than there is in your own home or office. Principle is either everywhere evenly present and active, or it isn't a principle. An unpleasant environment is a challenge to us to see God in action at that place in the universe. Jesus had the ability to see God everywhere and in all people. He knew and demonstrated omnipresence. We, too, must make this demonstration right where we are, and we also know how to do it.

WHERE I am, God is. The presence that fills every great cathedral fills my home and my place of business today. There is no confusion where I am, for the peace of the Almighty surrounds me, and I know it. I live and move and have my being in the one Mind which is forever thinking rightly, thinking lovingly. The harmony and the order of the universe now fill my life and world with good. I am surrounded by it. I am filled with it. I sense it in all things and find it in all people. I joyously acknowledge God where I am at every instant. The life, love and perfect action of truth are mine now. My environment is saturated with the presence of good, and I live in peace this day.

October 7

There Isn't God and Man, There Is Only God as Man, and I Am That Man Now

I will praise thee; for I am fearfully and wonderfully made: marvelous are thy works: and that my soul knoweth right well. How precious also are thy thoughts unto me, O God! how great is the sum of them.
Psalm 139:14, 17

WE believe in the divinity of man. We believe that man is the individualization of all that God is. Infinite Mind is forever thinking by means of its beloved creation—man. Each of us stands in the midst of an omnipresent intelligence, which seeks to express through us, and as we recognize (re-cognize, to know again) this relationship we become valuable instruments for good. Man is God in action, and we must know this, believe this and act from this premise. Then, we never plead with God to do something for us; rather, we rise in the integrity of our own being, and thinking rightly move into action to produce the good we need. As we perceive this eternal process of our inner self as God thinking through us, we become conscious of great possibilities—and become co-creators with the Almighty of a good world, filled with good people living in justice, peace and love.

ALL that God is, is now in action through me. Infinite Spirit fills me, infinite love surrounds me, infinite Mind directs me. There is no fear in my thought, for God's thoughts are now my thoughts, and they are perfect. The law of Mind produces my word into form right now. I declare that I am a perfect expression of God, and only God's thoughts function in me this day. No evil can come nigh me, for God is all there is in my world. All is good for all is love. The peace that passeth all understanding is my peace now. I rejoice in my divinity and dedicate myself to its full expression in this hour.

October 8

I Am Surrounded, Upheld and Maintained By a Perfect Mind

The spirit of God hath made me, and the breath of the Almighty hath given me life.
Job 33:4

THE people in all ages who have lifted up their eyes unto the hills of God have felt a surrounding presence and a sustaining life. They have been aware of an indwelling power that was more than body, more than material living. It has surged up within them and has given them the power of accomplishment. Because this presence is eternal, we can find it and let it use us today, as it did the prophets and wise of old. The living presence which surrounded Abraham, Moses, Isaiah and Jesus is around us now, and it asks that we behold it and think of it. The glory of God is upon us. We, too, can lift up our thoughts and become its vessel of expression. Infinite Mind surrounds us and is in us; infinite life sustains us; infinite power flows through us. All fear is removed for we are certain of who we are and of what we are doing. We arise from the "I can't" belief into the "I will" knowing.

I AM surrounded, upheld and maintained by Mind. This Mind is God, forever thinking through me. It knows no impossibility, no weakness, no lack. It loves to live abundantly by means of me. It loves to express power through my hands and my heart. I am strong in the strength of the Lord. I am sustained in all my ways by the indwelling action of truth. I am upheld in righteousness and justice, for all that I am God is and ever shall be. I walk the highways of Spirit, knowing only the good of my fellowman. I rejoice in the Spirit which fills and floods me with peace. This day is the day of good, and I accept with joy new and finer experiences of life.

October 9

The Words of My Mouth, the Meditations of My Heart and the Activities of My Hands Are Acceptable to Infinite Mind

And that ye put on the new man, which after God is created in righteousness and true holiness. Wherefore putting away lying, speak every man truth with his neighbor, for we are members one of another.
Ephesians 4:24, 25

THE inner life of man is his most priceless possession. In the center of our beings, we decide whether we shall be worthy of the divine life with which we have been endowed by the creative Mind of the universe. When the inner life is creative, orderly and growing then our outer activities are fine and true. We know the law of Mind, and to be the sincere and creative people we hope to be, we have to be truly consecrated within. We are equipped to speak the kindly word, to pray for others in the depths of our heart, and to do those things in the world which are constructive. The equipment we have, but the impulse must arise within us to use it rightly. God seeks through each of us to express all that Mind is, all that love is.

I BELIEVE that I was created by a perfect intelligence to be its means of expressing thought and feeling. I, therefore, dedicate myself this day to the original purpose of my being. I cleanse my mind of all that is unworthy of a spiritual being. I dedicate and consecrate the words of my mouth, the meditations of my heart and the activities of my hands to Almighty God. Nothing shall cause me to be unkind, unloving or mean. I believe that God indwells me as Mind, and this eternal Spirit is now blessing the world by means of me. I know that all my inner capacities are now quickened for good. I am strong in my determination to speak the truth, love my fellowman, and act as the son of God.

October 10

I Am Alive With the Clean, Fresh Life of Spirit

Therefore if any man be in Christ, he is a new creature: old things are passed away: behold all things are become new.
II Corinthians 5:17

THE Bible reminds us that it is the essential nature of God to ever renew and ever revitalize His creation. "Behold, I make all things new." This great healing, energizing activity is around us as a vital presence and within us as a vital life. We did not create it, neither does our food, nor our exercise and play create it. It is an impersonal gift from the universal Spirit. Our food habits, our sleep, and our times of exercise merely keep the channels open for It to function through us more efficiently. We are endowed with life, health and vitality by the creative principle of being. It is ours. We either use it rightly and are healthy and fresh at all times, or we misuse it and are sick and depressed. It is our individual responsibility. Knowing the power of thought, we keep our minds filled with the idea of a fresh, clean life that is forever welling up within us and seeking release by means of us.

DIVINE life can never grow stale, grow old, or wear out. I know that God's life is in me as my life now. It is an endless stream of clean, fresh, vital energy. It fills every cell and organ of my body with its healing presence. I am renewed this day by the life of Spirit working in and through me. I am refreshed as I speak this word and know this truth. I joyously respond to fresh life, and it joyously responds to me and is working in every part of my body. I dedicate my thinking to this youth-giving life of God. Old conditions have now passed away, and fresh life is pouring through my being. I am energized and vitalized by God.

October 11

There Is Nothing in My World But the Life and Love of God

The earth is the Lord's and the fullness thereof; the world, and they that dwell therein.
Psalm 24:1

OUR world offers us the opportunity to cooperate with it on a spiritual basis, or to argue with it on a material basis. If we do the first, we have an abundant life with great peace. If we resist and argue with circumstances we find our troubles heap themselves upon us in even greater measure. The Bible states that man has dominion over his world if and when he assumes it from a spiritual premise. It also states that the world is a spiritual organism. Putting these statements together we have the key. The conscious can always control the subconscious; therefore, we can control the conditions of our world when we see it as the creation of God-Mind. If God created it, then His life and love must dwell in it. This we believe, and for this we look on every side. We agree with life and with love. We expect these qualities of Spirit to be in our present environment and experience.

THERE is nothing in my world but the life and love of God. I refuse to believe otherwise. I live this day abundantly and lovingly, for I accept and express God's life and love. Wherever I go and whatever I do I am surrounded, upheld and maintained by this perfect good. I behold good in every situation, every person and every place I go. I walk in God's presence upon God's world and greet my fellowman as God's beloved creation. I expect more life and more love to be mine today than I have ever known before. My body is filled with perfect life, my world is filled with perfect love. I declare this, I believe this, and I know this is true right here and right now.

October 12

I Am Poised and Established in the One Mind

Thou wilt keep him in perfect peace, whose mind is stayed on thee: because he trusteth in thee.
Isaiah 26:3

THE assets of a spiritually minded person are his ability to remain untouched by the confusion of the world around him, and to instigate a creative process which will bring order out of chaos. It may seem easier to exist in a panicky state of mind, telling all whom we meet how difficult life is, than to remain poised and say nothing at all. Yet, we are assured that there is a way of thinking wherein we can handle every situation with ease, stability and poise, by becoming still, and from a center within ourselves, find a peace which has never been disturbed. God in the midst of us is instantly available as peace, order and harmony. All that is required is to turn within and think in His terms, His ideas. As we do this the panic flees and order is born. We are already in the Mind of God which always operates in peaceful, and perfect ways.

MY thought is stayed on the Christ-Mind within me and from It I drink the waters of peace. There is nothing to fear for my God indwells me; His Mind thinks through me; His love enfolds me. Every idea I need to meet any situation is already given unto me by my indwelling Spirit. I know what to do, and how to do it, and I do it with ease and efficiency. Nothing can disturb me, for His perfect presence fills my world and all things now work together for good. I radiate peace and receive peace, for God is peace. I am poised and established in the one Mind and nothing can disturb the calm and peace of my soul. I give thanks for perfect spiritual poise in handling my world and the people in my life.

October 13

Whatever Needs to Be Done, It Is Being Done Now by the Action of God, the Action of Mind

The Lord will perfect that which concerneth me.
Psalm 138:8

PATIENCE in spiritual demonstration is not only a great virtue, it is also a definite necessity. We must believe that the word we have spoken does accomplish that whereunto it has been sent. Too often we pray and then immediately look to see if the result has appeared. We fail to realize that a process is involved. Our word has set the law into activity, and the result will take place when the process in demonstration has been completed. Having spoken the word, we then rest in the knowing that the law is doing the rest. This takes the strain and stress out of metaphysical practice. It brings calm assurance, which is the mental atmosphere necessary for the seed to take root and become the full-blown flower. Declaring the truth is our work. Producing the demonstration is God's work. The word is always made flesh when we let it evolve in its own way.

I DECLARE the truth, for it is that which is true of God. I believe the law of Mind is now in action in my consciousness bringing forth the good I need and desire. I rest in complete confidence that all through this day the invisible Mind of the universe is working for me and through me in perfect ways. There is no sense of hurry or impatience, for God is at work. Whatever needs to be done in my life, is being done now by the activity of the Spirit. I relax and rest in the one presence and the one power. All is order, harmony and intelligent activity. Great events of good are being born into my world and I rejoice, give thanks, and am glad.

October 14

God Is My Employer: My Work Is Efficient, Creative and Right

For we are laborers together with God:
ye are God's husbandry, ye are God's building.
I Corinthians 3:9

LIVING in a universe of activity we are expected to be efficient and creative. Our work, whether in office, factory or home is that part of the universal activity which we have selected to do. Therefore, we should do it with ease, with efficiency and with pleasure. We confuse issues and think we are earning money, instead of seeing our true position as a center through which the universal activity of Mind focalizes itself by means of us. The Mind of God is our employer. It asks that we be receptive to Its Ideas, Its plans and Its purposes. The inner Spirit knows what to do, how to do it, and does it when we believe in It. As we turn to the indwelling presence of God and affirm Its action through us as our true employment, we work easily and efficiently. Then we can render service to God and to man.

TODAY I work for God, and His Mind directs my every move. I dedicate my thoughts, my hands and my heart to divine intelligence and divine love. All my activities take place in the one presence and are the outpicturing of one power that is forever releasing Itself through me. Every idea I need for efficient service comes to me from the greatest universal Mind as and when I need it. I refuse to worry, for I have complete trust in the Mind of God which does all work by means of me. I refuse to shirk responsibilities for I do what needs to be done under divine inspiration, and every task is light and easy. God is my employer, and my work is efficient, creative and right.

October 15

God Around Me, God Within Me, All Is Well

One Lord, one faith, one baptism, One God and Father of all, who is above all and through all and in you all.
Ephesians 4:5,6

WE live in the midst of an unlimited presence, forever in action as an unlimited Mind. It created us, and it sustains us. It operates through us. All It asks of us is our recognition of It. As we affirm the presence and power of God in our lives, something happens within us to improve us. This can be tested by anyone who wishes to see what will happen when God works in his experience. It requires no advanced study, no educational background, no particular vocabulary or posture. The process of approaching the deity is merely one of knowing It is, and that It abides within. What we affirm, we become. As we affirm God, we actually become the sons of God and heirs to all that God is and has. "Draw nigh to God, and He will draw nigh unto you."

THERE is only one presence, God, and I am in It. There is only one power, God, and It acts through me this day. There is only one Mind, God, and it is my mind now. All around me at every instant is the same presence that enfolded Jesus. The same Mind which acted through him is now in action through me. I am the heir of all that God is and has and I know it. I live in a spiritual universe governed by a spiritual law that is always working for my good. I am safe for God is with me. I am wise for God is in me as my consciousness. There is nothing to fear. God around me, God within me, all is well with me today.

October 16

I Refuse to Worry, I Trust God and Man

> *Take therefore no thought for the morrow:*
> *for the morrow shall take thought for the things of itself.*
> Matthew 6:34

THE most insidious thing which the student of truth must handle is worry. We do not consciously set aside times for worry, as we do for right thinking, and often we are startled to find that we have been wasting an hour fussing over some problem or fear. We immediately say "But, I know better than to do that," and we start making positive statements of truth. This is what Jesus meant when he said "Watch and pray, that ye enter not into temptation." Like sentries of an army, we must watch hourly over the trends of our thinking and the deep feelings of our souls. To start the day with a firm resolve not to worry is to practice the teachings of truth. To follow this resolve with a constant watch of the mind and its activities is the fulfillment of the teaching. This is a friendly universe and God interpenetrates it as a loving presence and all-intelligent Mind, so we fret not and go ahead.

BECAUSE I know that I am the operation of a perfect God, I do not worry. I let that Mind be in me which was also in Christ Jesus. I acknowledge It in all my ways. I trust Its guidance, Its plan and Its purpose. I believe that Spirit is in me seeking to express through me. I walk this day in full confidence that my good is seeking me, and I shall know it as it appears. Hour by hour, my every need is met on time and in order by divine Mind and divine love. Never late, never delayed, always at the instant I need God and His intelligence, it is with me and thinking in me. I refuse to worry, for I trust God and man, and I live in peace.

October 17

I Have No Enemies, I Have Only Sons of God Expressing Love Toward Me

See that none render evil unto any man: but ever follow that which is good, both among yourselves, and to all men.
I Thessalonians 5:15

DISAGREEABLE people are a problem to all of us, and it is a problem that has to be met. It is easy to go through life feeling that we are the victims of other people's thought and actions. We all have an adequate vocabulary to describe just how vicious and mean the other fellow is. One of the essential teachings of Jesus was a spiritual way of handling our fellowman. He, also, had vicious and unkind people in his world, but he understood that the people who were unkind needed his love and understanding more than all the others. They needed healing. We are practicing his teachings, and we know that all that needs correction is our own thought. The other man's actions and words fail to register in our consciousness, when our minds are sustained in a spiritual concept of what he really is. God is in the so-called enemy. God's life is his life, and God's Mind is his Mind.

EVERYONE in my life is blessing and benefiting me. They are spiritual beings expressing toward me the love and justice of Almighty God. I do not have an enemy. I have only God's people in my world. No one is vicious, mean or unkind to me, for my consciousness cannot receive such wrong ideas. I believe that man is the individualization of God, and as such the people in my world are good, loving and kind. No one can hurt me but myself, and I refuse to do that. I keep my thoughts worthy of the infinite thinker that is expressing through me. I believe in the Christ in my fellowman, and I see him as he really is.

October 18

The God in Me Loves the God in My Fellowman

Let us love one another: for love is of God:
and every one that loveth is born of God, and knoweth God.
I John 4:7

THE word "love" when used to describe the nature of God can be easily understood by everyone, for we are always responsive to love. Rich or poor, religious or nonreligious, we know the word and feel an expansion within us when it is used. Believing that God acts through man, then love must act through man. It is easy to love the people who agree with us, but Jesus had the knack of loving the people who didn't agree with him. We must make a sincere attempt to love those who oppose us, who disagree with us. If we realize that within them is the love of God, even as it is within ourselves, and we salute it and thus bring it forth, we shall be worthy of the teachings of the Man of Galilee. We may not love the outer actions of our fellowman, but we can love the fact that God dwells in him.

I BELIEVE that divine love indwells all the people whom I meet this day. I salute that love within them and expect good in some form from each one. No one dislikes me, and I dislike no one. I seek until I find some good in everyone. I am loving, kind and courteous to all. I show through the words of my mouth and the unseen thoughts of my mind that love is in my heart and joy is in my soul. To all who would irritate me I say, "The love of God in me loves the love of God in you." The world is alive with divine love and I abide in it as a loving and gracious expression of Spirit. I give beauty and peace to my world and, therefore, I can only receive beauty and peace from my world. I give thanks that God loves by means of me.

October 19

I Am Free to Express All That God Is

Ho, everyone that thirsted, come ye to the waters, and he that hath no money: come ye, buy and eat: yea come, buy wine and milk without money and without price.
Isaiah 55:1

IN the realm of Mind there are no limitations save those which are self-imposed. In our everyday living we seem bound by time, space and money. Often our health limits our living freely, or our hurts and pride keep us from pleasant experiences. Isaiah, like other biblical teachers, reveals to us the freedom of the Spirit. He tells us that there is a way of living mentally where we are unbound, unfettered, free. This is the same teaching which Jesus gave us in his concept of the kingdom of heaven as being possible here on earth for those who will think rightly and aspire greatly. Freedom begins and ends in our consciousness. As we turn in thought to the unlimited possibilities of what we are in God, we begin to be freed from the limitations of matter and material laws. This must be done mentally, and we who love God do it and prove that freedom is a reality.

I HAVE faith that I am a citizen of the kingdom of God on earth. This kingdom is one of perfect Mind, and all its perfect ideas now function in me, delivering me to greater good and greater service to my fellowman. I am free to select the good, the right and the true, and I do this joyously for my own Christ Self urges me now to do just that. There is nothing to bind me, limit me or make me afraid. God is the only real presence and the only real power, and I am the living representative of God. I freely express all that God is, and I love to do it. I am free, praise God, I am free. I know the truth, and I have been set free to live wisely, lovingly and justly.

October 20

This Is a Happy World and I Am Joyous In It

A merry heart doeth good like a medicine; but a broken spirit drieth the bones.
Proverbs 17:22

IT is sometimes difficult for people to believe that God wants us to be happy. We have been taught that to be spiritually minded usually meant to be burden-minded. This incorrect idea is fast disappearing, for which we can give thanks. There is no reason why any of us who will live rightly and love greatly cannot be happy right here. The Mind which created us gave us the ability to laugh and smile. These are healthy mental states. They relax us and give us peace. We like people who are gay and light, as long as we know their motives are right. We want to be with them and share in the warmth and cheer which they radiate. We want to be like them, and the Bible states that we should be. We need to accept the fact that the universe is planned for creative joy, and that we possess the ability to be happy in it. God wants us to be happy people, and His Mind has given us the capacity to know joy and to express joy. As we do this we fulfill our inheritance.

MY world is filled with the joy of Spirit, and I see happiness everywhere. Today, I express the joy of the Lord. I refuse to be discouraged and unhappy, for I know these states of mind are not of God. I have a God of joy and good cheer. I have a God who created me to smile and laugh and be lighthearted as I do my work. I am determined to have a song in my heart and a smile on my face. Everyone I meet senses this inner happiness which God has placed within me. They respond to it and are blessed by their contact with it. Divine love made this world a happy place to be filled with joyous souls rejoicing in good. I am loving, joyous and free. I respond to the joy of the Spirit in all and through all.

October 21

Divine Prosperity Is Working In All My Affairs

If they obey and serve him, they shall spend their days in prosperity, and their years in pleasure.
Job 36:11

PROSPERITY is the result of a mental atmosphere of faith and order induced within us through right thinking. We should believe that the universe is planned for abundance, and that we as a living part of the universal intelligence have a share in the general riches. Lack of supply to meet our needs is an indication of lack of spiritual development. The more we understand ourselves as spiritual beings living in a spiritual universe the more that supply flows to us easily and naturally. The disciplined mind can demonstrate prosperity, for it has provided the orderly channels necessary for it. A disorderly mind usually has financial troubles as a result of its scattered thinking. We know that man's mind is God's Mind in action, and we know that the divine Mind is always orderly in its processes. Jesus stated this as "first the blade, and then the ear, and then the full corn on the ear." He knew that we have to provide a mental atmosphere of order and harmony in which the living ideas can grow.

I LIVE in a world that is filled with God's abundance, and I now claim this as my own. The riches of the universe are open to me, and I partake of them in wisdom and joy. All my affairs are under the law of prosperity. Increased good flows to me from all directions and through all people. There is no lack in my consciousness, for God's ideas fill my thought and all is richness and opulence. I am orderly in all my ways. I am loving, kind and gracious. I speak this day in terms of abundance. I expect increased prosperity to take place in my world, for I know that God's activity is alive in my affairs. I now give thanks that the riches of God are mine to use and to enjoy in right ways.

October 22

Freely and Joyously I Let Right Action Take Place In My Life

Now the God of hope fills you with all joy and peace in believing that ye may abound in hope, through the power of the Holy Spirit.
Romans 15:13

THE law of life is a law of cooperation with all that is fine and true. Believing that life is God in action, we must accept its processes with a firm conviction that in the long run all things will work together for good. Resistance brings contraction; cooperation brings expansion. God's Mind is already in perfect action. We cannot start It working for us, for It is already trying to bring forth good by means of us. However, It does require that we accept Its methods, Its ideas and Its plans. Today, the infinite has arranged more good for each of us than our finite thinking can comprehend. With joy we open our whole body of consciousness to the divine inflow. We expect this spiritual presence to be in us as an accomplishing power for demonstration. Nothing can prevent the truth from appearing in our world, for omnipotence itself is in action at every instant.

FREELY and joyously I let right action take place in my life. I know that God's Mind is thinking through me at this moment, and greater results than I have ever dreamed are now appearing. There is nothing in my thought to block the action of God. I am willing to let my little thoughts go, knowing that the great thoughts of being guide me into paths of pleasantness and ways of peace. I accept without reservation the abundance that my Father has for me today. Every hour brings me the fulfillment of all my needs and desires. I believe in God. I love God. I have faith in God's processes. I live in the joy and the right action of Spirit.

October 23

Within Me the Spirit Is Alive and Vital

Thou gavest also thy good Spirit to instruct them, and withheldest not thy manna from their mouth, and gavest them water for their thirst.
Nehemiah 9:20

THIS is a universe of activity and vitality, and if we would live in it effectually, we must be actively and vitally alive. The Mind that created and sustained the universe, must have as its essential nature vitality and activity. We are the sons of God, the expressions of the creative Mind, and our inheritance is the capacity to express life with a punch, a zest and a joy. To do this we must be aware of our inner divine potential and through cooperation with it, let it act through us. Thus, we pray and treat to know that God is the energy, vitality and essence of our lives. From a center within ourselves there springs forth all that we need to live in creative ways and be a blessing to the world. The followers of Jesus were given by him a strong message to be vital and definite partners with life. Christianity must develop a mass of right-thinking people who demonstrate this energy of Spirit in creative ways.

WITHIN me is a part of God, it is my own true self. This inner spirit releases through me the energy, vitality and joy of the Lord. My whole body is now filled with God's vitality. I am not fatigued this day, for God's energy, working in every cell of my body, renews and maintains me in complete perfection. I am alive and vital for God's ideas fill my consciousness. New creative channels open for me this day in my business and family life. I look forward to new ways of service, new ways of expressing love. I dedicate all that I am to being vitally alive with the life of God. I shall be a blessing to all who contact me this day.

October 24

Today, My World Is God's World, and All Is Well

The Lord reigneth, let the earth rejoice; let the multitudes of isles be glad thereof.
Psalm 97:1

OUR mental attitudes are our most priceless possessions. No material security is actually secure, but the deep issues of our thought can make or unmake us. Like the psalmist of old, we should realize that our world is of God, therefore its essential nature must be good. That which seemingly opposes us in the world can be overcome and dissolved by right thinking, if our motives are right. This universe is our field of opportunities. It is the great laboratory in which he who knows the power of mind can work miracles. It says unto us that we can have and become whatever we desire, providing we can establish great ideas within our subjective areas of consciousness. To look out upon our world and expect only good from it is true spiritual living. Then, security is assured for our own right mental attitudes will produce it. The intelligence that created us requires our cooperation with the laws of right thinking based on right motives.

I BEHOLD my world today as the expression of God's intelligence. Everywhere I walk this day, I walk in the presence of good. Everyone I meet today, in business or at home, is the incarnation of Spirit. I joyously cooperate with the good in every man. I look out upon my world as God does and call it good. I expect today to be a day of fulfillment. I dedicate my thoughts to God's ideas and walk through His world seeing only that which is perfect, loving and beautiful. The glory of God fills my world and all the people in it. I rejoice in this day, for in it I shall find more of truth than I have ever known before.

October 25

God Is the Health of My Body, the Inspiration of My Mind, and the Good of My Universe

Then shall thy light break forth as the morning, and thine health shall spring forth speedily; and thy righteousness shall go before thee: the glory of the Lord shall be thy reward.
Isaiah 58:8

WE believe in the omnipresence, omnipotence, omniscience and omniaction of God as Mind, life, truth and beauty. Therefore, all that we are, or ever shall be, is a part of the universal being. Our health is God in action. Our consciousness is Mind in action. Our good is the manifestation of Spirit. If we believe this then it becomes our experience for the law of Mind produces it. Disease falls away from the person who is thinking in Godlike terms. Confusion melts from the thought of him whose mind is stayed on God. The universe becomes a friendly creative atmosphere to all who love the good and live rightly with their fellowman. Thousands have proven the truth in this way of life. The healed, the inspired and the successful bear witness to this truth we love, for the law is impersonal, it works for all who cooperate with it. We now blend with all that God is, and the demonstrations of good appear.

MY health is the automatic expression of my consciousness. No illness can hold me in its clutches, for I rise on the wings of God's thoughts, into perfect health of body and mind. I am inspired with the living, pulsating ideas of Spirit. The inspiration of the Almighty is mine today. I am led into paths of perfect activity bringing good results. My universe is saturated with divine love and order, and it returns to me the good I am now believing to be mine as a child of God. God is the health of my body, the inspiration of my mind, and the good of my universe at this moment, and all through the day.

October 26

I Cannot Escape Heaven, for I Am Already in It

Wither shall I go from thy Spirit? Or whither shall I flee from thy presence? If I ascend unto heaven, thou art there; if I make my bed in hell, behold, thou art there.
Psalm 139:7, 8

TO think that any person is outside of God is an absurdity. We know that God as infinite Mind is the only real presence and power there is, and all men are in It and of It. That our material troubles prevent us from knowing this all the time is obvious, but the disciplined soul can cause heaven to appear in the midst of every problem. When we pray, or treat a negative condition we set in process a divine idea which brings heaven to pass at the instant. As we recognize and affirm the omnipresence of Spirit, we are causing heaven to appear. All evil fades as truth is asserted by the determined son of God. Eternally, we live in heaven, the presence of pure being, the life everlasting. As we lift up our eyes unto the truth our minds are transformed. With a new viewpoint we look out upon our world and like God we, too, can say "behold, it is very good," it is heaven.

GOD made my world, and He called it good. I now link my mind with the Mind of God and look out upon my world from a new viewpoint. I see God in every person and every situation. All negatives are now cleansed from my consciousness. I am pure in heart and I see God everywhere. I see only the Christ Spirit in my fellowman. I look forward this day to the joy of living in the kingdom of heaven right here on earth. My home, my church, my office are locations in heaven, and they are filled with the atmosphere of good. Divine love absorbs my full attention and I release that love to all I contact this day; I cannot escape my heaven, for I am already in it, and all is well with my soul.

October 27

The Health of God Is My Health Today

Behold I will bring it health and cure, and I will cure them, and will reveal unto them the abundance of peace and truth.
Jeremiah 33:6

A FULL teaching of Christianity is impossible without the concept that God is the health of His people. We believe in spiritual mind healing, because we know that Jesus proved it as the action of the Spirit indwelling us. Health abides in us and is natural to us. Otherwise, the teaching of the man of Galilee is questionable, and this we cannot believe. We are reviving primitive Christianity and as a result the sick are finding health. This health which they find is not something created in them as a result of prayer. It is something revealed in them for it was there awaiting the call to come forth. This call which does the work is our faith and belief. William James called the truth teaching "The Religion of Healthy Mindedness." This is exactly what we are announcing. We believe that our bodily health depends upon our mental attitudes; that states of consciousness determine the health or disease of each of us. We acknowledge God as our health.

MY body is the temple of the living God. It is divinely created and divinely maintained. There is no lack of health in my body, for the presence of God is in every cell and function, and where God is, all is health. This word that I speak is awakening the perfect health of Spirit in me. My consciousness is filled with healthy thoughts about myself and my fellowman. I am strong, vital and perfect in every way, for I am a spiritual being living in a spiritually created body that responds to my thought. I think health, I appreciate health, I love good health. My whole being responds to this treatment. The health of God is my health today and forevermore.

October 28

I Am Now Open, Receptive and Obedient to All That God Has Prepared for Me

Eye hath not seen, nor ear heard, neither have entered into the heart of man, the things which God hath prepared for them that love Him.
I Corinthians 2:9

AS students of the Science of Mind, we should expect the impossible to happen, and the unexpected to be made manifest if we keep thinking in terms of God. The Bible has within it promises of what can happen when we let God work, and cease from our acceptance of limitation. Lack of time, money and power are feeble excuses to the person who knows that the Mind of God is within him, and that divine ideas are working through him. All the plans of the human mind with its time, space and money limitations are as nothing when God's thinking enters our consciousness. As we link our minds with the Mind of the universe, we start into action a liberating process which delivers us into greater good than we have ever conceived as being possible. Unexpected good appears, greater love flows through us, and the world becomes a vital creative place once again.

I BELIEVE in the Mind of God. I believe that this infinite Mind is my mind now. I know that this Mind thinks in unlimited and perfect terms. It has good for me far beyond my present human comprehension, and I now welcome God's ideas into my consciousness. I trust these spiritual ideas for I know they are for my increased good. I open my mind and heart to all that God is. I respond to joy, peace and new life. I drop all my reasons for my not being able to do greater things. I know that through the indwelling Spirit I can accomplish more and more. I am open, receptive and obedient to all that God has prepared for me.

October 29

I Am The Mind of God In Action, Therefore I Produce Only Good

To this end was I born, and for this came I into the world, that I should bear witness unto the truth.
John 18:37

THE nature of man is the nature of God, for there cannot be two, there can only be one. One Mind, one law, one life and we are expressing It, because we are the creation of It. As we begin to think of ourselves in heavenly terms, a new possibility arises within us. We see that our present mind is God's outlet. We become aware of a divine destiny for each of us; an eternal impulse within us to think rightly and well. We begin to speak as God would speak and to think as God would think. There is only the one Mind and that Mind is our mind now. The mind we are using to read this page is God's Mind and we are Its activity. "Beloved, now are we the sons of God." Knowing this we understand why all thought is creative, and we dedicate our thinking to right ideas. We are known by our works, and our works betray our thoughts, therefore, we must think as the divine Mind thinks.

THERE is only one Mind, God, and that Mind is my mind now. This Mind is thinking through me today, and all my thoughts are creative, producing under the law whatever I select to think. I choose with joy to think the thoughts of infinite Mind. I let larger and more loving ideas of God be the basis of all my mental work. All limitation is now destroyed from my consciousness, for God's Mind thinks in me and through me producing good. I see God everywhere and in all people. I think rightly, love greatly, and bring forth new good in myself and in all whom I meet this day.

October 30

The Light of the World Is the Light of My Life

That was the true Light, which lighteth every man that cometh into the world.
John 1:9

DARKNESS is always the symbol of ignorance, while light is the symbol of wisdom and truth. Darkness is always temporary, while truth is eternal. Our problems, which are our individual darkness, never long endure. At the most a problem could only endure ninety to a hundred years for any of us. But, it need not last for even a day if we can turn to the light of truth and find our peace. Within each of us, there is something that is saying, "I am the light of the world, if ye will follow me, ye shall have eternal light." This paraphrase of one of Jesus' great statements is true for all who will try it. It assures us that if we make the effort to look for the good in any situation, we shall find it, and having found it, it will increase, and the evil therein will decrease. Right where we are, God is: In the midst of our problem is the Mind and the idea that will solve the problem. We must know this and act upon this premise.

I WALK in the light of truth. There is no darkness on my pathway, for my God is with me, and my God indwells me. I am the light of my own world, and I let my light shine. I radiate divine love to all I meet this day. I speak the loving word to all I greet this day. I know that from a center within myself there flows out through me the light of healing. All my affairs are now illumined with infinite intelligence. I am wise with the wisdom of Spirit. The light of God fills my consciousness and I know everything that I need to know instantly. My pathway is radiant with good and I am divinely guided in all my ways. My world is alive with God, and my body is filled with the light of life.

October 31

I Am Not Fooled By Evil,
I Recognize It Only to Destroy It

For the evildoers shall be cut off but those that wait upon the Lord, they shall inherit the earth.
Psalm 37:9

THE sole value of evil is that it shows us the point of attack. The metaphysician attacks evil at its point of origin, which is the consciousness of the one experiencing it. We do not avoid it, we accept its evidence, for then we know how to treat it. If we are unaware of it, then we cannot erase it. We know that God is omnipotent, and that evil has no power to confuse us except as we believe it has. It can be destroyed through scientific prayer, when we have perceived its presence within us. Each attempt of error to manifest is a call to prayer. It is the battle cry of treatment. It is our opportunity to prove that God is all, and nothing can stop us when we are thinking Godly terms. We, then, make specific denials and affirmations regarding its unique form, and soon it has been eliminated from our experience. This is the better way.

I BELIEVE that God is all there really is, and that each attempt of evil to manifest in my world today is merely a call to prayer. I deny all evil, and affirm all good. Error is a lie and has no truth in it. It has no basis, no plan and no constancy. God alone is true, perfect and complete. I now destroy all negative thinking out of my consciousness through this word of truth. I live in a world of good, and all is well. God is where I am at every instant of this day, and I know this and rejoice in this. The peace of God is upon me. The love of God surrounds me. The joy of the Lord wells up within me. I live, move and have my being in a perfect Mind and a perfect presence, and all else is as nothing.

November 1

I Dwell In the Household of God

In my father's house are many rooms; if it were not so, I would have told you.
John 14:2

THE household of God is the household of perfection. It is the secret place of the most high. The inmates of this household are all divine beings. Nothing can enter the consciousness of any of these inmates which contradicts the unity of good. Each and every member of this household is at peace with all other members. There is a community of peace, of understanding, of fellowship, of love and unity.

In this household of God—which is any man's household who declares it to be such—there is no bickering, no jealousy, and no avenue through which any littleness or meanness may operate. It is not only a household of peace, it is a household of joy, it is a place of happiness and general contentment. Here is warmth, color and beauty. This earthly household symbolizes the divine harmony of the kingdom of God.

No one is a stranger within this household. Nothing is alien to it. It is protected from all fear, from every sense of loss. Nothing can enter it but joy, integrity and friendship. The same good I realize belongs to everyone else. I do not desire a good for myself which is greater than the good I desire for all people. Neither do I deny myself the good I affirm for all others. In this household, the host is God, the living Spirit Almighty, and all who dwell in this household are guests of the eternal host.

November 2

The Infinite Law of Good Brings Me Complete Satisfaction

Then your barns will be filled to overflowing, and your vats will brim over with new wine.
Proverbs 3:10

THERE is a power operating through me, a presence inspiring, guiding and sustaining me. Upon this power, I place my reliance. In this presence, I feel myself to be an outlet of immeasurable good. Because I am in this divine presence, and because it is in me, and because this Divine has all power, I know that my thought is made manifest in a perfect demonstration of health, of harmony and of success.

I know that the creative law of good is infinite and has all power to accomplish. I know its whole desire for me is freedom and joy. Therefore, I declare that freedom and joy are mine today. This freedom and joy spontaneously express in my experience, and there is nothing within me that can hinder this expression. Because this all-good is mine, and because it constitutes the only presence there is in the universe, I know that freedom and joy cannot be separated from me.

Realizing that the kingdom of love is at hand today, I enter into this kingdom with a song of praise, a hymn of joy. Knowing that God is hid in everything, I reveal this divine presence to myself and, to others, in sympathy; in love, in kindness.

I am conscious that there is an infinite wisdom directing me. Whatever I should know, I shall know. Whatever I should do, I shall do. Whatever belongs to me, must come to me. Because of the infinite intelligence which is mine and which is within me now, I am compelled to recognize my good; to see more; to understand and accept and express more. I know the infinite law of good is always bringing complete satisfaction into my life.

November 3

I Overcome Hate With Love

Therefore it is clear that Ignorance can only be removed by wisdom.
Raja Yoga Philosophy

I KNOW that there is but one power in the universe, and that power is God. That power manifests in and through all form, all people, all conditions, and so is at the very center of my being. This power is life itself, and its nature is love—all-good. I know that just as light dissipates darkness, just as heat warms the atmosphere, so a consciousness of good overcomes evil. I know that good constitutes the only power, presence and law, and the knowledge of good (the knowledge of love) overcomes the negation of evil (hate), dissipates it, obliterates it, blots it out.

I refuse to think of hate or any negation as a power and I know that it will flee from me. Its dissolution is its flight—it disappears. Hate cannot exist where love is recognized and knowing that good alone is real, I turn the searchlight of eternal truth upon every so-called evil in my experience, and these dark places of imagination are instantly dissolved into light. The dissolution of evil is complete; the manifestation of good is perfect. I know that love protects its own, and now makes clear the way before me, eliminating everything that looked like hate. I am guided into an ever-widening unfoldment of being, and my every thought, feeling and act is an expression of the God nature—love—through me. Continuously I overcome hate with love.

So I give back into the great and divine presence that which it has given to me, knowing that the gift will again be returned, but multiplied. So shall peace and joy come as a light from heaven, and in that light I walk.

November 4

Today I Meditate Upon My Divine Inheritance

*Every state of happiness that appears in the body
or the mind is said to be due to the quality of Goodness.*
The Mahabharata

"BELOVED, now are we the sons of God." The kingdom of God is at hand. I inherit everything that belongs to this kingdom. The riches and the power and the glory of this kingdom are mine now. I do not rob anyone by entering into the fullness of the kingdom of power, of joy and of abundance. I recognize that everyone inherits the same kingdom. There is no law of *human* heredity imposed upon me. Evil has no history. Limitation has no past. That which is opposed to good, has no future. The eternal now is filled with perfection. I always have been and always shall remain a complete, perfect and whole expression of the eternal Mind, which is God, the living Spirit Almighty.

All that the Father hath is mine. I am now entering into the kingdom of good which love has prepared for me. I am letting go of all the cares and fears of yesterday. I am looking forward to tomorrow in quiet confidence and with joyful expectation. And I am living today in the glorious fulfillment of the law of good.

Today I enter into the limitless variations which the divine Spirit has projected into my experience. I know that all things are good when rightly used. I perceive that all experience is a play of life upon itself. I enter into the game of living, then, with joyful anticipation, with spontaneous enthusiasm and with the determination to play the game well and to enjoy it. Today I enter into my divine inheritance. I have freed my thought from the belief that external conditions are imposed upon me by birth, through inherited tendencies or race belief. I proclaim the freedom of my divine sonship. I possess the kingdom of God today, in all of its fullness.

November 5

Today I Consciously Let Go of Every Discord

Be perfect, be of good comfort, be of one mind, live in peace; and the God of love and peace shall be with you.
II Corinthians 13:11

I DROP all sense of lack or limitation from my thought and every belief which I have ever had in lack or fear. I now have a belief in success and faith. I permit the Spirit within me to express Itself in perfect freedom, bringing increasing joy into my experience. There is that within me which is completely conscious of its unity with good, of its oneness with all the power there is and all the presence there is and all the life there is. Upon this power, presence and life, I depend with implicit certainty, with complete confidence and with absolute assurance.

There is a divine circulation flowing through me. The vitality and the energy of life flow through my every act. I am seeing in everyone around me the manifestation of perfect life. I am letting my mind dwell on joy and happiness, and I am knowing that this joy and happiness go out to others.

I allow the divine wholeness to flow through me into ever-widening fields of activity. Every good which I have ever experienced is now increased tenfold. Every joy which I have ever experienced is now multiplied. There is a new influx of inspiration into my thought. I see more clearly than ever before that my divine birthright is freedom, joy and eternal goodness. I perceive this same birthright is bequeathed to all people. All power is delivered unto me and this power I use for my own and every other man's good. This divine presence interprets itself to me in love and friendship. Peace, joy and goodness are mine now and forever.

November 6

At the Center of My Being Is Peace

They rise upwards who are settled in Harmony.
The Bhagavad-Gita

AT the center of my being is peace—the peace that is felt in the coolness of evening, when men have turned from their labor and the first star shines in the soft light of the sky. There is a freshness, a vitality, a power underlying this peace. It broods over the earth quietly, tenderly, as a mother watches over her sleeping babe.

Divine wisdom illumines me. Infinite energy activates me. All that I am and all that I have responds to the magnetic pull of divine life.

In this peace which holds me so gently, I feel strength and protection from all fear, all anxieties. It is the peace of God, and underneath it all, I feel the love of the holy presence. As I become more conscious of this love, all lack, all fear, all that is false, slips away as mist fades in the morning sunshine. I see God in everything, personified in all people, manifest in every event. The Spirit is not separated from the person or the event; It unites each to Itself, vitalizing each with the energy of Its own being, creating each through Its own divine imagination. I, too, am an instrument of Its divine imagination. I, too, am an instrument of Its perfection. I am one with deep, abiding peace. I know that all is well, I know that as I permit this peace to flow through my being, through my mind and heart, every problem is released. The way is made clear before me. It is filled with joy and harmony.

November 7

The Spirit of the Almighty Goes Before Me

*To those who are good (to me), I am good;
and to those who are not good (to me), I am good; and thus (all) get to be good.*
The Tao Te Ching

I KNOW that the power of good is an underlying principle of the universe and that it is a manifestation of God. I know that God is all-good. I know that good underlies all manifestations of thought and form because good is harmony, complete balance. Good is at the root of all manifestation, regardless of its seeming absence. I know that this good is the basic principle of my existence; that which I am is good. It is the vital, living force that supports my every thought and deed when they are in harmony with it.

The love of God fills my being and my life reflects the divine harmony which eternally guides my footsteps aright. Divine intelligence inwardly inspires and instructs that I may have the right ideas and the right guidance to do the good that I would do in my life.

Today I uncover the perfection within me. In its fullness I reveal the indwelling kingdom. I look out upon the world of my affairs, knowing that the Spirit within me makes my way both immediate and easy. I know there is nothing in me that could possibly obstruct or withhold the divine circuit of life and love, which good is. My word dissolves every negative thought or impulse that could throw a shadow over my perfection. Good flows through me to all. Good shines through my thoughts and actions. Good harmonizes my body, so that it is revitalized and manifests perfection in every cell, in every organ, in every function. Good harmonizes my mind, so that love sings joyously in my heart, and I am completely conscious of all-good in me, around me and in all that is. I am in complete unity with my good.

November 8

I Demonstrate Through the Perfect Law

And as He thinketh all things manifest, He manifests through all things and in all, and most of all in whatsoever things He wills to manifest.
Thrice-Greatest Hermes

ALL laws are laws of God. Whatever reality is, its nature is one. If I wish to demonstrate my good I must faithfully and fervently declare that the law of the Lord is perfect and that this law is operating in my experience now. I believe that it is the nature of thought to externalize itself, to bring about conditions which exactly correspond to the thought. Therefore, I turn resolutely from every sense of lack, want and limitation, and declare the perfect law, knowing that even though I am dealing with an invisible principle it will be made manifest in my experience.

Therefore, today I declare that the law of the Lord is perfect in everything I do. It will externalize happiness; it will bring every good thing to me. Today I am inwardly aware that there is a secret way of the soul, there is a secret pathway of peace, there is an invisible presence forever externalizing itself for me and through me. Today I believe in divine guidance. Today I believe that underneath are the everlasting arms. Today I rest in this divine assurance and this divine security. I know that not only all is well with my soul, my spirit and my mind; all is well with my affairs.

I sincerely believe that there is a divine presence and a law of good which attracts every person and everything to me, that belongs to me, and which, flowing through me, reaches out to everything in my life with love, with consideration, in joy and gladness.

November 9

Spiritual Substance Is My Supply

The Lord is on my side; I will not fear: what can man do unto me?
Psalm 118.6

I KNOW that Spirit fills all space and animates every form, therefore, Spirit is the true actor in everything. But I also know that Spirit can only act for me by acting through me. This means simply that God can give me only what I take. I am conscious that as I daily enter into my divine inheritance, in my thought and in the Spirit, I am entering into the realm of absolute causation and I completely believe that from this secret place of the most high within me, there shall be projected an objective manifestation of my every legitimate desire.

Hope rises within me and sings a song of joy. Love goes before me and embraces everything. Peace accompanies me on my way, while doubt and fear vanish as mist before the light.

Am I really accepting abundance? Is my thought really animating my experience with the idea of plenty? Am I affirming that divine substance is forever flowing to me as supply?

Today I praise the abundance in all things. I animate everything with the idea of abundance. I am remembering only the good, I am expecting more good, I am experiencing good. I acknowledge the good working everywhere. I give thanks that this good is flowing into my experience in ever-increasing volume. There is that within me that sees, knows and understands this truth, that completely accepts it. There is good enough to go around. Therefore I do not withhold this good from myself or others, but constantly proclaim spiritual substance is forever flowing to each and all as supply.

November 10

Every Atom of My Being Is Animated by the Divine Perfection

The Tao cannot be heard; what can be heard is not It.
The Tao cannot be seen; what can be seen is not It.
The Texts of Taoism

THE Chinese say that Tao (meaning Spirit) produces everything, nourishes everything and maintains everything. It spreads Itself over everything. It flows through everything and is in all things. Indeed, being all that is, there can be nothing outside It. There is a mystical presence which pervades the universe, and this presence, welling up in consciousness, evermore proclaims Itself as the source and root of all. The enlightened of the ages have said that it is this God within that recognizes Itself in everything.

I know that as there is one Mind, and that Mind is God and that mind is my mind, so also there is one body, that body is spiritual and that body is my body. Every organ, every function, every action and reaction of my body is in harmony with the divine creative Spirit. I have both "the mind of Christ" and the body of God. I could not ask for more and greater could not be given. I now seek to realize the spiritual significance of the one Mind and the one body.

Every function, organ and cell of my body responds to the magnetic pull of wholeness, of unlimited energy, of perfect life. As my thoughts are so put in order, all fear, doubt and uncertainty are banished into nothingness.

I live in the one Mind and act through the one body, in accord with divine harmony, perfection and poise. Every organ of my body moves in accord with perfect harmony. The Divine circulates through me automatically, spontaneously and perfectly. Every atom of my being is animated by the divine perfection.

November 11

The Law of Right Action Is Operating in My Life Now

*For then shalt thou have thy delight in the Almighty,
and shalt lift up thy face unto God.*
Job 22:21, 26

RIGHT action means that every legitimate and constructive purpose I have in mind shall be successfully executed. It means that I shall know what to do, how to think, how to act, how to proceed. I definitely declare that since my word is in accord with the divine nature, it actually is the law of God in my experience, enforcing Itself. Hence, there is nothing in me or around me which can limit this word. The power of this law is with me and the action which results from this power produces harmony, peace, joy and success.

Recognizing that there is but one power, one presence and one life, I so unite myself with this life that all things become possible to me through faith. Humbly, reverently, but with complete conviction, I accept the gift of heaven, that life which is complete and perfect, here and now.

I know that in this consciousness of reality is the supply for my every need—physical, mental or spiritual—and I accept that supply in deepest gratitude. I am thankful that this is the way life fulfills my needs, through the doorway of my inner self, and I am thankful that I know how to use this perfect law. I come to this great fountain of supply, in the very center of my being, to absorb that for which I have need, mentally and physically, and I am filled with the sense of the reality of that which I desire. As I am filled with reality I permit It to flow into my world of thought and action, knowing that it brings peace and harmony and order all around me. There arises within me limitless faith in the unconquerable presence, the perfect law and the divine action.

November 12

I Recognize My Identity With Spirit

Now faith is the substance of things hoped for, the evidence of things not seen.
Hebrews 11:1

MY knowledge that the great I Am is ever available gives me an increasing capacity to draw upon it and to become inwardly aware of the presence of Spirit. Through the quiet contemplation of the omniaction of Spirit, I learn to look quietly and calmly upon every false condition, seeing through it to the other side of the invisible reality which molds conditions and re-creates all of my affairs after a more nearly divine pattern. With a penetrating spiritual vision I dissipate any obstruction, remove all obstacles, dissolve all wrong conditions. Standing still I watch the sure salvation of the law.

Today I see peace instead of confusion. I entertain faith instead of doubt. I feel the impact of an all-enveloping presence. I know that there is a power of good operating in human affairs.

I now claim health instead of sickness, wealth instead of poverty, happiness instead of misery. In such degree as I gain mastery over the sense of negation, whether it be pain or poverty, I am proving the law of good. Every thought of fear or limitation is removed from my consciousness. I know that my word transmutes every energy into constructive action, producing health, harmony, happiness and success. I know there is something at the center of my being which is absolutely certain of itself. It has complete assurance and it gives me complete assurance that all is well. I maintain my position as a divine being, here and now.

November 13

Daily I Die to Everything That Is Unlike Good

When all desires dwelling in the heart have been quitted, then the mortal becomes immortal; (then) he enjoys here Brahma.
Brihad Aranyaka Upanishad

THE Talmud says that unhappy conditions arise when we mistake shadow for substance. Even the valley of the shadow of death causes no fear when we arrive at the consciousness of the psalmist who, from the exaltation of his divine deliverance, proclaimed, "… thy rod and thy staff they comfort me." The rod and staff of truth is the realization of the substantiality and the permanence of that which cannot change.

I am believing that we are identifying ourselves with success and happiness. This is what we are decreeing. This is what life is doing for us now. We know that goodness and mercy shall follow us all the days of our lives, and we will dwell in the house of the Lord forever.

We are ever renewed by the passage of the divine light through our consciousness. The revitalizing, regenerative power of Spirit flows from the consciousness of wholeness into our physical organism, and into every objective act when we give the realization of the divine presence free passage through our thought.

I know that every apparent death is a resurrection. Therefore, today, gladly I die to everything that is unlike the good. Joyfully I am resurrected into that which is beautiful, enduring and true. Silently I pass from less to more, from isolation into inclusion, from separation into oneness. The perfect law of good is operating through me. Joyfully I accept it. Joyfully I permit its action in everything that I do. I know that my recognition of good is the substance of the good which I recognize, and I know that this good is ever taking form in my experience. It is impossible for me to be separated from my good.

November 14

Today I See Him Reflected in Every Form, Moving in Every Act

*Now, when the thought of doing good has arisen in a man's mind,
though the good be not yet done, the good Spirits are in attendance on him.*
The Texts of Taoism

AFTER long meditation and much deep reflection, having passed through the confusion of human experience, Job finally arrived at the conclusion that the Spirit of God was within him and that the breath of God was his life. We all have traveled this same pathway of experience, the journey of the soul to "the heights above," and always there has been a deep inquiry in our minds—What is it all about? Does life make sense? What is the meaning of birth, human experience and the final transition from this plane which we call death? Somewhere along the line we too must exclaim with Job, "The spirit of God hath made me and the breath of the Almighty hath given me life." Nothing can be nearer to us than that which is the very essence of our own being. Our external search after reality culminates in the greatest of all possible discoveries—reality is at the center of our own being; life is from within out.

I feel that my search is over. I feel that I have discovered the great reality. I am not evolving into it, I am merely awakening to the realization of what it means. There is but one life. This life I am living. Today I speak this reality into every experience I have. Today I see Him reflected in every form, back of every countenance, moving in every act.

This is my deliberate choice. This is my secret desire. This is the sole ambition of my heart and mind and soul, that I shall walk with God, and walking with God, that I shall so manifest His nature that everything around me shall be blessed.

November 15

I Am Spirit Made Manifest This Instant

Infinite is that, infinite is this. From the infinite one proceeds the infinite one. On taking the infinity of the infinite one, there is left infinity.
                                        Brihad Aranyaka Upanishad

MY body, and every part of it, is made of pure substance—God. It cannot deteriorate. This instant this infinite substance within me, that is constantly flowing through me, takes form in the likeness of perfect, whole, complete cells. Every cell of my body is strong and healthy, filled with life and vitality, strength and cleanliness. My body (Spirit in form) knows no time, knows no degree; it knows only to express fully, instantaneously.

The divine presence, being everywhere and filling all space, must be in me. It must be that which I really am. I recognize it is within me and it is that which I am. I let this recognition of my indwelling divinity flow through my entire consciousness.

I know that my body is renewed, revitalized, remade. All the energy, action and vitality in the universe is pouring through it, and I know every action, every organ and function of this body is created in the wisdom of God and maintained by the power of God.

I let this thought reach down into the very depths of my being. I rejoice in my divinity. I am now made vigorous and hardy. I have the stamina of the infinite. I am sturdy and robust. I am fortified with God's perfection and right action. I am hale and able bodied. All the life of the universe is my life. All the strength of the universe is my strength. All the power of the universe is my power. Every breath I draw fills me with perfection, vitalizes, upbuilds and renews every cell of my body. I am born *in* Spirit and *of* Spirit, and I *am* Spirit made manifest this instant.

November 16

Today I Live

He who knows this grand completion does not seek for it; he loses nothing and abandons nothing; he does not change himself with regard to (external) things; he turns in on himself, and finds there an inexhaustible store.
The Texts of Taoism

THE wisest man who ever lived told us that the knowledge of truth shall make us free. All books of spiritual wisdom have taught us that it is not the one who makes the mistake whom we should seek to destroy; it is the mistake itself which must be erased. This means that evil has no existence in itself and has no history. No matter what the negations of yesterday may have been, the affirmations of today rise triumphant and transcendent over them. Thus all the evils of our yesterdays disappear into their native nothingness.

If we behold beauty instead of ugliness, then beauty will appear. If we persist in seeing the true rather than the false, then that which is true will appear. Let us, then, cease weeping over the shortcomings and mistakes and evils of our yesterdays, and steadfastly beholding the face of the great and the divine reality, let us resolve to walk in the light wherein there is no darkness.

Definitely I know that every negative condition of the past is cleared away from my consciousness. I no longer think about it, see it, or believe in it. Nor do I believe that it has any effect whatsoever in my experience. Yesterday is not, tomorrow is not, but today, bright with hope and filled with promise, is mine. Today I live.

I now surrender every doubt and fear, every thought of confusion or uncertainty, into the keeping of the divine Spirit. I lose all sense of limitation, lack and want into the divine abundance. I lift up the bowl of my acceptance and know that it is filled from the wholeness of plenty. I let God, the supreme intelligence, guide and direct me.

November 17

I Experience Complete Wholeness

And that ye study to be quiet, and to do your own business, and to work with your own hands, as we commanded you; That ye may walk honestly toward them that are without, and that ye may have lack of nothing.
I Thessalonians 4:11, 12

I KNOW that I am some part of the divine being, that the power and the presence of that Spirit is in the word I speak, and that word infinitely and perfectly and permanently makes whole. I know that I represent an individualization of the truth—the truth of wholeness, the truth of love, reason and of sound Mind; the truth of peace and joy; the truth and the freedom of the circulation of the Divine in every atom, in every function and every organ. I empty myself of any and every thought that denies this. I know that, silently but effectively, the divine power of the invisible Spirit is working here and now—this moment.

Realizing that God, the living Spirit, is the one final presence and power in the universe, I consciously enter into communion with the divine presence that is within me and within and around everything.

I hold this realization with complete certainty. I recognize that I am a perfect being, living under perfect conditions, knowing that good alone is real. I also know that good alone is the only thing that has any power either to act or to react. Everything that I do, say or think today, shall be done, said or thought from the spiritual viewpoint of God in everything.

My recognition of the power is sufficient to neutralize every false experience, make the crooked straight and the rough places plain. Definitely I know that this recognition establishes the law of harmony in my experience, the law of prosperity, the sense of happiness and health. I experience complete wholeness.

November 18

"I Know That My Redeemer Liveth"

Not to be separate from his primal source constitutes what we call the Heavenly man; not to be separate from the essential nature thereof constitutes what we call the Spirit-like man; not to be separate from its real truth constitutes what we call the Perfect man.
The Texts of Taoism

IT has been written that Christ is the redeemer; also that Christ is in us. We have been told that our redemption is at hand. We have been told to awake and that Christ will give us light. Therefore, I conclude that my redeemer lives and is now acting through me. Why, then, is not my redemption at hand? It is, but I have failed to see it. Can it be possible that I am using the creative power to produce the very limitation from which I so earnestly seek to extricate myself? Undoubtedly, this is true. There are not two powers; there is but one power.

Today I realize that life is truly a mirror of king and slave. Today I realize that my redemption is at hand. The Spirit within me refreshes me daily. I feel myself saturated with the life essence itself; I feel the same life essence flowing in and through me. I feel myself to be a perfect instrument in life's divine symphony, in tune with its harmony and perfection. My body is an instrument in, through and upon which life plays a divine and perfect harmony. I am not going out in search of another power but am going to use the power which I know already possesses eternity and is already at the center of my own life. I know that this will heal every condition, overcome every obstacle, break down every barrier, and free me from every false condition. My redemption is already at hand.

I look confidently into the future. I see new friendships, new opportunities. Everything in my experience is renewed. Everything is made glad and happy and whole. As I turn to the world around me, I see this same good evenly distributed everywhere, and operating through all people.

November 19

Constantly, I Partake of the Divine Bounty

There is nothing impossible of attainment by persons of virtuous behavior.
                                                        The Mahabharata

I HAVE within myself, as I sit here, the sense that though my body is real, tangible, with definite form and outline, it is at the same time somehow made of a living stuff which is saturated with God-life. I know that whatever the stuff is of which my body is made, though it is called material, it must really be made of the one stuff and essence of which all things are made. Therefore, I sense within the very cells and tissues of my body an eternality.

Realizing that the Spirit within me is God, the living Spirit Almighty, being fully conscious of this divine presence as the sustaining principle of my life, I open my thought to Its influx. I open my consciousness to Its outpouring. I let that Mind be in me which was also in Christ Jesus. That is the mind of truth, the Mind of God, carrying with It all the power of the infinite.

I am now inviting the Spirit within me to flood my mind with its wholeness, to bring warmth and color and feeling and love into everything I do, say and think. I believe that at the very center of my being there is the man whom God has made, a perfect man. Therefore, I lay aside all fear, all doubt, all misunderstanding, all uncertainty. I know that life has need of me or it would not have put me here.

I know and understand that good alone is real. I know that silently I am drawing into my experience today and every day, an ever-increasing measure of truth and beauty, of goodness, of harmony. Everything I do, say and think is quickened into right action, into productive action, into increased action. My invisible good already exists. My faith, drawing upon this invisible good, causes that which was unseen to become visible. All there is, is mine now, all there ever was or ever can be, is mine now.

November 20

I Have Confidence in My Understanding of the Law

Despise no man and deem nothing impossible; every man hath his hour and everything its place.
The Talmud

I BELIEVE that no matter what the experience through which I am going, good will come out of it. I believe that all poverty will be turned into riches; that all fear will be converted into faith. I believe that good finally will triumph over every evil and love will heal all hate. I believe that I have a silent partnership with the invisible; that this partnership has never been dissolved and never can be. I believe in the invisible presence of good in a universe peopled with perfect and eternal entities. I believe that all things are possible to him who does believe.

Knowing that the law of God is a law of love, and knowing that the law of love is a law of liberty, I see freedom, joy, happiness, peace and wholeness in everything I look at. I respond to the divine calm which is at the center of everything. Knowing that perfect love casteth out all fear, I am strong and confident because I know that the law of good goes with me and prepares the way before me.

I have complete confidence in my knowledge and understanding of the law of good. I not only know what is the law, I know how to use it. I know that I shall obtain definite results through the use of it. I realize that doubts about my ability to use this law are things of thought. What thought has produced, thought can change. Knowing this, having confidence in my ability to use the law, and using it daily for specific purposes, gradually I build up an unshakable faith, both in the law and possibility of demonstrating it. There is no doubt in me, no uncertainty rising through me. My mind rejoices in certainty and in assurance. I confidently expect that my word shall not return unto me void.

November 21

I Rely Upon the One Perfect Activity of God

Verily, verily, I say unto you, He that believeth on me, the works that I do shall he do also; and greater works than these shall he do; because I go unto my Father.
John 14:12

THE all-intelligent, creative presence is the source of all that I am. I believe in the ability and the willingness of this great source to sustain its own creation. The kingdom and the power and the glory of God expresses through me. I recognize myself to be a center through which the intelligence and power of the universe find expression. Infinite Mind, operating through me, now brings to me the manifestation of harmony, order and the highest good. The consciousness of peace and plenty is established within me. All that is necessary to my happiness and well-being now comes into my experience.

Tuning my mind into the Divine, I seek to draw into my own soul the essence of everything that is good, true and beautiful. I seek to draw into my own mind the realization of the divine presence and the power of good until my whole being responds.

There can be neither limitation nor lack for nothing has happened to the one perfect activity. It is in full operation for me. I am now free from any sense of bondage. All power is given unto me from on high. Knowing this, I am strong with the strength of the all-vitalizing power of the universe.

I am sustained and healed by a divine stream of Spirit-energy, which flows through me as radiant health and vitality. Every fiber of my being responds to this spiritual flow. I stand revealed as the perfect child of the perfect Father. Strength and courage are my divine birthright and I am now expressing my true self. All that the Father hath is mine. I draw from the spiritual treasure house all that I need.

November 22

Today I Bestow the Essence of Love Upon Everything

Love worketh no ill to his neighbour: therefore love is the fulfilling of the law.
Romans 13:10

"THE law of the Lord is perfect" and the law of the Lord is love. We are made perfect in the law when we enter into the communion of love with one another and with the invisible essence of life. Love is the fulfillment of the law, that is, we never can make the most perfect use of the law unless that use is motivated by love, by a sincere desire to express unity, harmony and peace. As the true artist weds himself to the essence of beauty, imbibing her spirit that it may be transmitted to the canvas, or awaken a living form from cold marble, so we must wed ourselves to the essence of love that we may imbibe its spirit, and, transmitting it, give loveliness to all events.

I desire that everything I think shall be from the heart as well as from the head. I wish to release kindness and love, sympathy and understanding, peace and joy. No condemnation, judgment or fear shall go from me to anyone or anything.

Today I bestow the essence of love upon everything. Everyone shall be lovely to me. My soul meets the soul of the universe in everyone. Nothing is ugly; everything is beautiful, everything is meaningful. This love is a healing power touching everything into wholeness, healing the wounds of experience with its divine balm. I know that this love essence, the very substance of life, the creative principle back of everything, flows through my whole being, spiritual, emotional, mental and physical. It flows in transcendent loveliness into my world of thought and form, ever renewing, vitalizing, bringing joy and harmony and blessing to everything and everyone it touches.

November 23

My Word Does Accomplish

The first step that the soul of the faithful man made, placed him in the Good-Thought Paradise;
The second step that the soul of the faithful man made, placed him in the Good-Word Paradise;
The third step that the soul of the faithful man made, placed him in the Good-Deed Paradise.
— The Zend-Avesta

SINCE thought is a definite, dynamic, creative, consciously directed and intelligent energy, then I know that a thought of truth will definitely neutralize a negative argument. I am on guard to protect my own word by knowing that it is the activity of Spirit through me and as such cannot be denied. In effective prayer, I realize that a power greater than I am consciously acts with creative intelligence upon my word. In this way, I free myself from a sense of personal responsibility, while, at the same time, remaining aware that even spiritual laws must be definitely used, if they are to provide tangible results in my experience.

Believing that there is one divine intelligence that governs everything, I affirm that this intelligence is acting in my mind, causing me to know what is best and to do what is best. I open my mind to new thoughts, new ideas. And I know that as I do this new experience shall come to me.

I seek to believe with absolute conviction that my word will not return unto me void, and I do this when I realize that spiritual laws execute themselves, just as do other laws of nature. I know that my word penetrates every unbelief in my mind, casts out all fear, removes all doubt, clears away every obstacle, and permits that which is enduring, perfect and true to be perceived by my mind.

I provide faith, acceptance, and a joyous expectancy that all the statements that I make in my prayers or treatments are not only true but that they will be carried out as I have spoken. As my work is done with this sense of reliance upon the law of good, I know that my word shall not return unto me void but "shall accomplish that whereunto it is sent."

November 24

I Accept My Own Spiritual and Physical Perfection

He is a rock, his work is perfect: for all his ways are judgment:
a God of truth and without iniquity, just and right is he.
Deuteronomy 32:4

MY body is the temple of the living God. It is spiritual substance. I have perfect confidence in my heart that God's lifegiving Spirit is my life. Since God is my life and God is eternal, my life is eternal. Therefore I cannot be separated from God, from good, from perfection. If I would renew body, mind and affairs, I must first cause my imagination to rise above them. The supreme ruler, omnipresent, therefore existing at the very center of my thought, the Christ within me, really has the power to make all things new.

The perfect life of God now expresses through me, and every part of my body expresses its innate perfection and wholeness. As the sun dissolves the mist, so does my knowledge of truth dissolve all pain and discord. I know the truth about myself as a child of God and that truth makes me free. I am free because the power of the living Spirit is my power and it remolds and recreates my body after the likeness of the perfect pattern of God. I open wide the doorway of my consciousness to a greater influx from the Divine. I know that the all-conquering power of Spirit is with me. I accept my privilege, as a son, of manifesting the life, love, peace, strength, harmony and joy of God—the Father Almighty who indwells me and incarnates Himself in me, as me.

Therefore, I rest in peace and in the quiet confidence that all is well. It is my sincere desire that the life and the love which God is shall flow through me to the whole world.

November 25

The Life of the Father Is My Life

*When Heaven and Man exert their powers in concert,
all transformations have their commencements determined.*
The Texts of Taoism

GOD could not withhold Himself from me. That which He is He has given fully unto me to enjoy. The life of God is perfect, it is eternal, it is the essence of all things. That life is God's gift to me. Therefore, this fullness is within me, ready to manifest through me as I partake of it. Since I am self-choosing, even though divinely endowed, I partake of my divinity only as I let it through; I am always in the midst of plenty everywhere. I know that I live in a changeless reality. I am not disturbed by the passage of time, the movement around me, nor the variations of experience through which I go. Something within me remains immovable and says, "Be still and know that I am God."

There is no here and there to the Spirit, for both are included within Itself, even as yesterday, today and tomorrow are but passing events in Its unitary wholeness, even as big and little are but outlines. The manifest universe is an expression of that which transcends time, overshadows eternity, encompasses all form, and remains stable within that which forever flows.

I now consciously draw upon the life which is mine. I now reeducate myself definitely, by whatever steps I may, to a belief that there is given unto me a fullness of life which is divine in its origin, eternal in its presence, and always fully available. The life of the Father is my life. The infinite richness of the Father is mine to enjoy. The vital good health, the wisdom, the peace of the Father are mine. All things which proceed from Him may be mine. I now claim them. The act of taking is my right and privilege. I exercise it now intelligently and in full faith.

November 26

Life Sings Through Me in Radiant Ecstasy

The footsteps of those who dwell with the god of Light are set free.
Book of the Dead

NOW and always I recognize that I live, move and have my being in God. I am part of universal Mind. I am one with universal substance. All the qualities and all the wealth of good and desirable things that exist in universal Mind are mine now. I perceive, accept and experience them. I know that all the beauty of form around me is the garment of God. I know that that presence which manifests in my heart and mind is God expressing Himself within me. As I feel this presence more and more I hear the song of joy deep within. Always when I am still I hear the song of life pouring through my consciousness, I have only to listen, for it is always there.

The Father and I are one. This I know to be the truth of my being. I open my mind and my heart to the inflow of the divine Spirit and know that the presence of God flows through my being with perfect action and in perfect unity with good.

With this knowledge, this assurance that the loving presence is always here—"closer to me than breathing, nearer than hands and feet"—I have nothing to fear. I feel this loving protection around me, and I know that it is not only a song of joy, but a song of love and protection. I tune out all dull, negative ideas, and tune in with the sunshine of life, with brightness and laughter, with the joyous presence that is life itself. I now lay aside all anxiety, all striving, and let the law bring my good to me. I joyfully anticipate greater abundance, more success and more joy. Joy wells up within my heart and life sings through me in radiant ecstasy.

November 27

I Will Fear No Evil

Are not the friends of God, those on whom no fear shall come, nor shall they be put to grief?
The Koran

TODAY my heart is without fear, for I have implicit confidence in the good, the enduring and the true. Fear is the only thing of which to be afraid. It is not the host encamped against us, nor the confusion around us, that we need to fear; it is the lack of confidence in the good alone which should concern us. Through inner spiritual vision, we know that evil is transitory, but good is permanent. We know that right finally dissolves everything opposed to it. The power of Spirit is supreme over every antagonist. Therefore, we should cherish no fear, and when we neither fear nor hate, we come to understand the unity of life.

I put my whole trust in God. I know that the Spirit will gently lead me and wisely counsel me. I know that the love which envelops everything flows through me to everyone, and with it there goes a confidence, a sense of joy and freedom, a buoyant enthusiasm for living, a zest for life. "For all thy ways are ways of pleasantness, and all thy paths are peace."

I realize that fear is not Godlike, since it contradicts the divine presence, repudiates limitless love and denies infinite good. Therefore, I know that fear is a lie, a fraud. It is neither person, place nor thing; it is merely an impostor that I have believed in. I have entertained it so long that it seems as if it really were something, and it attempts to make me believe that two and two are seven, that the earth is flat and that God is limited. Today I repudiate all fear. I renounce the belief in evil. I enter into conscious union with the Spirit. I accept the good as supreme, positive and absolute. With joy I enter into the activities of the day, without regret I remember the events of yesterday, and with confidence I look forward to tomorrow, for today my heart is without fear.

November 28

His Law Is in My Heart and I Delight To Do His Will

That in which he findeth the supreme delight which the Reason can grasp beyond the sense, wherein established he moveth not from the reality;
Which having been obtained, he thinketh there is no greater gain beyond it; wherein established, he is not shaken even by heavy sorrow.
The Bhagavad-Gita

I KNOW that the perfect life of the Spirit is my life, and I now permit It to radiate through my world of thought and action—to express in my physical form. As I relax my body, consciously and definitely—which I am able to do by mentally relaxing and dropping all strain—I feel flowing through me a vital energy, a dynamic force, a great surge of living power. I feel immersed in and saturated by a vital essence of perfection, which brings me into tune with life.

Today I let God's life live itself through me. I permit it to flow through me to others that heaven shall be joined with earth, that the Divine shall blend with the human, that love shall conquer fear, and a little child shall lead them.

Because my whole being is this perfect God-life, I have nothing to fear. Every person that I meet recognizes the love and peace and wisdom and courage within me. Each person I meet feels our common bond, knows that we are a part of the perfect whole, harmonious centers in the great unity of life, and so has faith in me. No one could wish to harm or hurt me in any way. I, too, can know only love and understanding for my fellow beings. I know, because I am God-life, God in expression, that every circumstance I find myself in, is right for me. Through my consciousness of love, which is the very essence of God-life, I transform any seeming imperfection into the perfect idea of my true self. God knows me only as a perfect idea, and that perfection I now manifest. His law is written in my heart and I delight to do His will.

November 29

I Have Dominion

Ponder the path of they feet, and let all thy ways be established.
Proverbs 4:26

I KNOW that there is a God-power at the center of every man's being, a power that knows neither lack, limitation nor fear, sickness, disquiet nor imperfection. But out of my personal experience come the negative suggestions which arise from the race consciousness. If I permit them to, they act as a mesmeric or hypnotic power over my imagination. They bring up arguments from every man's experience, declaring that impoverishment and pain must necessarily accompany every man in his experience through life.

But I know that there is a presence, a power and a law within me, irresistibly drawing everything into my experience which makes life worthwhile. I know that friendship, love and riches, health, harmony and happiness are mine. I know that nothing but good can go out from me, therefore the good that I receive is but the completion of a circle—the fulfillment of my desire for all. So, I refuse to judge according to appearances, either mental or physical, no matter what the thought says, or what the appearance seems to be.

Today I acknowledge the presence and the power of the living Spirit and I invite it to lead me into pathways of peace, of health and happiness and wholeness. I permit the divine Spirit to lead me into the Garden of Eden, for I know that in this garden there grows the fruit of peace and joy and happiness. And I know that the river that waters this garden flows from the heart of eternal love. As I bathe in this river of life, I permit everything to be washed away that does not belong to the kingdom of good.

There is always a higher power. Upon this power I rely with absolute confidence that it will never fail me. I have dominion over all apparent evil, which is merely a belief I no longer indulge in. I repudiate all its claims, cast out every fear accompanying the belief in it, and continuously exercise the dominion which rightfully belongs to me.

November 30

There Is an Inspiration Within Me That Guides Me Aright

Purity and stillness give the correct law to all under heaven.
The Texts of Taoism

THE disciple John tells us that "God is a Spirit: and they that worship him must worship him in spirit and in truth." Wonderful indeed is this conception of the union of all life, which Jesus proclaimed in the ecstasy of his illumination, "I and the Father are one." All cause and ill effect proceed from the invisible Spirit. Man is one with this Spirit and cannot be separated from It. His word has power because his word is the action of God through his thought.

I now clarify my vision, purify my thought, so that it becomes a mirror reflecting inspiration direct from the secret place of the most high, at the center of my own being. I do this by quiet contemplation, not through strenuous effort but by learning to fast to all negation and to feast upon the affirmations of spiritual realization. I know that I need never break before the onslaught of any confusion that exists around me. Today I walk in the light of God's love. All the creativity, all the power and all the joy that there is in the universe finds outlet through me. There is a song in my heart, the song of the open road that leads to complete fulfillment. And as I travel along this road with others, I find that my hand is in theirs. I have confidence in life, confidence in myself, because I first have confidence in God, the living Spirit.

Today I am guided and my guidance is multiplied. I know exactly what to do and exactly how to do it. There is an inspiration within me which governs every act, every thought, in certainty, with conviction and in peace. I know that the key that unlocks the treasure house, the key to the kingdom of God, is in my spiritual hand. This is the kingdom of God's creation, and is directly experienced by me today.

December 1

Before Me Is a Clear Road, and I Proceed

When one follows unswervingly the path of virtue it is not to win advancement.
Mencius VII.B.33

THE forward look is the Godward look. My heaven will never be unless I make it out of the materials of my own thinking. Today I set my sights on Him who fashioned me in His image and after His likeness. I stand at the door of the abundant life and I knock. All that I seek opens to me and beckons me to life's fullness. I enter into my Divine heritage and walk with the great and the true. My pathway is filled with ease, for I am thinking to take me to my goal. All of Mind urges me on, and all power is my strength to move. Idea after idea comes to my consciousness in right sequence at exactly the right moment. I am inspired to right action in every detail. I walk forward in ease.

There are no obstructions in my pathway of mind. The mistakes of yesterday are behind, and the future beckons with promise. God is where I am, and God will always be with me. His hand will never loose mine, nor will His love let me go. His listening Mind tells me good can be before me. The way is clear, and I never let my doubts create detours. I handle each doubt as it appears and declare it to be nothing. The way is straight, I walk in peace to my selected good. I am pushed from behind by the Spirit, even as I am led forward by true guidance. I walk in faith.

My decision to accept my greater freedom is a mighty power within me. It leads me, directs me and comforts me when doubts assail. I am undaunted by the problems I seem to face. Ahead of me is the royal road to good living based on Spirit and motivated by love. This is the day of progress; this is the day of demonstration. I walk in the dream of accomplishment, and my dream becomes a fact.

December 2

All Power Is Mine to Use and to Enjoy

Thine, O Lord is the greatness, and the power,
and the glory, and the victory, and the majesty.
I Chronicles 29:11

GOD known is power revealed. The unlimited power of the creative Mind is mine to use for the increase of blessings in my world. Such use will harm no one, and will make me a finer person, a greater instrument of the Almighty. By my right use of the one power I shall become what I ought to be. I know that only through my Spirit can this power be used in right ways. I am weary of the destruction and turmoil in my life. I now affirm that I use the power of God for right and intelligent purposes. I say farewell to all mistakes. I am power, for He who made me dwells in me as power. Using this power with wisdom and with divine direction, I cause good to appear on every hand.

The divine power rightly employed by me gives me joy in living. I know that my burdens are merely indications of my refusal to let God act through me. All weariness with everyday struggles is now dissolved, for I release the one power with definite intent. I know what I am doing, and I know how to do it. No pressures, no demands, just the right releasement of His Spirit within me in creative ways. This is easy to do, and I love to do it. As I see ideas unfold through the law into new and better conditions, I stand still and praise the power of truth. Seeking my demonstrations completed makes glad my heart. Infinite Mind knows me as a clear channel for Its operation, and power unlimited gives itself to me. Life is wonderful.

Being the only power, there are no obstructions to its purposes. Even I cannot block the power of God. It uses me as its vehicle of distribution, and I accept the responsibility of this birthright. My thought determines the use I make of God's power. My consciousness determines my experience. I now decide to use power rightly. I now create a new heaven and a new earth for myself. I give strength and power to all. I act as power in my world. I change whatever needs to be changed. God in me as power demands my right use of it, and this I do willingly. I accept my responsibilities and I live with joyous ease because I use power rightly.

December 3

There Is Always a Way Out of Trouble

As the Lord is called righteous and loving, so you be righteous and loving.
Sifre Deuteronomy 85a

JESUS proved that God in man is unlimited. I accept this and now proceed to demonstrate it. My troubles are no longer stumbling blocks. I accept them as challenges to prove that right thinking is the creative power of life. As I dismiss them, the solutions appear. Temporarily they have blinded me, but now I see through the eyes of Spirit, and the way out is clear. As I discipline my thought to God's ideas, I am divinely led to right solutions. No matter how great my problems may be, I dismiss them as unreal. God wants me to be happy, and that is why I want to be happy. I can be joyous, for Mind in me knows that my good is at hand. No delays, no obstacles—my good is where I am and I declare it.

The way is mental, not material. I struggle with matter, but I demonstrate with Mind. Letting go of my struggles to change conditions, I have faith that the Spirit within me generates what I need and what I want. Too long have I tarried in the halls of matter; I now enter the upper room of Mind action and take my place in the world as God's representative. Clothed with all power and all creative possibility, I see myself as victorious. The universe is my kingdom and I rule with authority. Never again will a trouble torment me. I have been resurrected out of all fear into power. I speak this word with assurance, for I know that the law of Mind does what I direct it to do. I have a way out, and a way upward.

The way is joyous and loving. The solution of my problems makes me a better person. It is easier to love my fellowman. It is easier to be a happy person. God acting through me transforms me, and my whole viewpoint changes. I now see that the word "impossible" is a lie. God's possibility is always within me awaiting my recognition. I am now victorious over troubles. Life spiritualized is life simplified. In quietness my purpose becomes clear, my divinity takes control and my troubles fade as mists before the morning sun. The way of truth is mine today. There is nothing to oppose me, and all of God is working for my victory.

December 4

Life Makes Me Conscious of My Responsibility

O ye who believe! You have charge over your own souls.
The Koran

THE creative process which gave me life expects me to use it rightly. My life is not my own making, it has a destiny and a purpose. I turn confidently to the source of my being and let it reveal why I am here and what it has planned for me to do. The life which gave me birth must know how to produce in me and through me what it has in Mind. I am not an accident of birth. My appearance in these times is part of a divine plan and a divine design. In my present world, right where I am, I have a mission and a purpose. I now let the Mind which created me out of Itself reveal to me my purpose and what I should do today. In the minutest details of today I shall fulfill the reason for my being.

I accept my responsibility to think rightly about myself, my fellowman and the world in which I live. Within me great ideas are being born, and I let them manifest in my mind, body and affairs. I do not pollute them with fear or doubt. I see them as divine in origin and possible in expression. Coming from God they move through me into form. I behold my fellowman as free, and I no longer impose my viewpoints upon him. I know that God in him will lead him into right ways of success and happiness. I have no condemnation for the world in which I live. God made it, and knows how to operate it. I live in the world with ease rejoicing in the good it has for me.

There is so much that is heavenly and perfect in my life. I see this, believe this and increase this. As I accept the responsibility to act and react as a spiritual being, I find all life cooperating with me. No more strain to succeed, no more trying to make things happen. My only duty is to let the action of God take place through me, and this I do. My right place is always where I am, and my right work is to do the will of Him who sent me. Freely I give my whole mind over to the divine wisdom and the divine power.

December 5

I Respect the Health in My Body

For I will restore health unto thee, and I will heal thee of thy wounds, saith the Lord.
Jeremiah 30:17

MY health is not self-created, for God is the health of man. This health is worthy of my respect. Only that which I respect do I value and handle with care. My body is a spiritual vehicle through which God's life flows. God's unlimited health maintains it in strength, vitality and ease of action. My thought definitely affects my health, and my spiritual responsibility demands that I stay positive and creative. As all illness and fatigue originate in my mind, I now eliminate their causes. Every spiritual thought of mine is a tonic to my whole system. Every joyous thought of mine helps the body to remain sound and whole. Such thoughts I have with ease.

No more fear and no more worry for me. I know their destructive actions, and I refuse to adulterate God's health in my body with such errors. I must not impede the health and vitality which God has planned for me. No hate is worth the toll it takes in my tissues. No anger is worth the destruction it causes in my body. What God made I use with all the wisdom I have and can claim. As I respect my body and declare that God abides within it, I feel an upsurge of life. Strength and power become my tools to use for right activities. All fatigue disappears and I do easily whatever needs my attention. God responds to me with all possibility, because I have rightly used His life within me.

The divine pattern of my health is now accepted by me. This includes a rich sense of well-being all the days of my life. I expect my body to react with ease, as my thinking acts with wisdom. Letting go of all beliefs in sickness, I never again experience disease. Even the slightest cold will be no more, for I now see God as my health. I respect the Divine enough that I dedicate my thinking to positives. I rejoice in my healthy body, because it indicates my healthy thinking. Today I am alive with health, vitality and the power of accomplishment. I eat with wisdom, rest with wisdom. I think only those thoughts which maintain me in health. I am alive now with the permanent and perfect health of the Spirit.

The Idea I Need Now Appears

To attain this subtle realization, you must completely cut off the way of thinking.
Mumonkan 1

I AM the creation of an all-knowing Mind, an infinite love and a divine law of action. As a mother feeds her child, so does this holy wisdom nourish my consciousness. Forever within me is all that I shall ever need. I seek without no more, for God in the center of me is my unfailing supply. All Mind is given unto me. All power is mine to distribute in creative ways. All love is asking me to release it unto my fellowman. Christ indwelling me is all that I want and all of the kingdom of heaven. I am the richest person there is, for all of God is offering itself to me in consciousness. I rejoice in my capacity to receive greatness.

What I need to know at this instant, Mind gives to me. The idea I need is now active within me. I draw from my own divine center the wisdom to handle my affairs. I do not question, I know. I do not seek, for I have found. God leads me with His ideas into success in all my ways. Where I am the Mind of truth is. The idea I select, the law will execute instantly. The new, the fresh and the different offer themselves to me now. I select new ideas, and I have new experiences. Weary of negatives, I select positives. The night of false conclusions is over, for the dawn of clear thinking has come upon me. I am prospered by infinite Spirit, and I am made glad by absolute joy.

Quickened by the one Mind, I freely use Its ideas. Now, I know what to do, how to do it, and when it should be done. No more doubts, for the certainty of God's inspiration is revealed to me. This is my hour of right decision followed by right action. The portals of my thought are open to truth and ideas of God enter my consciousness. My way is easy and my burden is light, for I am inspired at every instant. Decisions are clear, and my authority is of God. All that I can ever use is mine now. All this is good, and all this is true. Mind revealing Itself in me is my security. For complete inspiration at every moment, I rejoice and give thanks. I have every idea I need at the instant of time that I need it. God's action in me is wonderful.

December 7

A Light Is in Every Man, and I Behold It

> *Let all mankind be thy sect.*
> Adi Granth, Japuji 28, M.1

HUMANITY is divinity made visible. We are good people in the sight of our Creator. Knowing this, I see my neighbor as a part of the divine plan for all. His ideas may not be mine, but they are right for him. I may not agree with the outer man, but I must agree with the inner one. In him is the spirit of truth, the need for self-expression and the vision of what he can become. This I respect, and this I value. I no longer try to make him in my image and likeness. I now realize that his individuality is of God, and I adjust my thinking to this premise. A light born of love burns within him, and I cross the bridge of human opinions and embrace him as a son of God.

There is a goodness in my fellowman that needs my recognition. He is hungry for someone to see him as he really is. He needs my spiritual perception of his innate kindliness and I now look for every slight indication of God in man and praise it. In the midst of him is the Spirit, and I now see its many modes of expression. I appreciate and bless everyone I know. Family, friends and coworkers are God's means of peopling my world with love. No more need to be on guard, I lovingly and joyously accept every person as God made manifest. No one can harm me, no one can take from me any good. Others make me whole and loving. God in me reaches out to the highest and the best in everyone I know. Friendship and understanding await me in my home, my place of business and the neighborhood where I live.

People bless me, for they give me so much that I need. The hand of God is in every hand I clasp. I now see a beauty and a wholeness in everyone I know. No mistakes, no injustices, no more suspicions. I let God run His universe, and I let His law take care of all whom I know. I expect the best from my friends. I live in a friendly world, and all people are essentially good. There is light born of God within all people, and I expect this light to bless and benefit me. Today I release all human judgments. I behold the Christ in man. God is in me, so he is also in everyone I meet.

December 8

God's Mind in Me Is Clear and Definite

In all things ye have approved yourselves to be clear in this matter.
II Corinthians 7:11

I ALWAYS make right decisions, for within me is that which knows. The revelations of truth have come to others, so they now come to me. Eternal Mind is not restricted to a time, an era nor a certain religion. The infinite which released itself through the great people of all times now releases itself through me. All that the wise have known, I can know. All that the great have accomplished, I can accomplish. I, too, am an outlet for divine Mind and divine love. I accept this interior gift of the ages, and I let it determine my life this day. God's Mind in me is clear and definite. To me is given the knowledge to handle every situation this day may bring. Omniscience is mine.

Guided by a perfect Mind, I make right decisions and accomplish with ease. Life abundant offers itself to me, and I accept it. The wisdom I need for greatness is already within me, and seeks me as its outlet. I affirm divine wisdom. I affirm divine intelligence. I affirm my own capacity for success. No more hazy thinking, no more foggy questioning, I know what needs to be done, and I know how to do it. The cobwebs of confused thinking are swept out of my consciousness. Life is plain, clear and direct. As I think, infinite Mind thinks as me. As I create, the one Mind is creating through me. I am one with God and with all of God's clear ideas. Today my thinking is positive.

Demonstrations of every kind appear in my experience in the next few hours. This treatment guarantees my health, happiness and security. My thinking of God assures me of perfect action this day. Dwelling upon His wisdom, I am wise. Dwelling upon His life, I am healthy. I know what I want to accomplish, and I proceed to accomplish it. My thinking is straight, my intentions are right, and my procedure is scientific. I know God wants me to be successful this day. I know that all His Mind and His love are revealing themselves to me right now. Led by this inner divine compulsion I accomplish far more than even I expect. It is good to know Him whose ways I walk with certainty.

December 9

Money Is God in Action

The virtuous, excellent man cheerfully attains the state of the gods.
Uttaradhyayana Sutra 7.21

MONEY is God's means of giving me ease and freedom. It is the symbol of the divine supply forever maintaining me in comfort. I like money, and I appreciate the money I use. I like all people who have money, spend money and enjoy the use of money. I like the comforts and luxuries of life, and I believe God wants me to be happy and prosperous. I do not want another's money, because God gives me the ability to earn my own. My earning capacity depends upon my consciousness, and I now have a prosperity consciousness. I receive money with appreciation, and I spend my money with wisdom. I know that God is my source and that more money flows in to fill my every need. Money is God in action.

I think in large and generous terms. Realizing my thinking determines my experience, I now let money appear in all possible ways. My faith determines my fortune. All of God offers Itself to me, and my financial ease is a part of God's loving care of me. I rejoice when I pay my bills. I see each bill as an avenue for releasing abundance into a good channel. Everyone I owe has faith in me, and I am worthy of that faith. I pay my bills on time and with joy. I love to release the good which has come to me. Money is mine to use, but not to own. It circulates in my life with accuracy and ease. God's money comes to me in order that I shall pay it out. Money is God's ease in my life.

The universe supports me and maintains me in freedom, because God is the source and continuance of good. The Mind which created me sustains me. I use money for the glory of God, and good of my fellowman and the ease of my own experience. I do not worship it, nor overevaluate it. I see it as a means of exchange. I have not fear of lack, for always God prospers an alert mind. Recognizing the spiritual value in money, it increases in my world. Money received and spent with wisdom is the circulation of ease for man. I have a right to this ease, and I claim it. The things that money can buy will make my life richer and easier. I know my spiritual responsibility for the right use of money. Money is God's way of making my life free.

December 10

God Is Not Handicapped By Me

What knowest thou, that we know not?
What understandest thou, which is not in us?
Job 15:9

THE unlimited action of the Spirit works through me, and even I cannot hinder Its perfect results. The divine processes cannot be altered nor confused by me. The omnipotence of God cannot be stopped by my will. Its action can be directed, but its flow will never cease. I now direct it into constructive channels that bless and benefit me and my fellowman. All that God is happens to me. I now assume my rightful place in the divine order of life and let power move through me into beneficent action. I am never a handicap to God. Nothing in me can impede the perfect Mind. Divine ideas use me as a clear outlet for their completion. Heaven is happening to me at every instant.

I am a center in the infinite Mind and the love of God. Every time I am confused and hurt, I prevent the action of good in my life. Knowing this, I resolve today to cease from all such futile actions on my part. God needs me and wants me as His creative expression, and this I am. Every positive idea finds acceptance and clearance in my thinking. Every desire to love and to be loved finds a response in my soul. No more impediments within me, the allness of truth finds me and uses me for its perfect ends. The windows of my subconscious are ajar to let in the divine patterns which make me a whole person. I accept my heaven.

The stars at night shine upon the just and the unjust. The eternal goodness of the creative process offers itself to me without judgment. My past is not its concern. My present alone is sought by the divine wisdom and the divine action. Today it wants me to be like itself. This challenge I accept. I agree to let God be in me what His intelligence wants to be. I know that this will make me a greater person, a finer instrument for goodness, and a wider avenue of love. I place nothing in the path of the eternal. I fear no evil, for God is with me, and is what I am. All doors are open; all ideas are coming to me. Today is alive with truth and the future is secure. I am open and receptive to the divine inflow.

December 11

God Maintains Me in Balance

He has attendant angels, before him and behind him,
watching over him by God's command.
The Koran

THE creative power is a mathematically exact power. I may strive to have my own way, but in the long run God always has His way. The law of Mind cannot be broken, and the ways of Mind cannot be used for my own selfish ends. There is a divine law of balance forever maintained. My petty likes and dislikes have no power and no reality. The divine design of my life will manifest for me, whether I see the way or not. If I run roughshod over my fellowman in my greediness for more good, I shall only have a setback. There is nothing in God which allows me, as Its creation, to play with spiritual dynamite. The law remains undisturbed by my hysterics.

The balance of my thought and emotions is required by the universe. Creation refuses good to the unbalanced individual. Divine wisdom is forever in balance with divine love. In me this wisdom must be in balance with love. Is my present plan consistent with both wisdom and love? If it is, then I shall prosper. If it is not, then all my efforts are in vain. Balance will be maintained in me and my affairs, whether I like it or not. No individual can shake the foundations of this world which are set in law and order. I must be balanced to be effective, and now I let all the wisdom and love of God maintain me in balance.

I affirm right motives in all that I do. The infinite wants me to be happy, successful and at peace. My right motives will let divine action take place through me, and I now do just that. Receptive to the perfect will, I am inspired to perfect control of mind and emotions. This assures me of success and peace. Balanced in my innermost parts of consciousness, order appears at the circumference of my life. Now I can be what I want to be. This is the day of my demonstration. No longer do situations dominate me, for Mind is in charge and love is the power of my life. Intelligence directs me and feeling moves me through the mist of confusions into the answer I seek. I am balanced.

December 12

I Am Immersed in Intelligence and Love

To love is to know Me, My innermost nature, the truth that I am.
The Bhagavad-Gita

ALL of God is where I am, and all of good is offered to me. I waste no more time seeking the truth, for I am in it and it is me. The present moment is alive with God's intelligence and God's love. My present thinking is God's channel of action. My present mood is the way love acts through me. I now think as God thinks, and feel as God feels. The simplicity of this is hard to believe, but it is the truth. I need no mystical contemplation of a deity, I need only to think straight. I need no special mood or feeling, love is already flowing through my present emotions. I rejoice in my ability to let God out into His world through my mind and emotions.

Immersed in intelligence, I act as intelligence. Mind in process through me demonstrates what I select. Thinking in terms of what I want, the law of Mind now produces it. Feeling the goodness of life, I now experience it. It is right where I am, and is already in action. I only pray to recognize what is already being done, and to give my life right direction and meaning. My recognition of truth is the truth in action. As I know it, it is never apart from His omnipresence. Love does not suddenly come to me, for I have always been its vehicle. "Look unto me" is the way, and "This do" is the technique.

Immersed in divine love, I am loving. The infinite is no respector of persons, so I now love all my coworkers, my family and my friends. Life insists that I do this. Mind challenges me to do this. I know that faults are easy to behold, but I now train my consciousness to seek virtues. Everyone I know has great good within them. I seek this good, for it alone will endure. I now assume my rightful place in the scheme of things. Mind thinks through me, and love acts as me. The responsibility is mine to think this day with clarity, and to love this day with fullness. Nothing can hinder this decision on my part. Intelligence quickens me to seeing the truth in my fellowman, and to thinking rightly about myself and my world of affairs.

December 13

I Am a Friend to Every Man

In whose hand is the soul of every living thing, and the breath of all mankind.
Job 12:10

THE universe is a friendly system. Love offers itself to me through every person in my world. God gives of Himself to me through people. I can give of God to all whom I meet today. My face will reveal my inner peace and joy. My walk will reveal my sense of security in the divine presence. My smile will reveal the friendliness I have for my fellowman. Whoever sees me is richer by the sight. I radiate the qualities of the Spirit, and these alone are imparted to others. No one can find faults in me, because I have only good to give and only love to share. I am the representative of God walking among His beloved creations. God in me greets the God in them.

I refuse to sit in judgment upon my fellowman. I let his business be his business and not mine. I condemn no one. I have faith that each is doing the best he can at his own level of consciousness. I silently recognize the Spirit in man, and at the same time give him his freedom of self-expression. With my eyes fastened on God's possibility in man, I see that which heals and evolves him. Beholding the real man, my neighbor becomes him, and in this becoming I am raised to new heights. His opinions of me are not important, for I know my spiritual worth. I walk forward on the pathway of truth, whether my neighbor knows this or not. I create my own destiny.

Whoever contacts me finds good in me. I am a radiating center of creative intelligence and love. No one criticizes me nor condemns me. Everyone gives me the freedom to be myself. My friends increase my faith in God, and my conviction of my own worth. All people find the good in me, for I now release all self-opinionated beliefs. I know that I am only right when I am one with a divine purpose and a righteous activity. My friends are a joy to my soul, and I can only give them my highest thought and my greatest love. No one ever hurts me nor confuses me, for I behold the Christ in them. Outer actions never confuse me, because I am seeking the inner Spirit in all.

December 14

God's Effortless Power Is Mine to Use

See truth as it is and be forever free of opposition and contention.
Garland Sutra 11

I AM my only enemy. My wrong beliefs about life cause me to strain and struggle with my problems. I decide right now to let the effortless power of Mind act through me, and give me my freedom from struggle. No more weariness, no more "working for a living." This I have discarded. From now on I shall let the truth control my life. My burden is easy and my way is light because of this decision. My human thinking steps aside to let in God's healing thought. Weary of humanity, I now seek my own divinity. In me is the power of God. It created me to act through me, and I let it act. God knows no difficulties, nor do I. The universe displays an effortless action of intelligence and cohesion. This is true of my world around me, so it must be true of the world within me.

Infinite Mind has no useless ideas, so I am of value to this world. I now let God's purpose create me into the being it had planned me to be. Whither I go divine wisdom knows, and what I shall be the divine plan has prepared. This now takes over all my thinking and feeling, and I became the son of God that Mind intended me to be. Turning over all my human decisions to the divine knowing is easy, and its ways make my pathway clear. I no longer struggle to be my human self. I let God in me be whatever It has planned for me to be. Divine wisdom guides me, divine love enfolds me, and a success is all that can be before me. I let God decide.

The effortless power of the Spirit is mine to use and to enjoy. I give it directions to produce for me health, prosperity and happiness. This it does, because God acts at my level of consciousness. In me God loves to be healthy. In me God wants to be freedom in finance. In me God wants to be love. As an individualized outlet of the Spirit, I now take my rightful place in life. I cease all human efforts to be good, and I let the Divine in me be what it wants to be. God knows my next step, and reveals it. I relax and let Mind reveal Its next idea. God will produce my good, when I let Him do it, and this I now do.

December 15

My Present Experience is Good

The superior man by determined good conduct nourishes his virtue.
I Ching 4: Immaturity

TODAY is the day in which I prove that the power of Mind is greater than the power of material belief. What I face today, and the mental attitude in which I face it, will determine my experience today. I cannot blame my mistakes on the past. The subtle deceit of so doing entices me, but I refuse to believe it. I am not conditioned by my childhood, I am only conditioned by my present thinking. The past with all its combination of good and bad is now only a force of creative memory. What I have been, is merely an indication of what I should be and shall be. No false glamorization of the past, only my recognition of the now as potent with possibilities. My present world is good.

My future is not dependent upon my past. It is dependent upon my ability to think God's thoughts today. I know what I want to accomplish, and I know the way I shall go. Today, I think as cause to the tomorrow which will be in effect. My aims are clear, my goal is in sight. No airy dreams of impossibilities, no visions beyond the realm of logical possibility. I can become the person God intended me to become, and what I shall be will be good, creative and honest. Dreaming falsely profits me nothing, seeing clearly gives me what I want. I look forward to my full demonstration, and I think today in tomorrow's terms. I live now as though my dreams were true, for they are true.

God in me, acting through me, is the doer of the present moment. Right where I am, God is. In my thinking at this moment divine Mind is the real thinker. Around me is the plastic substance of all life, and I mold it this day to bring forth what I want. The law of Mind is mine to use and to employ. Today's thinking brings forth tomorrow's demonstration. So, I look out at my present experience and name it good. It is my only place to start, and I begin to give God to my day. Recognizing each hour as my possibility to prove truth, I think as Spirit and act as love. I do not hesitate to deny evil and affirm the good. I watch my thought and handle negatives. I see good in my present experience.

December 16

New Ideas Are Mine This Day

But there is spirit in man: and the inspiration of the Almighty giveth them understanding.
Job 32:8

INSPIRATION is the act of the infinite through man. I now open my whole consciousness to it. I let God give me the ideas I need to handle the questions of today. From early morning until late at night, I am directed to right action through His Mind which indwells me. Forever abiding in God's Mind, I cannot fail through His Mind which indwells me. Forever abiding in His love, I cannot fail but understand my fellowman. I look out upon a wonderful world alive with more good than I ever supposed. Every contact today is a blessing to me, and to everyone I bring a larger peace and a greater joy. Filled with the freshness of Mind, I give new impressions to my everyday tasks.

I refuse to believe that I shall meet problems. I see these as tests of my ability to inaugurate a new idea born of God. Each moment brings me the chance to live as a spiritual being of integrity. The idea I need at this moment of this day, I shall have. God meets me in the hour, the moment and the instant of my need. His inspiration is my security to handle all things rightly, and all things lovingly. What I see as a problem, God sees as an opportunity to release His intelligence. Knowing this, I am confident and serene. Neither a person nor a situation can confound me. I silently turn within and find the spiritual answer.

I welcome new ideas, for they mean a greater good for me. They press upon me, they draw nigh unto me. His knowledge is available to me now, and I let it be in me a vital source of ideas. Wisdom is mine to use, and I use it. I cannot make a mistake today, for God's omniscient Mind is my mind now. We are one, and in this oneness, I am led to right answers. Immediate right guidance is mine. I do not need to beseech, I only need to know that He in me is all in all. Rejoicing in this perfect supply of inspiration, I cannot fail. Where I am at every moment, His Mind is. This is my security; this is my peace. Conclusions born of God make easy my way. I am receptive to God's ideas.

December 17

I Am Mind in Action

According as one acts, according as one conducts himself, so does he become.
Brihadaranyaka Upanishad

IN the midst of me is the Spirit of the Lord. To me It offers Itself without limitation. "All that the Father hath is mine." It forever presses upon me all Its ideas and they find me a willing vehicle of expression. At every instant I am urged to be my greatest self. At every instant I am bidden to let God shine through as health, peace and creative self-expression. The unlimited action of truth is the true source of my life. I see this, know this, and act according to this. I let my mind be inspired by a wisdom greater than its present knowledge. I see ideas as the cause of all experience, and control them to produce what I want, when I want it. I am Mind in action.

Mind offers me all of Its being. Every idea in the universe is available to me. What I need to know today is already offered to me. I now receive the ideas of God and give them welcome. I open the doors of my thinking and let divine inspiration flow into my mind. New vistas appear around me, as new ideas are born within me. I have confidence, I have security. Nothing is withheld from me, and to me comes omniscience. I am consciousness knowing truth. I am the creative process through which God acts as Mind. I am a thinker in a universal medium of mental law, and as such I alone control my destiny. God wants me to be free, but I must accept His ideas in order to be free. I now do this.

I can be all things which I desire, for the ideas I need are already mine. My consciousness is inspired by the Mind from which all things proceed. Unto me is given the greatness of Spirit, and the way of creative accomplishment. I deny all barriers to my success. God sees none, and I refuse to accept them. I join my thinking with the divine thinker and experience happiness here and now. All that I have sought is found. In me now is the answer to every question, and the solution to every problem. I think clearly, act wisely and let my good happen. Inspired by Mind, I think success, peace and prosperity. I am Mind in action, for this is the inner meaning of the term "Son of God," and this I am named by Him who created me.

December 18

My Peace I Give to My World

I have no tact except the exercise of gentleness.
Oracle of Sumiyoshi

HARMONY is the automatic action of Spirit, and in me this action now manifests. The universe is order, harmony and peace. Despite my present affairs, I now acknowledge this, and act from this premise. If the sun fails to shine, the tide to rise and fall in the sea, then neither can my few matters be disturbed nor upset. God's universal law of order is now in me, through me and around me. It is my peace of mind; it is the order in all things I do. Having this peace, I now share it with others. My whole mental atmosphere is radiant with peace. My home, my office and my entire environment are bathed in it. This peace, born of God, is infectious and my fellowman receives it.

I have a poised, balanced mind in a poised balanced body. God's eternal harmony and order are mine, and I let them express through me. My family and coworkers sense this and are healed by this. Peace flowing out from me heals everyone I contact. It is a subtle, soothing balm to all their fears and doubts. They feel better for having spoken to me or clasped my hand. Every room I enter is alive with divine harmony and order. God's presence is made alive by the truth I know and the love I emanate. Power flows to the weak, positive conclusions flow to the uncertain, and God's omnipotence is made visible. The whole Spirit of God in every man is quickened into right action.

I walk this day as a divine creation. Nothing in me can confuse, for God alone is the center of my thinking. My divinity is obvious, my peace blesses all. Life flows easily, and all things work together for good. Radiating peace, I am a blessing to all and a problem to none. A warm welcome awaits me where'er I go. Joy greets me in every face, and cooperation appears everywhere. I see nothing but peace as I look at the people around me. They, too, are centered and grounded in the one universal order and harmony in God. Sensing the eternal good, my friends join with me in silently acknowledging it. We are all of one Mind now, and together we bring peace to all who are hurt and confused. This is my job this day.

December 19

Having Received Light, I Pass It on to Others

O send out thy light and thy truth.
Psalms 43.3

THE light of truth is within me, and I release it in every thought and feeling. This light of God has always been in me, yet only lately have I realized what it was. I now know that it is the Divine using me as a center of perfect operation. I know that it is the truth which I have sought and now found. I know that it is my highest self, and that I am it right here in my present circumstances. God in me at this moment illuminates my whole consciousness and I am free of all untruth. Alerted to the light, I give this light to others. Every word I speak is a light to men. Every thought I think is a treatment to all whom I know.

The light of truth cannot be dimmed. I may not see it some of the time, but it remains within me awaiting my recognition. This light is the light of my world. As I look out at my environment, I am looking though the eyes of light. I see all things clearly, easily and normally. Through my eyes the light of God flows out, and healing appears everywhere. I see only the good, the true and the eternal. I see God in every man and love in every heart. Others see this light in me, and rise to new heights of accomplishment. They see truth made manifest, the one Mind releasing Itself. By their sight of God in me, they are healed physically, mentally and financially.

There is a radiance that shines from me, for God's healing light is the true light of my soul. There are no dark corners in my thinking. Memories of the past, actions of the present and hopes of the future are all exposed to this light and are cleansed. The wrong is erased, and the right is amplified. I let my light shine to bless and benefit my neighbor, for it is God's light shining through me. Releasing the light, I am immersed in lights, and true perception is mine. I see God everywhere. I see God in everyone I meet. I see God in the little and the great. Omnipresence is manifested to me. Having received the light, I now pass it on to others.

December 20

Demonstrations Follow My Word

Where can I find a man who has forgotten words so I can have a word with him?
Chuang Tzu 26

THERE is nothing to obstruct the spiritual word that I speak. All the power of God is for me, and all the power of God is working through me. As I make these statements of truth, the truth happens in my world. I speak the truth, and the truth sets me free. This word is not dependent upon my will, for it is the action of God taking place through me. I now declare my own spiritual perfection as a child of omnipotence. I speak the truth and the truth happens to me. Health appears in my body for I know God as the health of my mind. Strength flows through me and vitality is instantly available. I am free in body to do all those things which need to be done. I am health.

My prosperity is definite, for God thinks his prosperous ideas through me. I now demonstrate permanent abundance. I live with wisdom, but I live with ease. All the substance of Mind is in action as my immediate and permanent prosperity. I use money for I see it as my immediate and permanent prosperity. I use money for I see it as God's means of maintaining me in freedom. This flow of good is right where I am, and is happening at this moment. I declare my freedom in finance. God is my supply right now. What I need, the one Mind provides this day. All life is backing me up as I make this statement. Even my own subconscious fears cannot prevent this demonstration. My word is a law unto that to which I speak it. It is God declaring Himself by means of me.

I accept demonstration as normal. God has offered Himself to me, and I let His Mind do what It desires. The infinite loves me. The infinite appreciates me. The infinite wants me to be at peace. This I now accept as my demonstration. My destiny has been given into my hands by the Spirit, and I select my world as carefully as I would select a gift. I choose what I want, and declare it. I let the law of Mind bring forth my decisions. Unlimited, save by my own wrong beliefs, I stand in a process divine which works for me, as I direct it. Demonstrations follow demonstrations hourly. Good appears on every hand. Love offers itself to me and God gives me what I want.

December 21

There Is a Glory in My Heart

I was a secret treasure, and I created the creatures in order that I might be known.
                                                                Hadith

WARM is the love of the eternal, and it glows within me, satisfying my soul. The heart of God beats within me its rhythmic harmony of glory. I am fed in all my depths of emotional need by this inner well of compassion. The universe glows with kindliness. Every man offers me the warmth of love and the joy of friendliness. The glory of God is upon me and I rest in its perfect action. I sense the divine friendliness of the world in which I live. All things work together for my good, and all people appreciate and love me. This deep inner sense of well-being is now forever established, and never again shall I feel loneliness. Glory abides within me.

The expanding power of God is the joy of my soul. Every mood of good increases and every feeling of goodness is accentuated. The holy Spirit of peace is upon me and resident in me. Glorious is my day, and rejoicing is my heart. God's wonderful life within me is not completely explicable. More than my outer mind can describe, more than my intellect can define, is the glory within me. Beyond all description is the inner peace and the inner glow. God in me is a terrific presence of power, love and peace. This inner deep feeling of greatness now takes control of my thought.

I not only know the Mind of God, but I feel the presence of the Spirit. I arise and shine, for the glory of God is within me, and peace does fill my world. The light of truth is within me, and a feeling of greatness arises. God in me is saying to me that I am His beloved creation. To me He gives all that He is and all He has. This is wonderful and this is heartwarming. Warm on the inside and wise on the outside I can accomplish my aims. The holy Spirit is in my mind now. Divine love floods my emotions. Glorious is my thinking, and glorious is my experience. God is my all, no more can I seek. Omnipresence warms me and omniscience guides me into a friendlier experience.

December 22

Heaven Is My Environment Today

What shall I render unto the Lord for all his benefits toward me?
Psalm 116:12

I EXIST in an eternal beneficence which seeks to give me what I want. What others label a material experience, I behold as the heavenly possibility, and put all my efforts to its demonstration. All of God is where I am, and all of Mind is giving of Itself through me. The doors of my thinking are open wide, and right ideas in perfect order reveal themselves to me. Guided by the divine Mind and prospered by the divine love, I work with certainty and with ease.

Good seeks me, and I let it happen within me. This inner compulsion to right action is welcomed by me, for I know it is divine in source. Following the urges of the Spirit, I find good on every hand.

I start where I am and I begin with what I know myself to be. I am in an unlimited field of Mind action, which responds to me in the terms of my own thinking. I now change my concept of myself. I am not material, I am spiritual. I am not struggling for heaven, I am letting heaven happen where I am. I am not depreciating myself, I know that I am God's intelligent creation worthy of all the good I can conceive. All that I want to be, I can be. All that I really want to own, I can own. I look out at my world and behold a beckoning good, and a friendly humanity. Life bids me walk forward. With my feet set on a holy pathway, I progress with ease.

My senses are alerted to the truth. I see God wherever I look. I hear the Lord's voice in every sound. I sense heaven at hand, and divine love in my heart. Joyously accepting my present day, I see the good before me, and love offering itself to me. I am not led astray by false reports nor by unwise conclusions. Heaven is where I am, and I declare it. If others fail to see good in their world, this bothers me not at all. My God and I together walk, and He leads me beside the still waters and into the green pastures. These twenty-four hours are pregnant with Spirit and vital with truth. Each instant is crammed with the one presence, and each hour is filled with power.

December 23

No Evil Fools Me

Hence evil is but an illusion, and it has no real basis.
Science and Health, 480

THE allness of God and the spiritual nature of man are convictions in my mind. I am not of the world belief, nor of the world opinion. "Thine is the kingdom and the power and the glory forever." Knowing one cause operating through one Mind upon one law and one substance, I deny duality and its wrong experience. I have no place for evil in my thinking. It cannot register within me, for I am single-eyed to truth. I am poised in an absolute conviction of the omnipresence of God as good. I cannot be persuaded that evil is in me, nor in my fellowman. God alone creates, and I have faith in what He creates. This world is good enough for God, so it is good enough for me.

No evil fools me. I recognize it as a face, but I know it will fall apart of its own false making. It appears strong, but it is really weak. It seems to have power, but it soon wears itself out. It tries to make me believe it is true, but only the truth is true. Evil is a lie from beginning to end, and I will not accept its demands nor its allures. Infinite Mind in me reveals to me the truth, and every possible evil is of no importance. I do not waste one split second in its belief, nor in its sway. My time is valuable, for every moment God thinks through me. Instead of wallowing in past errors, I now create present good. I am alerted to truth.

I am determined to be a creative person through whom flow God's ideas. False reports, though they seem valid, are still not the truth. God alone is real, and truth alone is eternal. In God I am, and by God I exist. His Mind is my mind now. No other mind can function in me, and no false belief has power over me. Evil has no existence in my consciousness, and no appearance in my world. Watching the doorway of my mind, I let in only that which accords with Spirit. All untrue perceptions are turned aside. Nothing in me can draw negatives, and nothing in me can create them. I rest in a perfect wisdom and a perfect love. I am surrounded by a wall of intelligence, and only good can enter my soul.

December 24

God's Action Through Me Is Complete

Rewards are obtained according to one's heart.
Garland Suttra 10

THE Lord God omnipotent acts through me. All power seeks release through me. All love uses me as its channel. My spiritual responsibility I now accept. Knowing that the one Mind focalizes Its ideas through my consciousness, I determine to let God alone think in me today. If I expect the law of Mind to produce increased good for me, then I must do my part in the process. I must affirm God's action in me, and act as a spiritual being. This means I cannot be a difficult nor unkind person. I must seek to understand my fellowman and each situation as it arises. If I do not always have my own way, I must see this as right action, and agree with it.

As I open my whole mind to the influx of truth, I must be willing to let go of all my petty beliefs. Much of my everyday thinking is not worthy of Him who created me. I cannot love truth and at the same time find fault with my work, my family and my friends. I now decide to live as though every spiritual belief I have were an actual fact. The teachings of Jesus were that I do this, and now I will. I refuse to be depressed and unhappy. I know that the action of God is taking place in me and producing for me my good, and I let it happen. No more pettiness for me. I think in terms worthy of the Mind that indwells me.

The whole action of truth is upon me, within me and around me. I give it full control of my thinking and feeling. The Lord is in His holy temple within me, and now expressed forth from me. God in the midst of me is mighty to produce right results around me. The labor is no longer mine, for He that is within me does His perfect work, and I rejoice in immediate results. Miracle follows miracle and glory appears on every hand. All men shall call me blessed, and all people everywhere shall rejoice in my presence. I move from good to more good, as I let God determine what needs to be done. God's action through me at this moment is complete, and beauty appears now.

December 25

The Christ Is Born in Me

Let this mind be in you, which was also in Christ Jesus.
Philippians 2:5

"HE that sent me is with me." The action of God in me is the Christ of my being, and on this Christmas Day, I pay tribute to Jesus who is the world's greatest example of God's action through man. Two thousand years have passed since a larger light came into the world and told man of his spiritual freedom to accomplish his heart's desires. These years have not been in vain, for gradually man has come to larger understanding of God and of his own Christ self. I now dedicate and consecrate myself to the teachings of the man of Nazareth.

On this Christmas Day I let Christ rule my heart, mind and affairs. I see the new birth of love in all people and in all events. All the beauty of Christmas is mine to behold. All the love of Christmas is given unto me. Each card and each gift brings me love, and they bless me with the knowledge of my own birth of truth. I shall be like the Wise Men and follow the eternal star of truth. I shall be like the shepherds and hear the voice of God in every harmony. I shall be like Mary and Joseph and watch carefully over this new inner dawning of true life.

I make of my mind a stable and welcome the Christ idea of perfect spiritual man. I give the gifts of my attention, my love and my substance to this idea born within me. I am open to the Divine this day. I let God be born into my thinking and feeling. I share this birth to a higher understanding with all men everywhere. I revere the memory of Jesus, and let His teachings be in me a light unto my world, and others seeing my good works shall find the light of truth within themselves. This is the day of Christ, the day of truth, the day of a birth into greater good.

December 26

His Will Is Done in Me

Do all things without murmurings and disputings.
Philippians 2:14

THE will of God is that man should be perfect. No longer do I think with reluctance that His will may mean my failure to demonstrate what I want. I know that all of God is for me, and all of Mind moves through me. What I decide will happen, as long as it is good and will harm no other person. There is a divine purpose to my life. My creation was not an accident. It was the fulfillment of a plan and a design. Mind could only know a perfect idea, and so His will for me is a perfect life here and now. Letting go of all visible evidence to the contrary, I accept this. God's will is done in me, and the world is richer because I am.

The will of God moves in me to accomplish my heart's desire. Without stint it offers me the full expression of life. To me it gives every hope, every vision, and every right desire. Out of the abundance of love it merely asks that I accept life and use it aright. Letting this divine design control my thinking, I find the good of the world at my hand. I am able to clasp that which I seek, and experience that which I have wanted. His will for me is wonderful, and I glory in it. I am the son which the Father intended I should be. I am life, love and his plan for all humanity. As I evolve spiritually, the whole human family benefits.

His will is done in me, and my permanent peace envelops me. It breathes through my consciousness bringing new and great ideas to pass. In this deep abiding security I know my own Christ self. I rest from all struggle, and let His action do the work. My hopes become possibilities, and my dreams unfold into facts. Life becomes glorious, and I do all things with ease. I expect the good to happen, and the true to appear. Mind thinks through me, love controls me, and I am the active expression of God. This is the will of the Father for the son, and I am that son now.

December 27

I Affirm My Own Divinity

> *Whatever then doth live, oweth its immortality unto the Mind, and most of all doth man, he who is both recipient of God, and coessential with Him.*
> Thrice-Greatest Hermes

I ACCEPT a divine purpose for my life. Intelligence brought me forth at the right time to do a right work in these present days. This is my right generation, and around me are my own people. I do not regret the past, nor do I postpone the future. I see now as the only time, and this day as my only opportunity to release god into my world through right thinking and living. These present hours are my tools of divinity. My thinking is in accord with the Mind of God. My actions are in accord with the divine plan of my life. I radiate love, live in peace and think God's thoughts. I fulfill my destiny, and be what God created me to be.

As a spiritual being, I live with wisdom and in health. I know that life will use me for the good of all, and at the same time for the profit of my own ventures. My own good limits no one, and makes me more able to help my fellowman. I do a better job when I am thinking positively. I give greater love and affection to others as I see my own indwelling Spirit in action. All my faculties are outlets for Him who creates me, and wonderful results appear right where I am. I am Spirit and I am truth. My mind is a holy vessel for the transmission of God's ideas. My body glows with God's victorious life. My environment is pregnant with good, and love flows to me from all whom I know.

I sense my spiritual importance. I lose my false sense of human importance. Knowing my divinity, my human ego retires to its right functioning. My only boast is that His Mind now acts through me. This is true consecration to truth. Letting go of all material pettiness, I become the greatness of God. Releasing the untrue and the unworthy, I accept ideas which transform me and all my affairs. I prosper as never before. I never again shall know illness or defeat. All that is nothing, for God in me is all in all. I have the victorious attitude, and I bring forth my demonstrations in order and ease. God made me, and I like His creation.

December 28

My Right Thinking Is Contagious

Every being has the Buddha Nature. This is the self.
Mahaparinirvana Sutra 214

MY thinking is my gift to the world. Consciousness alone is the gift of life. What I do for my fellowman is important, but what I think about him is more important. My every mood is noted by those around me. They sense my peace, but they can also sense my fear. Today, all men shall find good in me and peace emanating from me. To this end I think rightly of God, of my fellowman and of the world in which I live. I affirm every man's right to be himself. I affirm a spiritual wisdom in all people. I affirm an essential goodness, born of God, in all people I know. I forgive easily, for I see the unimportance of evil. I know a temporary hurt will always fall away.

A right mental attitude arises within me, and flows out from me to bless all who are in my world. God is in my mind and heart and all things work together for good for me and for all others. I am a radiating activity of truth. I share the joy of the Spirit with all I meet. I let out the good, the positive and the worthwhile. I am a tower of strength and a citadel of peace. I share all that God is through my right thinking. Dedicated to truth, light and love, I let my light shine before men and glorify my Father which is in heaven within me. All who contact me this day are healed, blessed and prospered. They find in me an example of a true spiritual enthusiasm.

God's joyous Spirit in me prevents any emotional depression. There is no gloom where divine ideas act with authority. My smile is sincere and my handclasp is firm. I walk uprightly and face God in every face I see. My work is easy and my burden is light, for I am relying on God's truth at the center of my being. I cause no fear, and reveal no inner tension. There is peace in my soul, and I reflect it automatically. Releasing good in all directions I rejoice, give thanks and am glad. All good is where I am, and I drink deeply of the living waters of truth. This divine completion makes the world a better place, and my fellowman a finer person. I radiate God.

December 29

Today, I Really Practice Right Thinking

Man is idea, the image, of Love; he is not physique.
Science and Health, 475

I SET apart the hours of this day which God has given to me to practice spiritual principles. I not only have good intentions to do this, but I really will do this. I am determined to prove Mind the only cause, and law the only process. I affirm my existence in a life which knows what to do, and a love which gives of itself through me. I behold my present world as the body of God alive with goodness and prosperity. I know that what I think will become a fact through the law. I now dedicate my whole thinking and feeling nature to the infinite Spirit. My thinking today brings to pass my heart's desire. The love I release today enriches the whole world.

Because there is but one Mind, God, infinite good, there is nothing to prevent me from demonstrating truth. All power is in full action through me. I now select what I want to demonstrate, and I subconsciously accept it as a present idea. I know it is not only possible, but having accepted it, it must take form in my life. The whole power and authority of the universal subjective now acts upon my selection and brings it forth immediately. There is no delay; God's action is full and complete, and my demonstration now takes place.

Certain of results from scientific prayer, I face the problems of this day with no fear. Within me and acting through me is divine intelligence forever producing right decisions and right results. I cannot be hurt, confused nor upset. I am a center of peace and poise is my only reaction. I have no criticism, no condemnation, no feeling of superiority. I know that He who indwells me also indwells my fellowman. I think straight, I feel love. I am a creative center in a universal Mind. My courage is complete, and my strength is sufficient. I am God's health made manifest. Today, I am on the beam. Today is the best day I have ever known. Today, I give thanks for truth.

December 30

I Determine My Own Demonstrations

For as he thinketh in his heart, so is he.
Proverbs 23:7

THE Lord God omnipotent created me as a free and full expression of Itself. I have the freedom of the Mind which brought me forth to express Its ideas. I choose, and divine law produces. There is no power to hinder me, and no law to refuse me. All of life is mine to use for good, and this I do. Backed up by omnipotence, I determine my own results. I have no one to blame for my mistakes, not even myself. I refuse to believe that the world acts upon me, for I know that I act upon the world. My thinking is my environment, and God is my heredity. I alibi no longer; I face the facts of my own conclusions. I am determined to demonstrate what I want.

Today I have unlimited health. His life in me guarantees this. As I praise life, health, strength and vitality, they arise within me and give of themselves through me. I shall not be tired at the end of this day, for I am constantly renewed by inner power. His Mind in me is my source of health, and this Mind never ceases thinking rightly about me. It never is defeated by my fears and confusions. It forever acts, and now I let Its action be my health and my vitality. Strong in the Lord, I accomplish without strain. All things are easy, and all work is a pleasure. I rejoice in my God-given health. I rejoice in the power and strength that are mine.

Today, I have peace of mind. It matters not what others believe, nor what others do. I know Him who created me, and I abide in His love. I refuse to let the material thinking of others influence me. I am not dependent upon the world, the world is dependent upon me. The contagion of evil will find no welcome in my consciousness. There is nothing in me to agree with it, therefore I cannot experience its falsities. I know a divine plan, a divine purpose and a divine law of action. This is my all-sufficiency. My peace comes from my knowledge of God as my source, my life and my deliverance. My demonstration is, because I know so deeply that it must be. I give thanks that this is so.

December 31

I Accept the Beauties of Life

Because it would never claim greatness, Therefore its greatness is fully realized.
　　　　　　　　　　　　　　　　　　　　The Tao Te Ching

RELIGION affirms the beauty of life, and that God fills this world with the beauty of His presence. Therefore, there is no reason why I should not experience this, and I now do. My mind is set on beauty, and it appears where I am. I need not seek it, for already its face is showing itself to me. People, places and things are beautiful when I look for details of loveliness. In minute ways harmony, order and right proportion catch my attention. All sight is glorious, all music is rich in tones of harmony. All food is God's substance served to me by intelligence in action. Even the glass of cold water symbolizes that cup of long ago which gave life a new meaning.

　　The beauty of Christ is the glory of my soul. In the commonplace Jesus saw God, and he bid me to do likewise. I look out at familiar walls, people and objects and I see them with a new light and a new meaning. I need not uproot the old to behold the glory of life. I only need to see rightly what already is and appreciate the Mind which brought it forth for me to see. The ugliest building is potent with harmony, order and balance. Its walls stand because a law is in action. Its presence declares a universal substance, and its form affirms a divine intelligence. I now see it anew, and appreciate an idea made manifest. The little becomes the great, for beauty is within it.

　　God's action always produces symmetry, and my whole world is filled with the divine Mind in action under Its perfect law. The beauty of Spirit is in me, and I acknowledge it in my brother. To me all people have qualities of greatness. Beauty is of the mind and heart as well as of appearance. These inner powers are the real beauty that no outer application can equal. The slightest kindness brings beauty to my heart. No good act is too small to be appreciated. God blesses me through all people and all situations. Wherever I look, beauty is at hand. God beckons to me in every face, every building, and every landscape. This is the day of harmony, order and balance. Beauty is mine.

RECOGNIZED as one of the foremost spiritual teachers of the past century, Ernest Holmes blended the best of Eastern and Western spiritual philosophies, psychology, and science into the transformational ideas known as the Science of Mind. Additionally, he formulated spiritual mind treatment, a specific type of meditative prayer that has positively affected the lives of millions.

Basing his techniques for living a free and full life on sacred wisdom, from the ancient to the modern, Ernest Holmes outlines these ideas in a collection of inspiring books. Written with simplicity and clarity, these books provide the means for every reader to live a more satisfying life. To learn more about the philosophy of Ernest Holmes:

Visit Science of Mind Online!
www.scienceofmind.com

The award-winning *Science of Mind* magazine delivers insightful and uplifting articles, interviews, and hard-hitting spiritual ideas each month. The magazine's Daily Guides to Richer Living provide you with spiritual wisdom and guidance every day of the year.

To subscribe, go to www.scienceofmind.com
or call 1-800-247-6463.

573 Park Point Drive | Golden, CO 80401

Made in the USA
Columbia, SC
04 April 2024